WORLD IN
THE BALANCE

WORLD IN
THE BALANCE

THE PERILOUS MONTHS OF JUNE–OCTOBER 1940

BROOKE C. STODDARD

POTOMAC BOOKS, INC.
WASHINGTON, D.C.

Library of Congress Cataloging-in-Publication Data
Stoddard, Brooke C., 1947-
  World in the balance : the perilous months of June-October 1940 / Brooke C.
Stoddard. — 1st ed.
      p. cm.
  Includes bibliographical references and index.
  ISBN 978-1-59797-516-2 (hardcover : acid-free paper)
  1. World War, 1939-1945—Great Britain. 2. World War, 1939-1945—Diplomatic
history. 3. Churchill, Winston, 1874-1965—Military leadership. I. Title.
  D750.S74 2010
  940.53'41—dc22

                                                              2010039433

Printed in the United States of America on acid-free paper that meets
the American National Standards Institute Z39-48 Standard.

Potomac Books, Inc.
22841 Quicksilver Drive
Dulles, Virginia 20166

First Edition

10 9 8 7 6 5 4 3 2 1

To the memory of

my father, Brooke Stoddard (1914–65), and

my mother, Gracey Luckett (1918–2009),

who lived through June–October 1940

and all it portended

ACKNOWLEDGMENTS

I am grateful to the following people and institutions for their assistance in the preparation of this book:

Excerpt from *The Gathering Storm*, by Winsion S. Churchill, copyright 1948 by Houghton Mifflin Company; copyright renewed 1976 by Lady Spencer-Churchill, the honorable Lady Sarah Audley, and the Honorable Lady Soames. Reprinted by permission of Houghton Mifflin Harcourt Publishing Company, all rights reserved.

Carl Gnam, publisher of *Military Heritage* magazine, in which portions of chapters 4 and 5 appeared in altered form.

Kevin Hymel for his expert assistance in photo research.

The Library of Congress and the National Archives, and their photo research staffs, for photographs and assistance.

Elizabeth Demers for taking a risk with the concept, for shepherding, for providing able guidance, and for editing.

Bob Diforio, a tireless and able agent, for never losing sight of the goal.

Marybeth and my supportive family, without whom this book would not have been possible.

A resounding and heartfelt thanks to you all.

CONTENTS

INTRODUCTION

May 1940 was no longer than May 1939 or any other month of May, though it seemed so to a Europe rent and ripped. Now as the wretched month lurched to its scorched conclusion, a world watched in shock. The armed forces of a rekindled and vicious Germany, having burst its borders on May 10 for yet the third time since autumn, grasped at neutral Luxembourg, neutral Belgium, neutral Netherlands (which received scant credit for sheltering Germany's former emperor Wilhelm II in the village of Doorn), and the nation with the largest army in Europe—France. Through mid- and late May, it engulfed Luxembourg, bombed the heart of Rotterdam to rubble, and battered Belgium into hasty surrender. It defeated a major French army at Sedan and knocked another, along with the British Expeditionary Force, back to a small strip of Flemish-French coastline, where the cream of French and British soldiers scurried weaponless to boats.

On May 28 Nazi soldiers of a Schutzstaffel (Protection Squadron, or SS) regiment received the surrender of eighty British and French soldiers near the French town of Wormhoudt. They proceeded to execute the wounded where they lay on the ground, killed scores of others with grenades after herding them into a barn, and shot the survivors.

This mass murder was not an isolated incident. Across France and Belgium, the common people of the towns and villages, fleeing the fighting on foot or with horse-drawn open wagons, were strafed by airplane machine guns and rent with bombs.

The atrocities fit a pattern. On the third day of the war (September 3, 1939), the Germans had rounded up fifty-five Polish peasants, including a two-year-old child; shot them all; and then burned their village of Truskolasy to the ground. As German troops spread across the Polish countryside, so did the horrors. The armed forces had orders to "be ruthless." Theodor Eicke, commander of three SS Death's Heads regiments, was not alone when he ordered his men to "incarcerate or annihilate" every enemy of Nazism using "absolute severity."

These offenses against humanity did not erupt with the crash of arms; rather, the medium for them had subsumed Germany and Austria for years. As early as May 1933, Nazis organized book burnings in cities and towns. Students hounded professors from their jobs, either because they were Jewish or were critical of Nazi culture. In 1935 the government stripped all "non-Aryan" people of the rights of citizenship. By 1940 the Nazis had sent tens of thousands of so-called undesirables—Social Democrats, Communists, Jehovah's Witnesses, labor unionists, homosexuals, Gypsies, and political opponents—to concentration camps or torture centers.

At the same time, the Nazis built up arguably the most powerful army in the world and, by most accounts, the largest military air force. At the helm of this European colossus was an energetic and charismatic fanatic, practically the founder of Nazism and supreme organizer of its rise to power in Germany, and a rabid anti-Semite and anticommunist who blamed the world's woes on Jews and revolutionary Russians and who vowed to crush them. This tyrant was Adolf Hitler.

Hordes of former German soldiers embittered by the 1914–18 war's outcome and millions of German citizens both disaffected by the shortcomings of democracy and battered by the ravages of economic depression cheered Hitler. A gifted and persuasive speaker, Hitler was going to remake Germany, regain its glory, and return pride and prosperity to those of "German hereditary stock." He called this movement Nazism, a form of fascism that had already sunk deep roots in Italy and Spain and was gaining traction in France and elsewhere, even Great Britain and the United States. Anne Morrow Lindbergh, wife of the celebrated aviator, wrote that fascist-like states were the "wave of the future," and many agreed. Resistance was futile. Hitler was emphatic about the movement's aggression.

Germany must have more European land, he wrote, and "what is refused to amicable methods, it is up to the fist to take."[1]

Now his word was made good. What he could not seize by intimidation—Austria and Czechoslovakia—he would take by the fist: first Poland, then Denmark, Norway, Luxembourg, the Netherlands, and Belgium. By late May the fist had closed upon northern France. British naval vessels, even ferries and sailboats, hauled wet and beaten British and French soldiers aboard in chaotic flight from the continent.

Their exit mimicked the demise of the liberal republics of Europe, one by one toppled and extinguished. Europe, the beating heart of the world, was being subsumed as had Germany in 1933 when Nazism seized its government. France looked to be next and Britain the target thereafter. But there would be a fight.

Everything would be thrown into the struggle: the courage and endurance of young men, the cunning of strategists, the insights of scientists, the oratory of leaders, the bravery of women, the output of workers, the ingenuity of engineers, the agility of diplomats, the resolve of civilians, the endurance of firefighters, and the intuition of code breakers. And all was vulnerable: infants and the infirm, schools, centuries-old churches, art masterpieces, and cities hundreds of years in the making.

The scales of fate now weighed an intolerant and vicious fascism against what was left of liberal democracies. The world was in the balance, and no one could yet say how the scales would tip.

CHAPTER ONE

PRELUDE

"Who is in charge of the clattering train?
The axles creak and the couplings strain; . . .
And the pace is hot, and the points are near,
And Sleep has deadened the driver's ear;
And the signals flash through the night in vain,
For Death is in charge of the clattering train."
—*Anonymous*[1]

In November 1918 Europe lay exhausted . . . and relieved. Exhausted owing to a debilitating and draining war and relieved because it was over.

What was then known in various stricken countries as the Great War, der Grosse Krieg, la Grande Guerre, la Granda Guerra, and Velikaia voina was the worst conflagration then known to humankind. Ten million soldiers and sailors had been killed and another six million crippled. Half of French men aged twenty to thirty-two had perished.[2] New and terrible weapons were unleashed. Both sides used chemicals—namely poison gas—to slay their enemies by the tens of thousands while common machine-gun bullets mowed down hundreds of thousands more. Germany bombed civilian London from the sky with blimps and fixed-wing aircraft. Submarines and mines from the silent depths of the oceans rent the hulls of warships, merchant ships, and passenger ships, blowing them to watery graves, all in the name of national advancement. The Great War was a war of empires, fought in a thousand places. Africans fought in the trenches for France and Hindus for Britain. English and German sailors died off the coasts of South America, Australians in Turkey, Siberians in European Russia, Belgians in Equatorial Africa, and Turks in Palestine.

Europe was relieved because it was over, at least on the surface. No war so horrific could be completely over. Civil war consumed Russia. Revolts and counterrevolts roiled Germany, where Communists tried to imitate the Bolsheviks, and violent men stormed just as hard to stop them. In the weeks after the armistice, violence, if not manifest, lay just beneath the quiet. By the tens of thousands, German soldiers were at first shocked and then outraged that they had fought so long and so hard only to lose their emperor, their government, and their comrades in vain; to have seen the deprivations of economic blockade wrench their families; and then to be told that they were to blame for the whole wretched mess. One of these soldiers, hospitalized near Berlin, had been blinded by chemical gas during a British attack at Ypres, Belgium. Although he had fought for four years and won his army's Iron Cross First Class for bravery, he broke down in anguish and tears at the news that Germany had asked for terms.[3] Just as thousands of his comrades, he believed a gigantic injustice had been done to the German people. Adolf Hitler would work for the rest of his life to avenge what he considered a gross and terrible travesty.

Older men, horrified by what the most advanced countries in the world could wreak upon one another, attempted by written word and organization to ensure that it would never happen again. The Versailles Treaty, as the various peace treaties are known, and the League of Nations were crafted to leash the ability of man to aggress against his neighbor. The principal treaty was meant to keep Germany—in many respects the largest, most technologically advanced, most militaristic, most envious, and thus most dangerous nation in Europe—from thrusting its armies out again in territorial belligerence. The Versailles Treaty, which was negotiated without German representatives present, stripped Germany of its colonies in Africa, China, and the Pacific and forbade it submarines, a military air force, a large navy, and a military draft. It limited the size of the German army to 100,000 men, which, without a draft, became an army of professional soldiers, and its officer class retained prestige and political influence. The treaty tore Germany in two, separating East Prussia from the bulk of the country and providing a corridor, known as the Danzig Corridor, for Poland's access to the Baltic Sea.

Moreover, the treaty called for huge war reparations paid to the victorious countries. To support this call for reparations, the Versailles Treaty included the so-called "war guilt" clause by which Germany would accept blame for the war. The German people, however, did not feel they had led Europe into the war, and so the clause gave no end of opportunity for agitators to stir resentment against the treaty, the countries that crafted it, and the German ministers unlucky enough to have eventually signed it. (One was murdered for his pains in 1921.) Germans in general did not accept the treaty, the borders specified in 1919–20, or even the amounts of the reparations finally presented by the Allies in 1921 as final. The recriminations against Germany sowed resentment among its people, most especially among the surviving soldiers. Even the Allies, after a time, felt some of the treaty's clauses should not be enforced.[4]

In addition the statesmen at Versailles in January 1919 and for the next year and a half had to deal with the dissolution of the Austro-Hungarian and Ottoman empires. They had to create entirely new nations, with the inevitable resettlements and resentments. For one, they created Czechoslovakia north of Austria and Hungry, giving it a sizable population of Germans along the western edges.

The defeated countries were not the only ones dissatisfied with the peace treaties. Italy felt poorly compensated for its war effort on the Allied side. China found nothing to like about the agreements. The Union of Soviet Socialist Republics (USSR) was shunted during the negotiations and resented the territorial outcome, let alone the notion of a cordon sanitaire of eastern European countries meant to buffer the threat of communism's spread toward western Europe.[5] The French were dismayed when the U.S. Senate refused to make any commitment for coming to France's defense in the event of another war with Germany.[6]

The Versailles Treaty and the League of Nations did collar Germany, but it could not leash the hearts of its people. German soldiers and their supporters could not accept that their nation's most magnificent instrument, the army, had been defeated on the field. So they lay their blame on the people and politicians in their own country who had called for the armistice and later agreed to the loathsome treaty. Theirs was the notion that the army, and thus the nation, had been stabbed in the back, and that without the perfidy of weak politicians, the army could have eventually triumphed. The German General Staff itself, however, had told the politicians that the German armed forces could not resist the Allies' armies should fighting resume and that they should therefore accept the treaty.[7] Meanwhile the blinded corporal, already a fierce racist since his early twenties who believed the Germanic people of the Austro-Hungarian Empire were meant to rule the lesser Slavs, was of like mind with thousands of other Germans when he vowed to renounce people believed to have betrayed the army.

Hitler was more or less a vagabond before and immediately after the war. In 1919 in Munich, Bavaria, he joined a small political association, the German Workers' Party, which one year later was known as the National Socialist German Workers' Party (NSDAP, or Nazi for short). Its goal was to build a mass movement stemming from the working class but without the international outlook woven into so many laboring-class political organizations. Rather, it would be fiercely nationalistic. The NSDAP was also committed to destroying democracy in Germany and returning glory to the army. In less than a year, Hitler had proven an effective speaker for the party and was in control of its propaganda. The party met in beer halls, attracting misfits and the discontented. In 1920 it enumerated twenty-five principles, among them a greater Germany that would comprise all Germans no matter what their present country, abrogation of the Versailles Treaty, and strong state control.[8]

The Germany in which the NSDAP fermented was a republic of more than twenty individual states, for example Prussia and Bavaria. It also advanced democratic law: universal suffrage for women as well as men, proportional representation, rights to referendum, and so forth. The people elected a president, who was the head of state. He in turn appointed the chancellor as chief executive, or the head of government. The chancellor ruled with the cabinet, which had to reflect the proportion of parties represented in the Reichstag, or the republic's congress in Berlin.[9] In national elections none of Germany's various parties could achieve a majority of representatives in the Reichstag, so a coalition government ran the country. On the left were Communists, and more to the center were the Social Democrats and the Catholic Center Party. On the right were various parties, including the anti-democratic NSDAP. The officer corps and the old aristocracy were generally rightists. The Weimar Republic, as political Germany was called, never enjoyed general support. The Communists looked to a revolution that would establish a dictatorship of the proletariat while many on the right despised democracy and favored a return of the Hohenzollern dynasty.

Two attempted revolutions rocked Germany shortly after the war. In December 1918 the Spartacists engineered a coup in Berlin on the model of the Bolshevik revolution in Russia. The republican government, the army, and an organization of disaffected former soldiers called the Freikorps fought back, killing and capturing the Spartacists. The two principal Spartacist leaders were then murdered while in police custody. The following year the radical Right attempted its own coup, with a Freikorps brigade occupying Berlin, later known as the Kapp Putsch. Trade unions called for a workers' strike, which took hold; Berlin ceased to function, and the effort failed.

Soon enough, however, rightists in Germany could look to a model of success. To their south Italy was wracked by war debts, depression, unemployment, and street fights between Communists and rightists. Benito Mussolini, a former Socialist and journalist, swept into Rome in 1922 and promised an end to the troubles. He set up what he called fascism, after *fasces,* a bundle of rods that was a symbol of state power in classical Rome. Mussolini's *fascisti* Blackshirts beat up striking workers and burned labor union offices. Mussolini rose to office nominally within the country's constitution, but upon achieving power, he wrested control for his party and himself (he called himself Il Duce, or the leader). Within a few years Italy was a one-party country whose government controlled the economy and fed the people less with economic progress than with illusions of recaptured glory.

France also struggled to rebuild itself and, ever mindful of a resurgent Germany, pressed persistently for reparations payments. Germany refused the French terms, so in 1923 the French army marched in to occupy the Ruhr Valley, where four-fifths of Germany's coal and steel were produced. German workers in the Ruhr struck, closing the mines and mills, and the German government supported them, going even so far as to print so much money that the country's currency, called the mark, became worthless. This move resulted in wiping out the debts of large industrial firms and thwarting reparations payments to France. For much of the country's middle and working classes, it also decimated their life savings and, worse, their faith in a republican government.

During these economic depredations, the Nazi Party gained favor. Hitler called the national government a "swindler and crook," adding, "We want a dictatorship."[10] Later in the year, when the national government called for accommodation with the French and a resumption of reparations, fresh cries arose against the ruling politicians. Thirty-four-year-old Hitler saw an opportunity to seize control of Germany just as Mussolini had seized Italy. First he would take over the government of Bavaria and then, with his bands of violent Nazis, march on Berlin. Hitler thus attempted the Beer Hall Putsch in late 1923. He and his band marched from a rallying point in a beer hall on to government buildings, but deadly gunfire from Bavarian security forces stopped them. Hitler was arrested, tried for treason in a trial that brought him and his ideas wide publicity, and was sentenced to five years in prison (though right wingers had a good history of having their terms reduced). He was sent to the Landsberg Prison, where he had a room of his own with a pleasant view of the Lech River and a comfortable life. He began to dictate to his aide Rudolf Hess what became known as the book *Mein Kampf* (*My Struggle*).

This work was a strange blend of autobiography, political philosophy, and commentary on history. To Hitler life was a struggle, and humans were fighters. Just as humans must fight for themselves, nations are fighting units and must strive for success among the other nations. To fight well Germans must keep themselves pure, that is, not mix with other races. In Hitler's view pacifism was bad. Jews, being international, tended to pacifism and had to be resisted. Youth had to be trained as soldiers; military-style obedience was to be more honored than intelligence. Communism was also considered international, like Jewry, and was thus an enemy. Italy and England were natural allies that could help in the struggle against Bolshevik Russia, from which Germany could expropriate lands. Selecting bits of nineteenth-century German philosophy, including parts of Nietzsche, Hitler espoused in *Mein Kampf* the notion of the superior person or leader—above common morality—who would guide the masses in the international struggle. Moreover people could be divided into two camps—the rulers and the ruled. Aryans were the greatest race and would be the rulers while others would live to support them, or so said Hitler in *Mein Kampf*. Most notably, when Hitler took office in 1933, *Mein Kampf* sold millions of copies. It was given as a gift for weddings and graduations, and its words were revered. From the time he wrote *Mein Kampf* to the day he died, Hitler did not deviate from the notions he committed to it.

When Hitler walked out of Landsberg Prison in December 1924, Germany was on the road to economic recovery. The disastrous inflation had ended, and new capital from the United States under the Dawes Plan was helping both to pay the war reparations and to rebuild industries.[11] Moreover the NSDAP was in disarray and many of its former leaders dispersed. Hitler kept writing *Mein Kampf*, but most Germans had little use for his Nazi Party. And in the ensuing months, the country's prospects continued to improve. In 1925 Germany normalized its relationship with the principal European powers by signing the Locarno treaties, which pledged peace among the nations. In 1926 Germany joined the League of Nations. Less than 3 percent of the nation's voters supported the NSDAP in the national elections of 1928.[12]

But the Nazi Party had a strong cadre, and its leader was more fanatical than ever about his destiny of leading Germany. Moreover Hitler had softened his radical image, no longer boasting of revolution by force but rather by working within the nation's constitution. He set about organizing a Nazi state within a state, establishing its own ministries and even its own army, known as the Sturmabteilung (SA, or roughly Assault Section). Indeed, by 1930, the SA, together with Hitler's Schutzstaffel (SS) "bodyguard," had more soldiers than the 100,000-man national army. And its propaganda was improving. Joseph Goebbels, an embittered man with a nimble mind and a limp, had a talent for using radio, symbols, and mass rallies to affect popular opinion.

Yet all of Goebbels's and Hitler's straining efforts to sway the German masses toward Nazi ideas would likely have come to naught save for the economic calamities that most notoriously erupted with Wall Street's collapse in late 1929. The misfortune was mirrored in Germany, where millions of people's life savings were wiped out and huge numbers of workers lost their jobs, with scant government programs to rectify either disaster. Businesses failed; hunger increased. No people suffered more at the hands of the economic hardships than the Germans.[13] But all this misfortune was a balm for Hitler, who wrote during the depth of the Depression, "Never in my life have I been so well disposed and inwardly contented as in these days. For hard reality has opened the eyes of millions of Germans to the unprecedented swindles, lies, and betrayals of the Marxist deceivers of the people."[14] Fear, uncertainty, and rage all welled in a populace desperate for a solution; Adolf Hitler offered himself as that solution.

Unable to stem the grim scourge of the Depression, in the summer of 1930, President Paul von Hindenburg dissolved the Reichstag and called for new elections that September. During the 1930 campaign, Hitler promised a stronger Germany, an end to reparations payments, a disavowal of the Versailles Treaty, a rooting out of corrupt officials (Hitler blamed Communists, Jews, and traitors), and a job and food for all Germans. These promises resonated among voters. More than six million cast ballots for the NSDAP (compared to 810,000 votes two years before), making it the second largest party in the new Reichstag and giving Hitler a prospect for the chancellorship. On the left the Communists also won increased support, with 4.6 million votes, while the center of the political spectrum shrank. Germany's politics increasingly narrowed to a conflict between the far left and the far right.

Now a successful rather than a marginal party, the resurgent NSDAP attracted the Prussian officer class, which welcomed the idea of a reinvigorated army, and the industrialists, who feared a Communist revolt more than radical nationalism. The officer class enjoyed prestige among the people, and the industrialists had money with which to fund the Nazi propaganda campaign among the citizenry. Both the officer class and the industrialists were wary of the Nazis' rowdiness and radicalism, but both groups believed they could keep Hitler under control for various reasons: the officer class was preternaturally arrogant, and the industrialists believed that their money and their boosting Hitler to power would make him beholden to them.

In a 1932 election, Hitler ran for president against the incumbent Hindenburg, although the old man's reelection was virtually assured. Hitler barnstormed the country, and the Nazis waged a tremendous propaganda campaign using film, posters, rallies, and loudspeakers mounted on trucks. Hindenburg received 49 percent of the vote to Hitler's 30 percent, while the Communist candidate received 13 percent. Because the president needed a majority of votes, a run-off election of the three candidates ensued. Hindenburg received 53 percent to Hitler's 37 percent. Thus the center and the republic were holding, if only barely, around the grand old Hindenburg, despite his slipping into senility. But the fragility of the republic was plain to many people, especially the principal politicians in Berlin. In back rooms they fostered various schemes for governing Germany, including ruling by presidential decree or bringing back a Hohenzollern heir. Communists and Nazis fought each other in the streets. In June in Prussia alone, street fighting claimed eighty-two lives, with four hundred wounded.

Reichstag elections, the third in 1932, were held on July 31. Hitler and the Nazis put on more staged rallies, with the result that the NSDAP took 13.7 million votes, or 37 percent. Now the largest party in the Reichstag, the Nazis had a plurality of members rather than a majority. Again the Reichstag and President Hindenburg could not form a working government, so elections were called for in November. The Nazis here polled 2 million fewer votes than earlier in the year while the Communists gained 750,000 more. In the ensuing weeks, two chancellors came and went. President Hindenburg was stymied and confused. In January 1933 he offered the chancellorship to the forty-three-year-old Adolf Hitler.

Hitler had long said he would gain power constitutionally and create the revolution second. Although the Nazis did not form a majority in the cabinet, or even fill its most powerful ministries, Hitler's first days as chancellor were ferocious. He outlawed Communist meetings and suppressed the Social Democrats either by decree or by SA-staged disruptions. The Nazis beat up trade union leaders and murdered people who actively opposed them. Old officials were removed from office and replaced with Nazi Party members.

Still this maneuvering was not enough. Hitler was constrained by the composition of the cabinet. He wanted dictatorial power, and to achieve that, he would have to claim an emergency. Within a month, he had one. Someone set fire to the Reichstag building. Almost certainly this arson was a plot hatched and executed by the Nazis, who were also ready with the response. Hitler and other top Nazis claimed that the Reichstag fire was the beginning of a Communist plot to take over Germany. The night of the fire, Hermann Göring shouted, "This is the beginning of the Communist revolution! Every Communist official must be shot where he is found."[15]

The next day Hitler persuaded the aging President Hindenburg to suspend civil rights. The decree allowed the national power (Hitler's chancellorship) to control the individual state governments and impose death sentences on people disturbing the peace. The SA, now many times larger than the country's army, broke into their enemies' homes, hauled them to prisons, and tortured and killed them. The Nazis stirred up a frenzy of fear about Communist insurrections.

Still, constitutional safeguards were in place. New elections were called for in March to assemble yet another Reichstag. In this election, Nazis polled highest, but more Germans voted against them—66 percent—than for them. The Nazis then teamed with some other rightists and arrested enough other delegates to pass an "enabling act" that gave Hitler's government extraordinary power for four years.

From that time Hitler was the dictator of Germany. He now had more control over Germany than Chancellor Otto von Bismarck or Emperor Wilhelm II ever had. No one could stand up to his concentration of power. Soon enough the other political parties were banned or had withered until only the Nazi Party remained. And still this consolidation was not enough. The Nazis invited the nation's important trade union leaders to Berlin for a Labor Day rally, then, while the unions' leaders were still in Berlin, shut down their offices around the country, appropriated their funds, and closed the unions. Many of the leaders were arrested. Collective bargaining was eliminated and strikes banned. Ordinary justice crumbled because the Nazis intimidated judges; murder went unpunished. Hitler also moved against Jews; he ordered a boycott of their businesses. In September and October, Hitler pulled Germany out of the League of Nations and the Geneva Disarmament Conference. Thus began the Nazi Revolution.

Brutal as this campaign was, many Nazi leaders wanted even more, the so-called second revolution. The Nazis had crushed the Left—the Communists and Social Democrats—and now some wanted to crush the Right, namely the industrialists, financiers, Prussian generals, and old aristocratic class. But here Hitler drew the line; he needed a modicum of order to consolidate his gains. Moving against such rightists would have been too risky. Moreover rearmament was already under way (begun under the previous government but championed by Hitler), and Hitler would have to sustain the army and industrialists if the rearming were to proceed apace. In fact it was his own SA that Hitler would have to fight. The SA's commander, Ernst Röhm, was a leader of the "second revolution" notion; moreover, he wanted the SA to supplant the old army and become a people's army under his control. The Prussian officer class was aghast; such an upheaval would be the end of them.

On June 30, 1934—known later as the Night of the Long Knives—Hitler, with the backing of the army, struck at the SA. More than 150 SA leaders were shot down. Röhm, Hitler's closest friend through the years of building the Nazi Party, was sent to prison and shot. Moreover, the nation's previous chancellor was shot dead, along with his wife, and the chancellor who had preceded this unfortunate saw his closest aides murdered. In a speech to the Reichstag later that summer, Hitler admitted ordering the bloody purge. Attempting to justify the execution of two politicians who had met with France's ambassador to Germany, he said, "When [such men] arrange . . . a meeting with a foreign statesman . . . and give orders that no word of this meeting shall reach me, then I shall have such men shot dead even when it should prove true that . . . they talked of nothing more than the weather."[16] Hitler acknowledged the summary execution of about eighty people, but the number killed possibly ran closer to a thousand. Men were murdered for knowing dark secrets of the Nazi past or to settle scores. A music critic was kidnapped and murdered because he was mistaken for a local SA leader.

When President Hindenburg died little more than a month later, in August 1934, Hitler arranged for the office of president and chancellor to be combined. He would be both the head of state and the head of government as well as the commander in chief of the armed forces. Then he abolished the title of president and had his title changed to Reich chancellor and führer. He required that all officers and men of the armed forces swear an oath of allegiance not to the country or to the constitution but to him, Adolf Hitler, personally. The code of honor for the officer class being what it was, such an oath was exceptionally hard to forswear or forsake. All of this accumulation of power was clearly unconstitutional, but much of Germany was beyond caring. The army and the industrialists supported Hitler; so did the discontented former soldiers and people thirsty for Germany to regain muscle in Europe. The rest were intimidated into submission.

Hitler and the Nazis set about making over Germany in their own image. In the fall of 1935, they imposed the Nuremburg Laws, removing citizenship from Jews—thus making them subjects—as well as outlawing marriage and intercourse between a Jew and an Aryan. The Nazis also applied race to science: if an idea stemmed from an Aryan German, it was good and right, but coming from a Jew, it was then bad and wrong. Even Albert Einstein's work was assailed. Stores often refused to sell Jews food or medicines. The Nazis cowed the Protestant and Catholic churches and arrested ministers who did not go along with these decrees. The Nazis burned books, not only of foreign authors such as Jack London and H. G. Wells, but also of such German authors as Thomas Mann and Erich Maria Remarque. Goebbels proclaimed at one book burning in front of the University of Berlin, "The soul of the German people can again express itself. These flames not only illuminate the final end of an old era; they also light up the new."[17] The Nazis replaced the paintings of Paul Cézanne, Vincent Van Gogh, and Henri Matisse with kitschy paeans to muscularity. The Nazi Party told the press what to publish and what editorials to write. Radio and film were leashed in order to serve Nazi aims. Textbooks were rewritten; teachers had to teach Nazi doctrine and take an oath of loyalty to the führer. The Hitler Youth indoctrinated teenage boys, training them in carrying heavy packs and marching with rifles.

In March 1935 Hitler announced conscription. Almost 600,000 youths were to be called up and trained in arms. The name for the armed forces under the Weimer Republic, or Reichswehr, was eliminated, and the reinvigorated armed forces under the Third Reich, or Wehrmacht, became "the school of military education of the German people."[18] Germany laid down the keels for the *Bismarck* and the *Tirpitz*, soon to be the largest battleships in the world. That same year Germany announced it possessed an air force as large as that of Britain. Understanding that the air, unlike the English Channel, was no difficult barrier to their enemies, the shaken British hastened to divert more resources to its Royal Air Force.

These were not the only storm clouds. Mussolini was moving from imposing fascism on Italy to expanding outside its borders. To avenge defeat at the Ethiopians' hands in 1896, aggrandize the country, and show increased muscle in the Mediterranean by puffing up its power in Africa,

Mussolini invaded Ethiopia from its colonies Eritrea and Italian Somaliland in 1935. The League of Nations attempted to stop the invasion but ultimately backed down for fear of a larger war. One result was that Italy, formerly an ally of Britain and France during World War I and a check against German movements south into Austria, became more allied with Germany. Austria and Czechoslovakia were thus caught between two fascistic states that were increasingly seeing themselves as allies. Germany looked less like a rogue country, and sunny Italy was becoming its close friend.

Elsewhere aggression was scorned but accommodated. Already on the Asian mainland, owing to its rule of Korea, Japan was eager for natural resources and seized parts of Manchuria in 1931. Faced with censure by the League of Nations, it quit that body in March 1933. Fascism gained ground, and democratic forms of government in Europe fell away. The ideals promulgated by the Versailles peace diplomats were crumbling. The examples of Italy and Germany showed that a nation could suppress social disorder and develop jobs for the unemployed, although at the price of restricted civil rights and of the jobs being in the armaments industry or military.

In early 1936 Hitler sent elements of the Wehrmacht into the Rhineland. Although this area belonged to Germany on the western side of the Rhine River, the Versailles and Locarno Treaties specified it as a demilitarized zone that was meant to shield France and Belgium from a German invasion. Here, on account of the military forces having seized the land, the Nazis violated the peace treaties even more flagrantly than before. And in doing so, they put more at stake than Germans marching on German land. If the army could fortify this border with France and Belgium, it would have little fear of attack from those quarters and could hold the fortifications with relatively few troops while attacking east or south. But the separate countries and the League of Nations did not order a military confrontation to roll back the Wehrmacht. Distracted by internal economic and political troubles and opposed to even the thought of another war in the region, they yielded.

Then in 1936 Spain fell into civil war, which quickly intensified into a struggle between fascist and antifascist doctrines. Republican Spanish had overthrown King Alfonso XIII and begun democratic and anticlerical reforms. Rightists resisted then took up arms after a 1936 electoral victory of

Republicans and leftists. The rest of the world was supposed to stay neutral in hopes of avoiding a spread of the fighting, but the rightists under army general Francisco Franco attracted arms and recruits from Germany and Italy while the leftists attracted arms and advisers from the Soviet Union. Spain became a testing ground not only for the weapons that industries were increasingly producing but also for the fortitude of competing political philosophies. Another effect was the strengthened ties among the nationalistic aggressor nations: Germany, Italy, and Japan. That October Germany and Italy formed the Rome-Berlin Axis, around which the world was meant to revolve. In November Germany signed the Anti-Comintern Pact with Japan aimed at containing communism. Italy signed almost a year later.

Through 1937 Hitler continued to build his military and strengthen the Nazis' grip on his country. Then late in the year he turned his attention to increasing the size of what he was calling Greater Germany, or the Third Reich.[19] The Austrians were largely a German people, so he would absorb Austria. An Austrian by birth himself, Hitler long advocated bringing all German people into one union, his Reich. Moreover, with Austria combined with Germany, Hitler would have Czechoslovakia half surrounded and would be pushing farther east and south in Europe. An Austrian Nazi Party had been at work in Austria for years and in fact had assassinated Chancellor Engelbert Dollfuss in 1934 during an abortive attempt to press Austria into the Reich that year. The Austrian government was friendly with Italy and quasi-fascist, though not especially popular, and many Austrians urged or would accede to a union with Germany. In early 1938 Hitler turned up the heat. The Austrian chancellor Kurt Schuschnigg tried to hold a plebiscite to judge the opinion of the Austrian people, but the Germans marched in before it could be held then conducted one themselves with predictable results. The Reich's seventy million people now included seven million more.

Hitler then set his sights on Czechoslovakia's German population, which was mainly living along the borders with Germany and Austria. Many of these ethnic Germans never felt much at home with the various other ethnic groups in the country and agitated for inclusion in the Reich. Indeed Czechoslovakia was a creature of the Versailles peace process, carved out of the old Austro-Hungarian Empire. Although self-determination—the opportunity for people to live in a country where they wanted to live—was a principle of the Versailles efforts, the Sudeten German problem was exceptional. Czechoslovakia was the most liberal and democratic country in the region. France had guaranteed its defense and so had Russia as long as the French acted. Moreover the Sudetenland had the second largest armaments industry in Europe at Skoda and tough mountain defenses against invasion. Giving the Sudetenland to Germany would give the Nazis the Skoda Works as well as the country's main border defenses, making a German invasion into what would be left of Czechoslovakia a foregone conclusion.

Negotiations proceeded through 1938 until Britain's prime minister Neville Chamberlain worked out an agreement with the Czechs in September. He presented it to Hitler, who then increased his demands. It seemed as if Germany and the surrounding powers would go to war over the defense of Czechoslovakia. Then Hitler invited Chamberlain, as well as representatives of France and Italy, to Munich for another round of negotiations. Neither Russia nor Czechoslovakia were asked to these negotiations or were represented. Neither Britain nor France, still lagging behind Germany in armed forces and the production of weapons, felt ready for war; in Britain especially, there was broad sentiment for a peaceful rather than a belligerent solution. Moreover Czechoslovakia, being in central Europe and half surrounded already by the Reich, would be difficult to defend. Accordingly Britain and France accepted Hitler's tougher demands for the guarantee that with most Germanic people back in the Reich, Hitler would then be satisfied and that his territorial aims would be finished. But the pact left Czechoslovakia practically defenseless. Three months into the new year of 1939, Hitler cast his army into the large remnant of Czechoslovakia, proclaiming that country a "protectorate" of the Reich. Now Czechoslovakia's entire manpower and other resources were his to exploit. The Sudeten Germans numbered about three million and the remainder of Czechoslovakia about seven million. Emboldened by these moves, Italy in April ordered elements of its military across the Adriatic Sea to seize Albania, a country in the Balkans northwest of Greece.

The March invasion of Czechoslovakia profoundly shocked Britain and France. They faced the ugly truth that Hitler was not the reasonable type of diplomat they were used to dealing with and that he would say anything and break any pact in order to expand the Reich. They saw his territorial ambitions were not quenched but still fevered and that what he had pronounced in *Mein Kampf* about slaves and masters and seizing land in the east were still his goals. The next time, whether France and Britain were ready or not, they would have to fight.

The next time came when Hitler agitated with Poland over the Danzig Corridor, the strip of land from the old borders of Poland to the city of Danzig (now Gdansk) on the Baltic. It gave Poland access to the sea, but it also separated East Prussia, which was historically and politically part of Germany, from the rest of Germany. Hitler wanted at least a portion of the corridor back, as well as the Germanic people within it, and to physically reconnect East Prussia to the Reich. Moreover he saw the Poles as Slavs, which to him were one of the inferior races that the master race of Aryans was meant to rule.

On the one hand, Poland was by no means a democracy—a "strong-man government" might be a better description—and it took a chunk of land from Czechoslovakia in the Sudetenland dismemberment as well. On the other hand, the sovereign nation of Poland had ties to France in hopes of confining German aggression. Indeed both France and Britain made guarantees for Poland's defense. In addition both had been in discussions with the Soviet Union, hoping that an agreement would box Hitler's aggressive impulses. But in late August, to the astonishment of the world (which believed them to be sworn enemies), Germany and the Soviet Union announced a nonaggression pact. The agreement renounced war between the two countries and secretly divided eastern Europe into German and Soviet zones of influence, leaving the Soviets a free hand for aggression westward into the Baltic states and Poland. Eight days later (September 1, 1939), Nazi Germany invaded Poland from Germany on the west, East Prussia on the north, and Czechoslovakia on the south.

Britain and France honored their word and declared war on Germany within days, but they could do little and in fact did little. Poland was difficult to reach. French troops advanced a bit into Germany from the west then retreated. Britain proclaimed a blockade of Germany and little more. Russia attacked Poland on September 17. The Poles fought for weeks, but the Wehrmacht and Russian attacks were too much. The German Air Force, the Luftwaffe (literally air weapon), smashed military supply points and towns. By September 15 the Wehrmacht had Warsaw surrounded. Two weeks later Poland was conquered by Germany and the Soviet Union.

Nor were these the only German successes during the new war. In September a German U-boat sank the British aircraft carrier *Courageous*. Another penetrated the main British naval base at Scapa Flow, Scotland, to sink the battleship *Royal Oak* in October. The German pocket battleship *Admiral Graf Spee* sank British shipping in the Atlantic.[20] The latter was especially troubling because Britain lived on imports. In 1939 the nation required fifty-five million tons of supplies from across the oceans. For this shipping it had the largest merchant fleet in the world, or more than three thousand ships, of which about twenty-five hundred were at sea on any given day. Britain imported all of its petroleum and half of its food, including huge amounts of North American wheat.[21]

After the Polish campaign of September and October and through the winter of 1939–40 was the Phony War, during which various countries tried to intervene and negotiate a settlement, though to no avail. Launching the Winter War, the Soviet Union invaded Finland on November 30 to broaden its defenses of Leningrad and gain an advantage on the Baltic, but the Finns resisted fiercely, and the Soviets' Red Army was seen to have been weakened by Joseph Stalin's 1937–39 purges of the officer corps. Meanwhile, the British sent four hundred thousand men and five hundred airplanes to France to bolster the French-Belgian border. Belgium was a neutral country, but it was generally supposed Germany would ignore that neutrality and attack through it anyway to reach northeastern France. Belgium, for fear of provoking Germany in what it already understood as a threatening situation, would not allow French and British troops into its country or coordinate its defense with their military forces. For their part the French and British armies were set to enter Belgium as soon as the Germans did so, breaking Belgium's neutrality. The former meant to defend France along Belgium's fields and canals. Thus, the best of two armies waited along the French-Belgian border, feeling that the Ardennes and the Maginot Line areas to the south were relatively safe. The Ardennes of Luxembourg and southern Belgium was rugged forest country with poor, narrow roads thought inhospitable to modern army movements, and the Maginot Line extending the length of the common border of France and Germany was an exceptionally strong line of man-made defenses. Furthermore, Britain and France worked on an agreement by which they were locked into an inseparable alliance. Neither could make a separate peace with Germany without releasing the other from its pledge. They signed this agreement on March 28 and set up what they called the Anglo-French Supreme War Council.[22]

Hitler had long set his sights on the West. The Soviets, at least for a time, were contented on the eastern side of Poland. As much as Hitler eventually wanted to crush Bolshevism, if he did so now he would leave his western borders open to France and Britain. He felt his best choice was either to knock France and Britain out of the war or neutralize them with negotiated settlements and then turn his attention east. Indeed he had a plan for attacking France through Holland, Belgium, and Luxembourg that was akin to the old World War I plan, with the benefit that it could gain territory from which the Luftwaffe's aircraft could intimidate Britain. Hitler also looked to attack Norway and, by virtue of being in the way, Denmark in order to secure delivery of their iron ore, which Germany needed to make steel for its armaments industries.

But just before the Wehrmacht was scheduled in January to strike through the Low Countries, two Wehrmacht majors flying near Germany's northwestern border became lost in bad weather and landed in Belgium with the battle plans on their airplane. The majors could not ignite the plans quickly enough, and the Belgians recovered them. Hitler was furious and delayed the attack on the West, but he launched the Denmark-Norway operation on April 9. Meanwhile he and his generals devised a new plan for the West. They would feint into the Low Countries, drawing the French and British armies northwest into Belgium. Then they would push their armored divisions through the Ardennes, bursting into France south of the Allied armies. They would then race for the English Channel, isolating the Allied armies from Paris and other French forces.

In April the Norway operation went well for the Germans. They occupied Oslo and made landings up the western coast. The British and French made counterlandings of their own, and the British threw in the Royal Navy against the German Kriegsmarine. But by the end of the month, both German goals—the rugged western coast, which would serve as a launching point for its warships to the Atlantic Ocean, and the iron ore region around Narvik in the north—were secure. Russia praised the invasion and helped the Germans in the vicinity of Narvik.[23]

This development was more than the British Parliament could stand. Support for Neville Chamberlain's war leadership diminished. Meanwhile, gaining popularity was Winston Churchill, a tested wartime administrator from World War I, a Cassandra who had warned against Nazi intentions since 1933, and the current chairman of the Ministerial Defense Committee.

On May 10, with about three million men and twenty-four hundred tanks, Nazi Germany invaded Luxembourg, Holland, and Belgium; the Allies could put up about one-tenth more men and one-sixth more tanks against them.[24] Belgian neutrality having been broken, strong elements of the French Army and the British Expeditionary Force (BEF) marched into Belgium to stop the Germans. The Phony War was over.

In Britain Parliament voiced an end of confidence in Chamberlain, who resigned. The candidates for the new prime minister were Churchill and Charles Wood, Lord Halifax, who shortly took himself out of the running because he felt that during this crisis the prime minister should be from the House of Commons (as Churchill was) rather than the House of Lords (as Halifax was). King George VI sent for Churchill.

Even by this early period of 1940, Churchill was a remarkable blend of soldier, politician, and man of letters. Born in privilege to a British politician and his rich American wife, he was educated at the Royal Military Academy at Sandhurst and became a cavalry officer in 1895. He saw combat in India and the Sudan, where he killed men in a cavalry charge. Captured in the Boer War, he escaped and became a minor celebrity in Britain. He ran for Parliament and won a seat in 1900. Soon he was appointed to higher offices: home secretary (1910), first lord of the Admiralty (1911–15), minister of munitions (1919–21), secretary of state for war and secretary of state for air (1919–21), and chancellor of the Exchequer (1924–29).

All the while he was producing memoirs, correspondence, speeches, and volumes of history. He had discovered a talent in school for crafting a sentence, and he memorized large swathes of poetry, even historical texts. His writing output was prodigious. He composed a two-volume history of his father, *Lord Randolph Churchill* (1905); a four-volume history of World War I, *The World Crisis* (1923–29); and a six-volume history of his ancestor the Duke of Marlborough, *Marlborough: His Life and Times* (1933–38). He was also at work on volumes called *History of the English-Speaking Peoples* when the war interrupted his writing.

All of his previous experiences and work served him well, especially his work with words, as he took the reins of office May 10, 1940. Even his minor efforts could be stirring. Several months earlier, in January 1940, he finished a speech in Manchester on the war in the North Atlantic:

> Come then, let us to the task, to the battle, to the toil—each to our part, each to our station. Fill the armies, rule the air, pour out the munitions, strangle the U-boats, sweep the mines, plough the land, build the ships, guard the streets, succour the wounded, uplift the downcast and honour the brave. Let us go forward together in all parts of the Empire, in all parts of the Island. There is not a week, nor a day, nor an hour to lose.[25]

Britain had learned where to look for inspiration during its time of exceptional trial.

The Wehrmacht's attack on the West was swift and effective. Paratroopers landed outside Rotterdam and the Hague, and in twenty-four hours they captured the key defensive work of Belgium, Fort Eben-Emael. The Luftwaffe made devastating attacks on Rotterdam. Still the first two days of the invasion went about as the French and British expected, with a general thrust into Belgium along the lines of the German invasion there in 1914. And, as on the 1914 model, the French and the British expected to stop the Germans in this region or at least slow them there so they could be stopped short of Paris.

But within another two days, the Allies could see that their expectations might have been illusions. On May 13 German armored divisions— they called their tanks panzers from an old German word meaning armor—having woven through the narrow roads of the Ardennes forest, crossed the Meuse River at Sedan, France. Allied eyes looked south at the breakthrough but had scarce manpower in the region. The following day the Allied air forces attempted to bomb the Meuse River bridges used by the advancing Germans, but German antiaircraft batteries destroyed almost half the force, and streams of German troops continued moving into France. In Holland, where Dutch resistance stiffened outside Rotterdam, the Luftwaffe brought home to northwestern Europe what they had visited upon Guernica, and Warsaw: the airmen carpet bombed the city, destroying about a square mile and twenty-five thousand homes, in a deliberate attempt to terrorize the Dutch into surrender.[26] The destruction of Rotterdam's core broke Dutch resistance, allowing the Wehrmacht to continue its advance.

On this same day, Churchill rose before the House of Commons for the first time as prime minister. After lamenting to the members that he had nothing to offer them "but blood, toil, tears, and sweat," he rumbled on:

> We have before us an ordeal of the most grievous kind. We have before us many, many months of struggle and suffering. You ask, what is our policy? I say it is to wage war by land, sea, and air. War with all our might and with all the strength God has given us, and to wage war against a monstrous tyranny never surpassed in the dark and lamentable catalogue of human crime. That is our policy. You ask, what is our aim? I can answer in one word. It is victory . . . victory in spite of all terrors—victory, however long and hard the road may be, for without victory there is no survival. . . . No survival for the British Empire, no survival for all that the British Empire has stood for, no survival for the urge, the impulse of the ages, that mankind shall move forward toward his goal.[27]

On May 15, the French premier Paul Reynaud telephoned Churchill to say, "We are beaten. We have lost the battle." Churchill was astonished, thought it could not be so, and made plans to fly to Paris. By May 16, as planned, the Germans streaming out of the Ardennes found themselves in a virtually undefended territory northeast of Paris. They could have raced toward the capital but instead turned northwest toward the English Channel. Churchill landed in Paris, where he could smell the smoke of state papers being burned. The British prime minister, still believing the Germans could be stopped short of Paris as was done in 1914, was shocked to learn from the French army commander, Maurice Gamelin, that no reserves could be massed against the Germans who were moving in a wide column south of the Allied armies in Belgium. Gamelin had instead placed his reserves behind the Maginot Line or in the north, where they had moved into Belgium.[28] Churchill flew back to London on the seventeenth. One of his measures when he returned that day was to appoint the Chamberlain loyalist and former foreign secretary Sir Samuel Hoare as ambassador to Spain, an exceptionally important post for which Hoare proved able.

Also on this day, the seventeenth, Col. Charles de Gaulle led a counterattack of French armor against the swift-moving Germans but could make little progress. The panzers were only temporarily checked and continued their drive toward the channel ports. In Belgium, Brussels fell to the Germans, who seized Antwerp on the eighteenth. On that day and two days later, Churchill telegraphed U.S. president Franklin D. Roosevelt, practically begging for war supplies. He also warned Roosevelt that a defeated Britain might have to bargain away its fleet, leaving the Atlantic to the Nazis.[29] On the twenty-first the British in Belgium counterattacked the German panzer thrust from the north; indeed, it began well but ended poorly. The next day Churchill again flew to Paris in hopes of helping coordinate a combined French-British counterattack set for May 26.

On May 22 the British Parliament passed the Emergency Powers (Defence) Act, making Britain a virtual dictatorship. The act stipulated that the government (at the will of the king) could enact laws "requiring persons to place themselves, their services and their property at the disposal of His Majesty, as appears necessary to defence or maintaining public order." The government could set wages and "direct any person to perform any service required." It could seize property, direct shipping, dictate what farmers could plant, and imprison people without trial. All these things the government actually did but in moderation. The government could control banks and demand access to a company's books. It set the tax rate for excess profits at 100 percent. Unlike federal law in the United States, parliamentary law in the United Kingdom is supreme and unchecked. People had no civil rights except by tradition. Reported Churchill, "Both the [House of] Commons and the [House of] Lords with their immense Conservative majorities passed [the Emergency Powers Act] unanimously through all its stages in a single afternoon, and it received the Royal Assent that night."[30]

These were dark days indeed. Those who knew the military situation—the French and British publics were not informed how desperate it was—could envision utter catastrophe, with France defeated and Britain stripped of its land army. They had to wonder what sort of terms Hitler might offer to end the fighting. Churchill believed his country was not yet to such a point and that to allow the public or the soldiers to think they were fighting only for negotiation points would have devastating effects on morale. At a cabinet meeting on May 26, Churchill said to the other ministers, "If this long island story of ours is to end at last, let it end only when each one of us lies choking in his own blood upon the ground." The cabinet concurred, and there would, for the time being, be no negotiation with Hitler on terms for peace.[31]

Meanwhile, the German panzer advance had reached the channel, cutting off 250,000 men of the French First Army and 250,000 men of the BEF from the bulk of the French armies to the south covering Paris.[32] Further north the Germans pressed the Belgian Army very heavily on the left flank of the BEF, which was commanded by Gen. John Verecker, Lord Gort. On the twenty-fifth, anticipating the Belgian Army's surrender and despairing of little organization for the combined French-British counterattack that had been scheduled for the twenty-sixth, Gort called off the BEF's participation in such an attack. He decided his best course was a retreat to Dunkirk and evacuation by sea.

Part of the best of the British Army held the ports of Boulogne and, closer to Dunkirk, Calais. When the Germans reached the sea between Calais and Dunkirk, the Boulogne defenders resisted for three days and then were evacuated by sea on the twenty-third. Holding Calais became critical because the Germans who were engaged in fighting its defenders could not turn toward Dunkirk. Day after day the Queen Victoria Rifles and other notable units held out in the old port city. Eventually Royal Navy destroyers were ordered to pull them out, but Churchill, in consultation with others countermanded the evacuation plan. Instead he ordered the British soldiers to fight on and give the men at Dunkirk more time. To commanding officer Brigadier Claude Nicholson, he sent a message: "Every hour you continue to exist is of the greatest help to the BEF. Government has therefore decided you must continue to fight. Have greatest possible admiration for your splendid stand. Evacuation will not (repeat not) take place and craft required for above purpose are to return to Dover." Churchill later reported he felt physically sick giving the order.[33] The defenders held out until overrun by the Germans on May 26. Many tried to escape to Dunkirk but were rounded up. Nicholson surrendered in the last fight and died in a prisoner of war camp in 1943.

The Germans, for centuries having focused on their land armies, believed they had trapped the French and British against the sea. The British, being an island nation, saw the ocean less as a barrier than a highway, with plenty of seamen at home—both naval and civilian—to offer transportation. Still, the situation was desperate. On May 27 Churchill "would not have wagered on more than 50,000 at a maximum" who could be taken back to England.[34] The call went out for Royal Navy destroyers to retrieve soldiers at the Dunkirk piers and for smaller vessels of any sort to take on men from the beaches themselves then ferry them to larger vessels at sea. Trawlers, torpedo boats, hospital ships, tug boats, and yachts—almost seven hundred craft of all sizes, four hundred of them small[35]—plied the waters toward Dunkirk.

That same day, outside the little town of Le Paradis, elements of the SS Totenkopf, or "Death's Head," Division captured a hundred men of the Royal Norfolk Regiment. The SS took the Englishmen outside a barn and machine-gunned them. Ninety-seven were killed in the massacre. Two escaped from under the corpses, and later a regular German army unit took them as prisoners of war (POWs).[36]

On May 28 about eighteen thousand men were carried off from the Dunkirk piers and beaches. The following day about forty-seven thousand men were rescued.

The evacuation was aided not just by calm seas but also by a two-day halt of German panzer attacks, suggested by one of the Wehrmacht's chief generals and approved in person by Hitler himself, who had left Berlin for military headquarters closer to the front. Various reasons are given for this halt, which otherwise may have allowed the panzers to capture the troops at Dunkirk. One is that Hitler wanted the bulk of the BEF to escape because he believed negotiations over peace would go better. Another was that Hitler feared the panzers might face unacceptable losses in the marshy ground near the coast. A third reason was that the panzers were already breaking down and needed refitting before turning south on Paris. Finally, some say that Hitler accepted Göring's argument that the Luftwaffe could destroy the trapped French and British using aircraft alone. Whatever the reason or reasons, the panzers' pause allowed the trapped British troops to strengthen their defenses and stream more men toward the waiting boats. While the British Royal Air Force (RAF) battled Luftwaffe bombers in the skies overhead, on May 30 the French and British evacuated fifty-four thousand men and sixty-eight thousand men the following day.

On May 31 Churchill, along with his chief military advisers, again flew to Paris. He reported that the Norway venture should be given up, and the French concurred. He said that his naval people told him that if they took 200,000 men out of Dunkirk, they could count it a miracle. He flew back to London the following morning.

Meanwhile, it was still hell on the Dunkirk beaches. Luftwaffe planes bombed the men on the sands and machine-gunned them in the water, where they waded in shoulder-deep water and waited for the boats to pick them up. The wounded were left in ambulances, abandoned and forgotten. What were known as Casualty Clearing Stations were overwhelmed.

One orderly found himself hoping some wounded would die so he could clear them out for others. Many did. The orderly reported, "I never saw any man who showed signs of fright, or who struggled to live. They just slipped away, as if they were relieved and happy to go. . . . One moment they were [lying] silent with grey tortured faces. The next they looked placidly up, and the pain vanished from their eyes."[37]

CHAPTER TWO

JUNE

Collapse

"Hitler knows he will have to break us in
this island or lose the war."
—*Winston Churchill, June 18, 1940*

Bright and clear weather opened June in northern France. The French First Army, the British Expeditionary Force, and elements of the surrendered Belgian Army huddled in an ever-shrinking perimeter around the piers and beaches of the channel port of Dunkirk. They were defeated, and they moved into evacuation vessels as fast as they could. The German Wehrmacht, toughened by six weeks of fighting in Poland, were everywhere triumphant. Bolstered by a military plan that was working perfectly, guided by tacticians who had wrenched warfare away from massed charges meant to gain mere yards per day into motorized strikes meant to gain kilometers per hour, and preceded by dive-bombers that wrecked enemy assembly areas and supply depots, the German war machine hammered the Allied defensive perimeter with increasing fury.

But the defenses, though shrinking, did not crack. Moreover, the Luftwaffe's bombing attacks were less severe than either propagator or target supposed they would be. The sands of the Dunkirk beaches into which the bombs fell absorbed much of the explosions, and casualties were low. Vessels large and small still boarded men from the quays and beaches, taking 26,000 on June 2, while the Luftwaffe and the RAF battled for air supremacy overhead. It was the last day men could be taken off in daylight.

On June 3 they were only removed at night. On the fourth, the Germans were practically on the beaches, but still boats boarded 26,000 French soldiers. In all, 338,000 of the more than 500,000 men caught in the Germans' trap escaped to the English shore.[1]

Here was a profound turn of fate. The British, the French, and the Germans all knew that but for a few shifts of events—the weather, for one, favoring the evacuation with calm seas, and the panzer halt order, for another—the Allied soldiers could have been forced to surrender. And at Dunkirk was the cream of the British professional army, including the officer corps trained through the 1930s. Bernard Montgomery commanded the Third Division and got away in the evacuation. So did the commander of the First Division, Harold Alexander, who later, like Montgomery, would become a field marshal. Alan Francis Brooke, later chief of the Imperial General Staff, commanded the II Corps and also escaped. Without the 250,000 regular BEF soldiers, England would have had few men of professional arms to resist a German landing. Further, without the professional officer corps represented at Dunkirk, the British army would have been far slower to build itself to any sort of offensive capacity against the Germans.

Still the Dunkirk toll was fearsome. The Germans sank by air bombing or naval attack 6 destroyers and damaged 19 of 39 engaged,[2] and in all they sank 226 vessels, including small craft. Far worse were the equipment losses to the British Army. The evacuation rule was "men before materiel," but it meant the savaged army arrived in England stripped of its vehicles and weapons. In the rush to rescue the men, the BEF abandoned 475 tanks, 90,000 rifles, 38,000 vehicles, 1,000 pieces of heavy artillery, and 400 anti-tank guns. The army was in England, but their weapons were in France with the Germans. Churchill wrote of it later: "Never has a great nation been so naked before her foes."[3]

Here indeed was a stunning Wehrmacht victory. It had not yet conquered France, but it had outwitted the premier fighting forces of the French and the British. It had driven them back to the channel and forced them to flee across it. The remainder of the French force between the Germans and Paris was accordingly weakened and demoralized. France, in possession of the largest army in Europe, was reeling. Its allies, the Dutch and Belgians, had surrendered. And the British were in full retreat.

On the last day of the Dunkirk evacuation, June 4, the British House of Commons assembled. Churchill had the task of strengthening its members' resolve. He was equal to it. He spoke to the people's representatives for twenty minutes, explaining the evacuation and putting as good a face on it as he could. He said Britain was prepared "to fight if need be for years, if need be alone." He concluded:

> Even though large tracts of Europe and many old and famous States have fallen or may fall into the grip of the Gestapo and all the odious apparatus of Nazi rule, we shall not flag or fail. We shall go on to the end, we shall fight in France, we shall fight in the seas and the oceans, we shall fight with growing confidence and growing strength in the air, we shall defend our island, whatever the cost may be, we shall fight on the beaches, we shall fight on the landing-grounds, we shall fight in the fields and in the streets, we shall fight in the hills; we shall never surrender, and even if, which I do not for a moment believe, this island or a large part of it were subjugated and starving, then our Empire beyond the seas, armed and guarded by the British Fleet, would carry on the armed struggle, until, in God's good time, the New World, with all its power and might, steps forth to the rescue and liberation of the Old.[4]

Indeed the New World was beginning to stir, if not jumping to the rescue. The day before, June 3, the U.S. Army chief of staff George C. Marshall approved a list of obsolete U.S. weapons to be sold to Britain. These included nine hundred field guns, eighty thousand machine guns, and five hundred thousand rifles manufactured in 1917–18 that had been packed in grease and stored ever since.[5] By June 11 British ships were loading them from the Raritan Arsenal docks southwest of New York City.

Meanwhile in Britain, there reigned a shallow euphoria. Once the men of the BEF were saved, the Dunkirk evacuation took on the aura of a sort of victory. Further, the evacuation was not seen as the end of the fighting in France. There was still the supposition that the French and British could stop the Germans short of Paris just as in 1914. Indeed French soldiers brought to southern England from Dunkirk were hastened to France further west and thrown into the front lines again northeast of Paris. In addition Churchill sent two divisions, the Fifty-Second Lowland and the First Canadian (neither of which had not been at Dunkirk), to France to bolster the French defenses.[6]

The situation on June 5 was similar to much of what occurred in World War I. The Germans were poised along the Somme River, which for fifty miles ran parallel to the Seine sixty miles to the southwest, and along the Aisne River stretching to the east. Opposing them were mainly the French Army with elements of the British. From the channel down to the northern end of the Maginot Line, the French still set 1.5 million soldiers to hold the Germans at bay.[7]

On June 5 the Germans struck in the northern sector of the Somme front opposite Paris. Pressing the attack were their panzers, refitted and repaired for this new offensive. On the same day, they broke the defenses on the far side of the Somme and pressed toward Rouen, which sits on the Seine between Paris and the channel port of Le Havre. The Wehrmacht pressed their successes. Its military units proved nimble and quick to respond to changing circumstances, while the British and French suffered from poor coordination. In the south two German panzer corps attacked toward Chalons to get behind the armies of the Maginot Line. Some French units fought stubbornly, but others cared little for the struggle and capitulated without much resistance.

On June 8 the German battle cruisers *Gneisenau* and *Scharnhorst* attacked and sank two destroyers and the British aircraft carrier *Glorious*, which was evacuating British men and supplies from Norway. Of almost sixteen hundred men, only forty-three survived. Lost as well on the *Glorious* were two squadrons of aircraft and all but two of their pilots.[8] The captain of the *Glorious* did not have scout planes up and was taken by surprise when the *Gneisenau* and *Scharnhorst's* guns started booming. He went down with his ship.

Near the channel the French IX Corps and the British Highland Division were in danger of being cut off from the remainder of the Allied forces after the German spearhead to Rouen. Days went by with no order that would have allowed them safe withdrawal down the coast to Le Havre. The Germans surrounded forty-six thousand of them west of Dieppe at Saint-Valery and within days forced their surrender. Thirty-eight thousand French and eight thousand British were taken prisoner along with four division commanders.⁹ Amid a series of military disasters for the French and the British, this one was a standout.

On June 10 Italy declared war on France and Great Britain, jarring again the balance of power and strategic outlook in Europe, the Mediterranean, and northern Africa. Western leaders had expected Italy's aggression for some time but had worked against it and hoped Mussolini would refrain from belligerency. Churchill had written to Mussolini in mid-May, reminding him of past British-Italian accord and urging him to a peaceful course: "Down the ages above all other calls comes the cry that the joint heirs of Latin and Christian civilisation must not be ranged against one another in mortal strife. Hearken to it, I beseech you in all honour and respect, before the dread signal is given. It will never be given by us."¹⁰ Mussolini's written answer two days later hearkened instead both to British offenses Italy suffered during the Ethiopian crisis of 1935 and to Italy's treaties with Germany, which he said guided Italian policy.

France had reason to fear war with Italy also. Italy would likely try to attack in the southeast when French armies were already severely pressed in the northeast against Germany. Italy would also threaten French territories in North Africa, and the Italian Navy would challenge the French Navy in the Mediterranean. On May 26 both Britain and France had asked President Roosevelt to appeal to Mussolini that he had more to gain by maintaining peace than by waging war. Roosevelt agreed and did so that day, but Mussolini rebuffed the message the next day. From this time on, Churchill and his military advisers thought Mussolini was likely to enter the war if he believed Germany was winning, thereby making it easier to snatch spoils at the peace table from France and perhaps the British Empire. Accordingly, the British looked to measures that would discourage Italy and get it to quickly cease activities if it ever entered the war. One move was to seize Italian warships, another to bomb industrial sites in Turin and Milan.

As soon as Italy declared war on Britain and France, it attacked French defenses both along the Riviera and farther north in the Alpine passes. Although French forces were stretched on account of the fighting around Paris and were outnumbered by Mussolini's legions, the Italians made no progress. Soon it was apparent that the French here had less to fear from the Italians on their front than the advancing German columns descending to their rear from behind the Maginot Line.

Britain could well dread war with Italy. Britain's route to the Suez Canal—that is, its principal route to India, Singapore, and Hong Kong—was compromised not only by the now dangerous Strait of Sicily but also by Italian Libya, which neighbored British Egypt in North Africa; by Italian-conquered Ethiopia along the Red Sea; and by Italian Somalia at the Gulf of Aden. Britain seized what ships it could at British naval stations, then bombed Turin and Milan. On the eleventh Italy bombed British-held Port Sudan and Aden at the mouth of the Red Sea from Italy's possessions in East Africa, and from the home country it bombed the British island of Malta near the Strait of Sicily.

Italy's entry into the war caused vexations in the United States as well. Presidential and congressional elections were less than six months away. Roosevelt had not yet decided to run for a third term—no previous president had ever served more than two—but he well understood that the Democratic Party and the Democratic nominee would be loath to lose the Italian American vote. To this time Roosevelt had been reluctant to speak harshly about Italian saber rattling, but when he received the news about Italy, he was on his way from Washington to the University of Virginia in Charlottesville to address the graduating class. He inserted into his speech, "On this tenth day of June, 1940, the hand that held the dagger has struck it into the back of its neighbor." The president went on to say, "We will extend to the opponents of force the material resources of this nation, and at the same time we will harness and speed up the use of those resources in order that we ourselves in the Americas may have equipment and training equal to the task of any emergency and every defense."[11]

These words were heartening to the British and French and encouraged them to think that the United States might soon enter the fighting, which from the Allied side grew increasingly dismal. Paris was threatened, and on the day Italy declared war, the French government abandoned the capital, setting out for Tours about 120 miles southwest on the Loire River. On the same day, Premier Reynaud cabled Roosevelt, asking for American aid in its fight against Germany.

On June 11 Churchill flew to France for the fourth time since May and headed to Briare, near Orléans, about halfway to Tours from Paris. Accompanying him were Secretary of State for War Anthony Eden and Churchill's two prominent military advisers, John Dill and Hastings Ismay.

They met Reynaud, Marshal Henri Philippe Pétain, and seventy-three-year-old French commanding general Maxime Weygand in a chateau that had a single telephone, which was in a bathroom. Also attending was the young Charles de Gaulle, whose spirited armored attack two weeks earlier had helped elevate him to undersecretary of national defense. The French briefed the British on the military situation, which they said was grim indeed. Churchill urged the French armies to defend Paris house by house because doing so would grind down German armies. Pétain rejected this notion, saying a ruined Paris would not affect the outcome. Weygand, too, was pessimistic. Indeed, later in the day Weygand ordered Paris an open city and began pulling French troops out.[12] Reynaud talked of a French redoubt in Brittany, to be supplied from the sea by Britain, and of holding out against the German army.[13]

Weygand argued that the Brittany redoubt idea would not stand militarily. He said the critical time of the battle against Germany had arrived. He asked the British to send every available aircraft, particularly the best British fighter aircraft, of which there were two types: Hurricanes and the faster Spitfires. Churchill had to refuse. The British cabinet had recently agreed with the man in charge of the RAF's Fighter Command, Air Chief Marshal Hugh Dowding, that Britain had to retain at least 25 fighter squadrons (of about 12 aircraft each) to defend itself against German invasion. In any event, Britain was losing 75 of 261 fighter aircraft sent to France since June 5. Another 120 had to be destroyed on the ground by British crews for lack of parts or fuel. Since the German attack toward the Seine on June 5, the Royal Air Force had lost 25 percent of its strength.[14]

Churchill urged greater resistance to stop the Germans as the French had done in 1914. But the French military chiefs said the roads were so loaded with refugees and government and military control were crumbling so rapidly that a stiffening resistance was practically impossible. Churchill suggested continuing the fighting in the country's mountainous regions or from North Africa. Reynaud told Churchill privately that Pétain believed France should call for an armistice. Weygand tended that way as well. Both Weygand and Pétain were of an officer class that feared a collapsed and undisciplined army, such as the one in Russia in 1917 that fueled the Communist revolution, and that also fostered Weygand and Pétain's mistrust of Britain.[15] Churchill continued to urge French resistance until the United

States could join the battle. But he was also anxious about the French fleet. Before he left for England, he took aside the commanding French admiral, Jean Darlan, and said, "Darlan, you must never let them have the French fleet." The Frenchman vowed he would never allow it.

Churchill took off for England in the morning. Below, he could see Le Havre burning, and his aircraft had to dodge German planes.[16]

The next day, June 13, Churchill flew back to France again. This time the French government had reached Tours. Weygand reported that the French Army was exhausted and just about broken. Reynaud, saying France had given its all, asked the British government to release France from its pledge not to seek a separate peace with Germany. Churchill conferred for a half hour with two British ministers who had accompanied him, then told Reynaud that Britain could not grant this request. He suggested Reynaud cable Roosevelt again and ask for U.S. intervention as the only way to save France. Reynaud agreed and a cable was sent.

Before the meeting ended, Churchill asked Reynaud for a favor. France held more than four hundred German pilots shot down by French and British fliers since May 10. Churchill wanted them turned over to the British so British fliers would not have to face these experienced men again in the skies over England. Reynaud promised he would deliver the pilots to the British, although in the speed and confusion of the ensuing ten days, he never did. Churchill with his entourage flew back to England.

When Churchill landed in London, U.S. ambassador to Britain Joseph Kennedy showed him President Roosevelt's reply to Reynaud's similar appeal of June 10.[17] The president said the United States would do all in its power to supply the democracies with matériel to continue the struggle. The message was not a declaration of war, but it was far more than a strictly neutral country could declare, and Reynaud wanted the letter made public. Churchill cabled Roosevelt in support: "Mr. President, I must tell you that it seems to me absolutely vital that this message should be published tomorrow, June 14, in order that it may play the decisive part in turning the course of world history. It will, I am sure, decide the French to deny Hitler a patched-up peace with France. He needs this peace in order to destroy us and take a long step forward to world mastery."[18] In the same letter, Churchill again appealed to Roosevelt for several dozen old U.S. destroyers—he had first done so in mid-May—because the British fleet was stretched thin while protecting both the southeast coast against invasion and the shipping lanes to the west for supplies and food.

Roosevelt agreed to make his reply to Reynaud public, but then his State Department talked him out of it as being too radical for a neutral country and too forward for a country whose Congress, not its chief executive, held the power to go to war. On June 14 Roosevelt replied to Reynaud's appeal of the thirteenth: he had gone as far in support as he could at that time. Thus it was a dark day for France. Its last grasp for the straw of a U.S. declaration of war, or even a strong public statement of support and supply, was gone. At dawn German troops entered the heart of Paris, marching down the Champs Elysées in an obvious imitation of the French victory parade at the end of World War I. Late in the day Alan Brooke, the commander of British troops still fighting in France, urged Churchill to evacuate Brooke's forces to England. Churchill agreed and ordered the 136,000 soldiers to ports in Normandy and Brittany for sealifts home over the next several days. Twenty thousand Polish soldiers came with them.[19]

June 14 was a dark day on the Baltic also. The Soviet Union demanded that Lithuania, an independent country since 1918, allow in Soviet troops, which then marched in on the fifteenth. On the sixteenth Estonia and Latvia received the same treatment.

Now the endgame was approaching for France. The hope of a Brittany redoubt having evaporated, the alternatives were to make peace with Hitler or flee to North Africa and carry on the fighting from there. Churchill, Reynaud, and Charles de Gaulle favored the latter. The advantages to the democracies' cause for doing so were considerable. The powerful French fleet would elude Hitler's grasp. Together with elements of the British fleet, the French fleet could hold at bay or overwhelm the Italian fleet. Italy would be far less a threat or nuisance in Libya. What remained of the French Air Force could fly to North Africa for use against Italy and later Germany. Soldiers from the shattered French Army who made their way to North Africa could reform, fighting the Nazis along the margins of their occupation and stimulating internal resistance in France proper.[20]

Hitler could see this possibility as well as anyone. To him a negotiated peace would render a relatively docile occupied area and a compliant government in an unoccupied area. The French fleet would be, at worse, neutralized and, at best, within his grasp. The French colonies would not be able to mass forces against him; further, the peace-signing government would keep them under control and administer them without consuming German resources. Thus he would offer terms that were stiff but also tempting enough for the French to cut their ties with the British and bargain with him.

On the fifteenth Reynaud and General Weygand, having moved again with the government to Bordeaux near the southwest Atlantic coast, quarreled over the next step. Weygand for days had believed that the French had to give up and make accommodations with the Germans, but he would not call for a cease-fire, which would be tantamount to surrender by the army. This move, he said, would bring shame upon the army; rather, the nation would have to call for an armistice and negotiate politically. Conversely Reynaud also had the example of other nations overrun by the Nazis to consider. The governments of Poland, Holland, Belgium, and others had fled in some form and continued their resistance against the German occupation.[21] But the negotiation movement was strong among the French ministers and politicians and getting stronger. Pétain was its leader, Weygand was sympathetic, and behind these two lay the opportunistic former premier Pierre Laval, who intended to move France closer to a German-French friendship and indeed to accommodate France to the Nazi New Order in Europe. To the men in the negotiation movement, it seemed better to accommodate a victorious country and maintain their empire than to maintain an alliance with defiant Britain that itself might fall to the Nazis by August. In the evening Reynaud again cabled London, asking that France be released from its word not to negotiate a separate peace.

Meanwhile a new notion was receiving considerable attention in Britain. Two days before, Jean Monnet and Arthur Salter, both officials of an economic warfare group called the Anglo-French Coordinating Committee, devised an idea that Great Britain and France should form an economic union and coordinate their combined resources. If accomplished France could not drop out of the war, and all of its resources and remaining colonies after the German advances of the last month would continue to be applied to the war effort. Charles de Gaulle liked the notion and strongly recommended it to Churchill, who agreed to put it to the British War Cabinet's meeting on the sixteenth. De Gaulle believed the union scheme would give Reynaud the flash of encouragement he would need and persuade the French ruling body, the Council of Ministers, to keep up the fight. It might not be as good perhaps as a declaration of war by the United States, but it would provide firm backing nonetheless.

Under the proposed merger agreement, the long history of Britain and France as separate and sometimes warring nations would end. Part of the short declaration as presented on the sixteenth read: "The two Governments declare that France and Great Britain shall no longer be two nations, but one Franco-British Union. The constitution of the Union will provide for joint organs of defence, foreign, financial, and economic policies. Every citizen of France will enjoy immediately citizenship of Great Britain; every British subject will become a citizen of France." There would be one War Cabinet, and the two parliaments would be "formally associated."[22]

Churchill at first was not enthusiastic, but, as he wrote later, "in this crisis we must not let ourselves be accused of lack of imagination."[23] Moreover on June 15 he found the general cabinet receptive to the idea and the War Cabinet receptive on the morning of the sixteenth. Getting wind of support, an enthusiastic Charles de Gaulle telephoned Reynaud from London about midday. Weygand, suspicious of the civilian government, had Reynaud's telephone tapped; the conversation has survived. De Gaulle told Reynaud of the scheme. Reynaud replied, "It is the only possible solution for the future. But it must be done on a large scale and very quickly—above all very quickly. It is a question of minutes. I give you half an hour."[24]

Reynaud had his own council meeting coming up that evening, and he knew this one would decide whether France would remain in or withdraw from the war. De Gaulle begged for a few hours, by which time he hoped to have formal approval from the British Cabinet. De Gaulle received it and telephoned Reynaud at four o'clock. Reynaud said the council meeting was scheduled for five; De Gaulle said he would bring the Declaration of Union by plane. Reynaud replied, "That will be too late. The situation has deteriorated seriously in the last few minutes."[25] The declaration was not even translated yet into French. In order to present it to the French Council, de Gaulle had it translated and then at 4:30 p.m. phoned Reynaud, who copied it down with pencil while an aide passed him sheets of paper. Churchill made plans to bring the heads of the three British political parties to a naval rendezvous off the Brittany coast and effect the union. Reynaud was greatly encouraged, and he set out with the one-country declaration for the council meeting.

But the meeting opened badly. The French ministers argued over the idea of a union. They had not yet heard the British answer about being released from the pledge forswearing a separate peace, which might have stiffened their resolve in the face of tough German terms. Indeed, the British early in the afternoon had cabled Reynaud that Britain *would* release France from its word against negotiating a separate peace so long as the French fleet sailed immediately to British ports, but the notion was never debated at the meeting. They did, however, discuss the one-country proposal. Yet those who favored a combined country with Britain could not persuade others and were themselves baffled over some of the proposal's points and implications. Ministers of the defeatist faction, led by Pétain, refused to seriously address the notion at all. They considered it a surprise, and some felt the pact would make France a mere dominion of the British Empire. The French naval secretary said, "Better to be a Nazi province. At least we know what that means."[26] Pétain argued that a union with Britain was like "fusion with a corpse." Reynaud countered, "I prefer to collaborate with my allies rather than with my enemies." But much of the will to resist the Germans had crumbled. A major military person, perhaps Weygand, was advising the council that "in three weeks, Britain will have her neck wrung like a chicken."

The council turned to consider approaching Germany for terms. After three hours of this debate, Reynaud saw he could not prevail upon the ministers to keep up the fight. He resigned. The council never formally discussed the British reply concerning the separate peace and rescue of the French fleet. The Reynaud government merely went out of existence. In effect, the French Republic moved to break its word about pursuing a separate peace and made no guarantees about the fleet.

Marshal Pétain immediately formed a new government of which he was the head. Weygand was made minister of defense, Admiral Darlan minister of marine. The fascist-leaning Pierre Laval would be a prominent player, though his position was uncertain at the moment. Before the night was over, the new Pétain government asked the Spanish ambassador to determine what terms the Germans proposed for an armistice.

As if Pétain's assumption of power was not enough, Admiral Darlan's ascension to the Ministry of Marine was yet another blow in Churchill's eyes. Churchill had some mistrust of Darlan. In November 1939, just after the war began, Darlan had visited England and was feted at the Admiralty. He reminded the British naval officers that British sailors under Adm. Horatio Nelson at the Battle of Trafalgar had killed his grandfather, leading Churchill to believe Darlan was one of the French officer class who hated England. Churchill also thought Darlan ambitious and self-seeking, if capable.[27] On the June 17, according to Churchill, Darlan could have given the order for all French warships to sail to British or American ports, or to the French colonies, and that Darlan had told France's field commander General Georges he would do so. When Georges asked him about it the next day, Darlan said he had changed his mind. Why? Georges asked. Darlan said that he had become minister of marine in the new Pétain government, which was entering negotiations with the Germans. According to Churchill, Darlan could have been the hero of France, sailing the ships out of the reach of the Germans and continuing the war against them. He would have far outshone the young, unknown Charles de Gaulle. Instead, he had joined the Pétain government.

Meanwhile tens of thousands of British, Canadian, and Polish soldiers were loaded onto ships bound for England. They sailed from Cherbourg, Brest, Saint-Malo, and Saint-Nazaire. The effort was almost as great as the one at Dunkirk but without the immense pressure from the Nazis by land. Still, a blow fell on this first day of the evacuation, June 17. Five thousand soldiers and civilian refugees boarded the Cunard/White Star ocean liner *Lancastria* in Saint-Nazaire. Fully laden, it was struck by a Nazi bomber not far from the harbor. The ship sank and four thousand people perished (compare to the *Titanic*'s toll of 1,517). When Churchill heard the report later in the day, he forbade the news from reaching the press, saying, "The newspapers have got quite enough disaster for today at least." He thought he would lift the censorship within several days, but the rush of events overwhelmed his intention until he forgot it. Six weeks later, news of the tragedy reached the United States and then Britain.

The evening of June 17, owing to the collapse of resistance in France and at the cabinet's request, Churchill addressed his country by radio. Churchill spoke for only about two minutes. His address ran in part:

The news from France is very bad, and I grieve for the gallant French people who have fallen into this terrible misfortune. Nothing will alter our feelings towards them or our faith that the genius of France will rise again. What has happened in France makes no difference to British faith and purpose. We have become the sole champions now in arms to defend the world cause.[28]

Living in exile in German-occupied Holland, the former kaiser Wilhelm II of imperial Germany sent a congratulatory telegram to Hitler. Although the former emperor generally despised the lowborn Nazi upstart, he praised Hitler and what he called a "victory granted by God."[29]

The House of Commons met on June 18, and Churchill faced his peers. They knew the calamity of the French withdrawal from the war and all that it implied. Churchill again had to brace the collected representatives of the British people. However, he was speaking not just to them but also to a world that wondered if, now that so many countries had been beaten by Germany, Britain would too call for negotiations. Churchill declared that under his administration, Britain would not. He told his listeners that the nation's chief military advisers believed there were solid grounds for ultimate victory. He said that the leaders of the four dominions—Canada, Australia, New Zealand, and South Africa—supported his decision to keep fighting the fascists and would share the burden. He pointed to the despair of the years of World War I and how it had been replaced, almost quickly, with a suitable outcome. Then he spoke words he had carefully crafted just that morning:[30]

However matters may go in France or with the French Government or other French Governments, we in this Island and in the British Empire will never lose our sense of comradeship with the French people. . . . If final victory rewards our toils they shall share the gains—aye, and freedom shall be restored to all. We abate nothing of our just demands; not one jot or tittle do we recede. Czechs, Poles, Norwegians, Dutch, Belgians, have joined their causes to our own. All these shall be restored. . . .

What General Weygand called the Battle of France is over. I expect that the Battle of Britain is about to begin. Upon this battle depends the survival of Christian civilisation. Upon it depends our own British life, and the long continuity of our institutions and our Empire. The whole fury and might of the enemy must very soon be turned on us. Hitler knows that he will have to break us in this Island or lose the war. If we stand up to him, all Europe may be free and the life of the world may move forward into broad, sunlit uplands. But if we fail, then the whole world, including the United States, including all that we have known and cared for, will sink into the abyss of a new Dark Age, made more sinister, and perhaps more protracted, by the lights of perverted science. Let us therefore brace ourselves to our duties, and so bear ourselves that, if the British Empire and its Commonwealth last for a thousand years, men will still say, "This was their finest hour."[31]

In the evening Churchill gave the speech again, over the radio, to the British people.

The prime minister was not the only person making important broadcasts in London. Charles de Gaulle had flown there from Bordeaux the day before. He would not accept his nation negotiating with Hitler and dropping out of the war. He would help organize Frenchmen to actively fight from wherever they might be. He broadcast in part: "France is not alone. She has a vast Empire behind her. She can unite with the British Empire, which holds the seas, and is continuing the struggle. She can utilize to the full, as England is doing, the vast industrial resources of the United States."[32]

Other like-minded Frenchmen attempted to flee France. Some were restrained. Others reached North Africa, but officials there detained them and kept them from sparking or joining a resistance movement. Georges Mandel, who was Jewish and one of the most vociferous ministers favoring a North African resistance, suffered such a fate.[33]

On the eighteenth Mussolini, having journeyed through the Alps by train, met with Hitler in Munich in the very rooms (the Führerhaus) where Hitler had hosted Neville Chamberlain and Édouard Daladier during the Sudetenland crisis less than two years earlier. Hitler outlined to Mussolini the armistice terms he would present to the French. The Italian dictator thought them too lenient, but Mussolini was frustrated in any event. While he wanted large chunks of France, he was not going to get them, for Hitler did not want the Pétain government balking and returning to the fight or the colonies breaking away in disgust. Further Hitler would not share Germany's moment of triumph over France. Germany would conduct the meetings alone, and Italy would hold separate meetings later. Mussolini's foreign minister, Count Galeazzo Ciano, saw how wily Hitler's terms were. He noted in his diary after the meeting: "Today he speaks with a reserve and perspicacity which, after such a victory, are really astonishing. I cannot be accused of excessive tenderness toward him, but today I truly admire him."[34]

In Moscow the Soviet foreign commissar Vyacheslav Molotov summoned the German ambassador Count Friederich Werner von der Schulenburg and, in the ambassador's words, "expressed the warmest congratulations of the Soviet Government on the splendid success of the German armed forces."[35] Although the exact words were not known to the British, the general tenor of the relationship between Germany and the Soviet Union was well understood: each gained something by an amicable trading partnership. Theirs was a mutually beneficial affiliation.

The Wehrmacht's success on the continent came more rapidly than most German planners had supposed. They had no particular plan for what would happen next and certainly not an operational plan for crossing the channel in force to wage land warfare on English terrain. The German army had no experience in amphibious warfare, its closest approximation being assaults across rivers. Naturally a cross-channel landing seemed daunting. At some time in June, Göring offered an alternative to invading England: occupy Spain, then hop to North Africa and drive the British out of the Mediterranean. Gen. Heinz Guderian, the celebrated commander of the XIX Panzer Corps that had knifed through France, concurred with Göring. He urged Hitler to postpone the armistice with France so he could push on to the Spanish border, rush across it, and seize Gibraltar in southern Spain. Gen. Alfred Jodl, chief of the Wehrmacht's Operations Staff, drew up formal plans for capturing Gibraltar, North Africa, and the Suez Canal as a way to knock Britain out of the war rather than attempt a cross-channel invasion.[36]

All through June 18 and 19, the German army, led by its panzers, rolled through France. On the eighteenth they overran Cherbourg, Rennes, Le Mans, and Colmar. The more land Germany occupied the stronger its position would be when presenting the armistice terms. Although the battle was essentially decided, the fighting was by no means cursory. Moroccans fighting for France and defending a rearguard position blocked an SS unit moving south. The SS soldiers, full of their notions of racial superiority, refused the option of surrender and wiped out the Moroccans to a man. Two days later an SS unit accepted the surrender of twenty-five white French soldiers but slaughtered forty-four "Negro" Moroccans.[37]

And although the Minister of Marine, Admiral Darlan, was equivocating, some under his charge were not so hesitant. On June 19, as German troops were closing on the Brittany ports, Capt. Pierre Jean Ronarch managed to work the powerful French battleship *Jean Bart* out of dry dock in Saint-Nazaire and set it on a course for Casablanca in French Morocco.[38]

On June 20 a French delegation to the armistice negotiation, having been first told to report to a site near Tours, was escorted northeast of Paris. Hitler wanted the French to sign the armistice in the same railway car and at the same location—a forest near the town of Compiègne—where the Germans had signed their bitter armistice with the French in 1918. Hitler himself is said to have come up with the idea of humiliating the French this way on the day Wehrmacht panzers reached the English Channel. For twenty-two years he had lived for this revenge, hoping to reverse what he considered a most horrible travesty.

Journalist William Shirer, author of *Rise and Fall of the Third Reich*, was present on the afternoon of June 21, 1940, when the railway car meeting took place. He recalled a lovely summer afternoon. Hitler, Göring, and an entourage of the highest-ranking Nazis and Wehrmacht generals and admirals pulled up in their Mercedes automobiles. German war flags draped over the Alsace-Lorraine statue, normally depicting a sword of victory piercing the limp eagle of the German Empire. But another monument remained uncloaked, a granite block to which Hitler and Göring strode. They read its lettering: "Here on the eleventh of November 1918 succumbed the criminal pride of the German Empire—vanquished by the free peoples which it tried to enslave." Shirer wrote in his diary of that day that as Hitler read the lettering, his face was "afire with scorn, anger, hate, revenge, triumph . . . his eyes meet ours, you grasp the depth of his hatred. But there is triumph there too—revengeful, triumphant hate . . . a burning contempt for this place now and all it has stood for. . . ."[39]

Shirer noted also the French delegation arriving, not having been told the spot to which they were being taken. Upon discovering where they were, "they looked shattered," Shirer wrote. All went inside the rail car to make the armistice official.

As expected, the Germans would occupy a major portion of the country, including Paris and the whole channel and Atlantic coasts, or in all about three-fifths of the landmass of France. The new government of France would administer the remainder. The French delegation balked at some of the lesser terms, but the Germans—Hitler had walked out after the reading of the preamble—insisted nothing could be changed. The French protested the requirement to turn over to the Germans all anti-Nazis who had fled from other countries to either France or her territories, but to no avail. Another clause required any Frenchman fighting with another country against Germany to be immediately shot, an obvious attempt to thwart de Gaulle's efforts in London and Africa. Another condemned French prisoners of war to captivity until the war was over, which most men in the railcar believed would be a matter of weeks or months, not the five years it turned out to be.[40] In addition France had to turn over all its military supplies to Germany and pay for the cost of Germany's occupation. It also had to release to Germany the four hundred pilots it held. Seemingly it was not many men, but this condition was a bitter pill to the British, who expected to suffer because of them shortly and did.

A vital section concerned the French fleet. Hitler was determined to keep it away from the British. He lacked a navy to seize it, and much of it had fled from mainland harbors, so the terms dictated that the French fleet would have to sail to designated ports in French waters, be demobilized, and disarmed "under German or Italian control." There they would remain under German and Italian supervision but never be seized by these countries' forces. Negotiations on small points continued into the next day when the Germans demanded a signing. At 6:50 p.m. the French signed and departed. Immediately the Germans began hauling the railcar to Berlin.[41] Within three days Hitler had the armistice site's granite commemorative to the French Great War victory dynamited to bits.

On June 23 Hitler motored into Paris with an entourage. He had admired Paris and its architecture since his youth. Now it lay prostrate before him on his first and only visit to the City of Lights. He arrived near dawn and was gone within hours. But in that time he visited the standard sights: the Opéra, the Eiffel Tower, the Arc de Triomphe, and more. At Napoleon's tomb in Les Invalides, he stared down upon the sarcophagus of the French military genius and declared, "This is the finest moment of my life." To his companion on the tour, architect Albert Speer, he said later in the day, "Wasn't Paris beautiful? In the past I often considered whether I would not have to destroy Paris. But when we are finished in Berlin, Paris will only be a shadow. So why should we destroy it?"[42]

He would ransack it, however. On the last day of the month, Hitler, instructed the German military in Paris "to take into custody all objects of art, whether state-owned or in private Jewish hands."[43] These pieces were to be used as bargaining chips in case of subsequent peace negotiations.

The next day in Germany, the Ministry of the Interior began the systematic murder of Jews in mental institutions and of any child considered mentally defective. The murder of adult Jews in mental institutions also began; they were gassed.[44]

Meanwhile the French had signed an armistice with the Italians on June 24, but because Mussolini's troops had conquered so little of France, scant territory was involved. All fighting in France ended the next day. Germany's campaign through the Low Countries and France, which began on May 10 and whose success was virtually assured by June 12, had lasted six weeks. French losses were steep: 92,000 killed, 250,000 wounded, and 1. 5 million captured. By comparison, British losses were minuscule: 3,500 dead, 14,000 wounded, and 41,000 taken prisoner. Belgian losses included 7,500 dead and 16,000 wounded; the Dutch, 2,900 dead and 7,000 wounded. The Germans suffered 27,000 dead, 18,000 missing, and 111,000 wounded.[45]

Here was a truly astonishing turn. After seeing Germany swallow Denmark and Norway, people everywhere expected Nazi Germany to attempt France. But France had a huge army, and it had stopped Germany through four anguished years in 1914–18. Britain ruled the waves, and the British and French empires spanned the globe. Yet in six weeks, France was as utterly defeated as the hapless Poland. It was gone, under the Nazi jackboot, with its surviving government a Nazi dominion, its vast industrial capacity and manpower set to the Nazi tune, and its City of Lights waving the Nazi flag from the Eiffel Tower. The world was stunned.

■

Churchill continued to work on Roosevelt and the American government. In a June 24 cable to Canadian prime minister Mackenzie King, he wrote:

> I shall myself never enter into any peace negotiations with Hitler, but obviously I cannot bind a future Government, which, if we were deserted by the United States and beaten down here, might very easily be a kind of Quisling affair ready to accept German overlordship and protection. It would be a help if you would impress this danger upon the President. . . .[46]

This entreaty was not enough. Four days later he wrote to the British ambassador in Washington, Philip Kerr, Lord Lothian:

> Never cease to impress on President and others that, if this country were successfully invaded and largely occupied after heavy fighting, some Quisling Government would be formed to make peace on the basis of our becoming a German Protectorate. In this case the British Fleet would be the solid contribution with which this Peace Government would buy terms. Feeling in England against United States would be similar to French bitterness against us now. . . . What really matters is whether Hitler is master of Britain in three months or not. I think not. But this is a matter which cannot be argued beforehand.[47]

Nevertheless the British government took measures to ship its gold and foreign exchange reserves aboard a battleship, two cruisers, and other ships to vaults in Montreal and Toronto. If it had to flee the island, it could fight the war from its trans-Atlantic dominion.[48]

Churchill wanted the issue of the destroyers kept alive as well. He had first asked Roosevelt for destroyers on May 15, five days after becoming prime minister. Britain had begun a program of building destroyers, but they would not be ready for a year. Churchill wanted thirty to fifty old ones from the United States to shore up the island's defenses until Britain's new ones could be finished. Roosevelt was wary, believing congressional opposition would be significant. In addition neutrality acts had been passed within the previous five years, severely restricting shipments of supplies and arms to "belligerent nations." But even if these acts could be evaded, the world would see the transfer of several dozen destroyers, even ones of World War I vintage, as a non-neutral act and move the United States from a "neutral country" to a "non-belligerent" one. Sending arms to a warring nation would perhaps set the United States on the slippery slope to a declaration of war. In any event Hitler could well view the United States sending dozens of destroyers to Britain as a hostile act and declare war on the United States for that reason. But Churchill kept making appeals. On June 11 he noted that with Italy in the war, Britain would be facing more submarines, not only in the Mediterranean, but also in the Atlantic if the Italians based submarines in Spanish ports. As France fell Churchill kept reminding Roosevelt of his request, all the more desperate after losing British destroyers during the evacuations from Dunkirk, Brittany, and Normandy.

Indeed in the United States arose one of the vital struggles of the new summer: to which cause would opinion and power swing—to the interventionists, who favored sending supplies to Britain if not joining their side as an ally, or to the isolationists, who wanted to keep the United States out of the European war? Variations on the interventionist-isolationist debate had brewed for decades, notably since the struggle over whether the United States should join the League of Nations, and warmed up again in the mid-1930s when isolationists presented the public with new material supporting their opinion that the United States should never have intervened in World War I. A result was the neutrality acts of the mid-1930s, one hope being that if the United States was not making arms deals with one belligerent in favor of another, it would less likely be drawn into war. Hitler's annexation of Czechoslovakia and then invasion of Poland stirred the interventionists, but the isolationists intensified their own efforts.

As the latter part of June approached, these struggles roiled the Republican Party, whose convention to nominate a presidential candidate would meet in Philadelphia June 24–28. The leading contenders were Thomas Dewey, a New York City district attorney, and Senator Robert Taft of Ohio. Both were isolationists of one stripe or another. But suddenly poised against them was, until two years previous, a registered Democrat who had never run for public office and who had not entered any of the Republican primary elections. This candidate was Wendell Willkie, a lawyer-businessman who admired parts of the New Deal. He also favored as much aid as possible going to Britain, short of war; in fact his foreign policy stance was about the equal of Roosevelt's.

The crush of neutral Denmark and Norway in April; the brazen and terrifying invasions of Holland, Belgium, Luxembourg, and France in May; and the collapse of France in June convinced thousands of Republicans that Taft had the wrong outlook on the international situation and that the thirty-eight-year-old Dewey was too young to lead the nation during this crisis, but they thought that Willkie had the energy and spunk for the job. A tremendous grassroots effort sprang up to nominate Willkie, and his supporters packed the convention galleries. Dewey won the first ballot, with Taft second, Willkie third, and Michigan senator Arthur Vandenberg, a leading isolationist, fourth. The standings remained the same on the second ballot, but on the third Willkie overtook Taft. On the fifth ballot, Dewey was well out of the running, and the nomination clearly was going to go to Taft or Willkie, the isolationist or the interventionist. The upstart Willkie won it on the sixth ballot. Roosevelt's secretary of the interior Harold Ickes opined in his diary: "Nothing so extraordinary has ever happened in American politics."[49]

The great import of this process was that isolationism did not enjoy the forum of the presidential campaign through the summer and fall of 1940. Roosevelt, who had decided by early July to run for a third term, could feel somewhat free to continue his support for Britain without fear of losing votes to the Republican candidate. Neutrality laws continued to constrain him, and the isolationist movement still enjoyed powerful currents among the populace, especially across the Midwest and West (the South being a stronghold for interventionism).[50] Roosevelt, however, would not have to lean back from his favoritism of the democracies against fascism on account of the approaching November elections.

■

On the last day of June, Hitler was settling into his new headquarters, called Tannenberg, near the Black Forest north of the Swiss border. He mulled over General Jodl's report "The Continuation of the War against

England." Jodl's view was that the war was as good as won, and if Britain did not acknowledge that fact, it would merely need a good shove to make it give up the fight. Jodl recommended attacks against the RAF and British shipping as well as on storage depots and factories, "terror attacks" against civilians, and a landing on the English shore. He placed top immediate priority on crippling the RAF, but he thought no part of his program would see much difficulty. "Together with propaganda and periodic terror attacks, announced as reprisals, this increasing weakening of the basis of food supply will *paralyze and finally break the will of the people to resist, and thereby force its government to capitulate.*"[51]

Jodl thought that a landing would merely be a coup de grâce to a teetering Britain. It might not even be necessary if the shipping to Britain were crippled or the bombing caused the people to howl for peace.

CHAPTER THREE

THE RACE TO READ THE CODES

"Dilly" Knox: "Which way does a clock go 'round?"
Respondent: "Clockwise."
Knox: "Not if you're the clock, it doesn't."
—*remembered of Dillwyn Knox, leading cryptanalyst*
at the Government Code and Cipher School,
Bletchley Park, Buckinghamshire, England[1]

Having been stung in World War I owing to the decipherment of the Zimmermann Telegram, Germany was intent on developing codes that its enemies could not read. The German foreign secretary sent the infamous Zimmermann telegram in January 1917 to the German ambassador in Washington, D.C., for forwarding to the German ambassador to Mexico. The Germans were about to resume unrestricted submarine warfare the following month, and they feared doing so would cause the United States to declare war against Germany. The telegram authorized the German ambassador in Mexico, if it appeared the United States would declare war on Germany, to approach the Mexican government and propose a military alliance: Mexico would war on the United States—therefore detracting U.S. efforts against Germany—in return for financial aid and the restoration to Mexico of the Texas, Arizona, and New Mexico territories lost to the United States in the nineteenth century. The British intercepted the telegram and managed to decode it. The British showed the telegram to the Americans, who then released it to the press. Americans naturally were outraged, and Congress declared war against Germany several months later. Decoding the telegram had been the key to having it utterly backfire on Germany. America's entry into the war, and the manpower it eventually applied against the German armies the following year, was a major cause of Germany losing the war.[2]

The Germans wanted some way to keep their messages secret. Sending messages by hand or over telephone cables only behind their own military lines would help keep them from enemy hands. Transmitting them by radio, however, had undeniable advantages: it was quick, it could span long distances, and it could leap over enemy forces, for example, from a naval headquarters to submarines far out in the ocean. But the Germans had to assume that enemy listening posts would record the transmissions and turn them over to cryptanalysts, who would try to uncover the plaintext messages. The trick was coming up with a method that was so complex a cryptanalyst could not decipher it or at least not within such time to make it useful to enemy commanders. But such a method also had to be simple enough for ordinary soldiers and sailors to use, easy enough to decode swiftly so that receiving commanders could understand and execute their orders in a timely fashion, and free of heavy or burdensome equipment because the coding operation would be needed on submarines and by rapidly moving army military units.

Immediately after World War I and into the 1920s, Dutch and German inventors believed they had developed such a machine. In particular a German engineer named Arthur Scherbius worked on a design for a cipher machine that would keep messages secret. He expected that business corporations would want them to keep their communications from competitors. These Enigma machines, as his company called them, did not attract much business, but Germany's military leaders were bent on secretly building up their forces in violation of the Versailles Treaty. By the mid-1920s the German navy thought the machines—about the size of a typewriter—had potential, bought them, and began to develop them.[3]

People have been writing ciphers for thousands of years to conceal their communications from those whom they wanted to keep ignorant of them. Ciphers take the form of substituting one letter or symbol for another letter or symbol, for example, writing *k* in the cipher text for every *a* in the plaintext. Each letter of the alphabet would be assigned a corresponding letter in the cipher alphabet so that the cipher text appeared to be gibberish. "I love you" might read "r olev blf" or, to confuse the reader further, "rolevblf" when the plaintext alphabet is transposed letter for letter into a cipher alphabet (in this case, *abcdef* . . . is set against a reverse alphabet, *zyxwvu* . . .).

But such ciphers are crude and cause little trouble to those who want to decipher them. If you read, "tl gl all," and you suspected that *l* represented a single letter, it might not take you long to figure that the message said, "Go to zoo." In fact, centuries ago the Arabs realized that because certain letters were used more often in a language's words, in a one-to-one letter substitution cipher—called monoalphabetic substitution—they could crack the cipher by first counting which letter is used most often and guess it is the letter used most often in the language of the plaintext. In other words, there would be a kind of "ghost" of the original message within the cipher message, and if you were clever enough you could urge the ghost out to read the original message. In English, *e* is the most common letter; so if *v* is the most common letter used in a cipher message, you might guess that *v* represents *e*. If you knew statistically how often each letter of a language appeared in normal writing, you could count the letters in the cipher, match them use for use with plaintext letters and make reasonable guesses at the cipher substitutions. The longer the cipher message you were trying to decipher, the more likely your guesses would be correct, and the shorter the cipher message, the less likely statistics would help you.

Cryptanalysts also used a method of guessing at words as well as letters. If certain words are used often in a language, a decipherer could guess that oft-repeated gibberish words were common words. There is a story of an Arab who deciphered the message of a Byzantine emperor because he suspected the first words were "In the name of God"; indeed, they were, allowing the Arab to use the revealed true letters from these five words to unlock the remainder of the message. If cipher writers always begin their messages with the date, they give decipherers openings with which to discover several letter substitutions and go from there.

The answer to the failings of monoalphabetic substitution is a polyalphabetic substitution. In this method each letter of a message is translated using a different and uniquely scrambled cipher alphabet. If, in "go to zoo," the first *o* is converted into *l*, the second *o* might be converted into a *k*. Instead of reading "gl tl all," in which the ghost of the plaintext message is evident, under a polyalphabetic substitution the message might read "ul nk wfb." Certainly this method would complicate the work of the decipherer, but so long as the message's intended recipient knew each substitution alphabet, the work of deciphering would not be difficult.

The heart of the German Enigma machine was the rotor system that Scherbius developed. The machine resembled a small typewriter in a wooden box. It had three rows of letter keys at the front that could be depressed like typewriter keys. At the rear were three rows of circular flat letter "windows" set in a wood panel, each window over a small glow lamp. When an operator depressed one of the letter keys at the front, battery current flowed through rotors in the machine to illuminate a single letter at the rear. Depressing c might illuminate k, for instance.

An Enigma machine was simple to operate, but the complexity within was immense. Inside the machine were three rotors, or flat cylinders, that were each about four inches in diameter and about a half inch thick. Each rotor had twenty-six electrical contacts—one for each letter of the German alphabet—on the outside of each face. Inside each rotor was a unique wiring pattern, linking each contact on one side to one contact on the other. Even these contacts could be shifted owing to a sliding disk alongside each rotor called the ring. Three rotors were set in a row, with the electrical contacts around their faces touching. When an operator pressed a letter key, an electrical charge traveled from the key to the right side of the machine, where it passed from a plate of contacts to the right side of the rightmost rotor. The electric charge moved right to left through the wiring of the rightmost rotor to the rotor's left contact plate; then into the middle rotor, where it received equal treatment (the second rotor's wiring was different from the first rotor's wiring); and then into the leftmost rotor (whose wiring was yet again different). From there it went into a reflector rotor at the left side of the machine. The reflector was called a rotor, but it was really stationary. It had its own wiring that connected pairs of electrical contacts on its face so that the signal passed behind it, emerging at another one of its electrical contacts. The electric charge then traveled back through the leftmost rotor, back through the middle rotor, and then back through the rightmost rotor to one of the glow lamps beneath one of the letter windows. The operator would see the illuminated letter and write it down as the cipher letter. As in the example above, depressing *c* might illuminate *k*. The reflector rotor was an ingenious stroke, because under these very same conditions, pressing *k* would illuminate *c*. The machine, or another machine with the same settings, could decipher a message as well as cipher one.

But if this work was all the machine could do, it would not create a difficult code. Linking one plaintext letter to one cipher letter results in a mere monoalphabetic cipher and is easy to crack. The machine's real complexity came in other ways. When the operator pressed a key, the current would illuminate a letter on the window board, but owing to cogs in the machine and on the rotors, it would also rotate the first rotor one twenty-sixth of a revolution. Now, if you pressed *c* again, another letter other than the letter *k* would be illuminated; thus, *c* would be enciphered by a second cipher alphabet all together. A third press of the *c* would use yet a third cipher alphabet and so on. After twenty-six pressings of letters, the first rotor rotated the second rotor one twenty-sixth revolution, and after this one had shifted twenty-six times, it moved the third rotor. The first rotor was therefore the "fast rotor," moving at every keystroke while the others turned far less frequently.

There were further complications. The rotors could be removed and replaced in a different sequence. The operator of the deciphering machine would have to have the identically wired rotors, set in the same sequence left to right and in the proper initial setting. This adjustment could be done because the edges of the rotors had letter markings, revealed when the rotors were in place by another set of three small windows, and the operator could rotate the rotors at will. An initial setting might be *htu*, for instance, and on the edges of the three disks, these letters would show in the three windows. Another complication was a board at the front of the machine that resembled a small telephone operator's switchboard with more than a dozen lettered contact jacks (*steckers*). These jacks could be connected with push-in wires; that is, an operator could connect, say, the *r* jack with the *l* jack. The ring setting of the rotors, the sequence of the rotors, the position of the rotors (represented by which letters on the rotor edges appeared in the windows in the top), and the manual wiring of the steckers made up the ground setting (*grundstellung*) for a message.

But there was more. The operator himself added his own setting. Having established the ground setting from codebooks that dictated it for a

given day or other time period, the operator would then choose three letters at random as his "message key." Say they were *tyu*. The operator would
first make sure that his ground setting was correct—with the accurate ring
settings, rotors in the correct order, rotors showing the proper letters in
their windows, the steckers set to the proper jacks—and then he would tap
tyu as the first letters of his message. The receiver of the message would
see the first three letters converted according to the ground setting; that is,
they would be three different letters, say *bnv*. Then to ensure that there was
no mistake, the sender of the message would tap in his three chosen letters
tyu again, but they would come out differently, say *rfd*. The operator would
then shift the three rotors from what the ground setting showed in the
three windows to his message settings *tyu* in the windows. Then he would
tap his message as he or someone looking over his shoulder recorded the
letters that lit up, and this output would be the ciphered message.

Indeed someone calculated that the different permutations for a single
letter were greater than the estimated number of atoms in the universe.
Someone working through all of the permutations in order to see if intel-
ligible language came out would be long dead before making the slightest
headway.

A code breaker attempting to decipher an Engima message would be
at a great disadvantage if he did not have the machine in order to examine
the wiring. For example, if he did not know what the wiring in rotor 1 was,
he would not know how the signal traveled. The same would hold for the
other two rotors and the backside of the reflector rotor.

Obtaining a machine even without the rotors would be of immense
value because a code breaker could examine the wiring behind the reflector rotor. Getting possession of one or more of the rotors would also be
extremely valuable because he could understand the wiring within it. But
even having the machine and the three rotors, he would not in any reasonable time be able to use it to decode a message without knowing the order
of the rotors, their initial settings, and the discretionary stecker wiring.

But if the code breaker were desperate, even hopelessness was a poor
deterrent to trying to crack the code. And Poland felt desperate. Poland
for two hundred years had much to fear from Germany to the west and
Russia to the east; it had been divided and obliterated several times by
this pair. If it could read Germany's military messages, it could prepare for

its neighbor's intentions. Accordingly, the Poles were especially keen on cryptanalysis and were pretty good at it, but in the late 1920s, they could not read any German military radio messages they plucked out of the airwaves. In fact, at first they thought what they heard was mere random test lettering. They could not discern any ghost of any plaintext message in the lettering they were copying down.

Then one day in January 1929, a crate arrived at the customs office in Warsaw labeled "radio equipment" and addressed to a German business in the city. Two Germans arrived and demanded the crate, saying it had been shipped from Berlin by mistake and should be surrendered before going through customs. Suspicious, the customs officials said that no one could do anything over the weekend but that it would be surrendered to the Germans on Monday. Over the weekend, the Polish Biuro Szyfrow (Cipher Bureau) carefully opened the crate and found an Enigma machine inside. They painstakingly did what they could to copy and photograph it, probe its secrets, and then reassemble it before the German agents returned to retrieve it.

Months later professors at the University of Poznan in the western part of the country, where many students spoke German as well as Polish, recruited twenty promising mathematics students into a cryptanalysis class. Most eventually dropped out, but three showed much promise: Jerzy Rózycki, Henryk Zygalski, and Marian Rejewski. Eventually the Biuro Szyfrow gave over much of the work to the twenty-seven-year-old Rejewski. The biuro had been trying to read the new kind of German messages and could get nowhere, so they thought they had nothing to lose showing the young man what they knew of the Enigma machine and letting him have a try.

The Poles ordered commercial versions of the Enigma machines, but as they had suspected, the Germans had modified the commercial models to greater standards of security. They still could not read the German military messages. Rejewski attempted to figure a way to mathematically determine the internal wiring of any single German military Enigma rotor, the reflector rotor, the ground setting for any particular message, and then the operator's setting. He made some progress but not enough.

Then the Poles were rewarded with a piece of luck. In 1931 a disgruntled employee of the cipher section of the German Foreign Office, Hans-

Thilo Schmidt, contacted a French cryptanalyst, Capt. Gustave Bertrand. Schmidt resented his more successful brother and had a taste for money and women, so he was willing to sell manuals about the Enigma to Bertrand. The Frenchman readily agreed and gave Schmidt the code name H. A., which soon transformed to Asché. Bertrand's own colleagues in the cipher section of French intelligence thought the manuals of little value. Without knowing how the rotors were wired and without being able to discern the ground setting and operator setting, decipherment would be too difficult. But Bertrand was not deterred. Owing to the fact that France feared Germany as much as Poland did and that the two were coordinating defensive measures, Bertrand offered the Enigma manuals to the Poles.

Ignorant for the time being of the manuals, Rejewski detected what he thought might be a weakness in the Enigma system as the German military used it. The operators were told to enter their three-letter message key twice. Thus, if the first six letters of an enciphered message were *opx ngl*, the underlying plaintext letter of *o* and *n* would be the same. Likewise, the underlying plaintext letter of *p* and *g* would be the same, as would *x* and *l*. Rejewski understood that no matter what three letters an operator chose, each would travel through a monoalphabet unique to the day's (or the month's, or whatever period's) ground setting. If he could assemble enough messages—he thought eighty might work—from that day or time period, he could look for patterns and apply permutation theory mathematics to discover what any single monoalphabet was. He began to record and categorize the patterns—there were more than 100,000 of them—and it took him a year to do it. But with these patterns, he at least had an opening in attacking the polyalphabets he confronted.

There were still too many unknowns for his mathematical formulas, however, and Rejewski was stumped until the Biuro Szyfrow gave him the Asché manuals, which contained the ground settings for two months in 1932—September and October. This information moved him along, but he still could not decipher messages. Then it occurred to him that the Germans perhaps had scrambled the wiring between the keys that were depressed and the contacts facing the first rotor. This possibility was indeed a large barrier; the Germans could have wired them in any manner, with the number of permutations being astronomical. In the commercial Enigmas, the top left keys were set as a modern English typewriter keyboard in the *qwert* pattern, and the wiring connected *q* to the first contact position, *w* to the second, and so forth. Rejewski, believing the German mind often ran to the orderly, in a flash of intuition and good fortune guessed that in a rewiring the letter *a* was connected to the first contact, *b* to the second, and so on. He tried this combination . . . and began to read messages. Soon Rejewski had also figured out the internal wirings of rotors 1, 2, and 3. With this information and the help of a radio manufacturing company in Warsaw, the Biuro Szyfrow began to build its own versions of the German military Enigma machines.

Rejewski's application of mathematics to the Enigma problem was impressive, but luck indeed had played its hand. If the Germans had decided to signal the first six letters, or the operator's key, "in clear" rather than run them through the ground setting, they probably would have been better off. But because these letters were run through the ground setting, it opened insights into what the ground setting was. In addition, if the "fast rotor" had not been the first rotor, Rejewski's problem would have been immensely harder. If the Germans had not wired the *a* key to the first contact position and so on down the alphabet and if Schmidt had not had a weakness for money and women and a resentment of his brother, Rejewski would have been stuck.

Reading radio messages ciphered by the German Enigma machines was still by no means easy. Rejewski, again working with Rózycki and Zygalski, needed about eighty messages sent with the same ground setting to crank them through myriad permutations until he and his colleagues could uncover what the ground setting was. With that knowledge, they could then read messages. To speed up the operation, they worked out a technique of combining two of their Polish-built Enigmas together and sending signals from one to the other and then back until one of the permutations began producing not gibberish but German. They called these connected Engimas *bombes,* named after an ice cream dessert Rejewski was eating when he came up with the idea. Eventually, they built six bombes, one for each possible wheel order. They sent signals through each, the wheels turning by electric motor, until something made sense. The wheels whirred, and the three young men began reading German messages on the day they were sent.

From 1933 to the middle of 1938, the Polish Biuro Szyfrow read many German military messages, learning about German military logistics, organizational structure, and other useful information. Then in September 1938, the Germans changed how the initial settings were made. Now an operator had to add three letters to the normal six, with the three letters specifying a new wheel order for the soon-to-be-transmitted message. Owing to this new complication, the Poles could no longer read the German messages. This development was not the only bad news. Three months later, in December, the Germans introduced two new rotors, 4 and 5, each wired differently from rotors 1, 2, and 3. The Enigma machines would still use three rotors, but the ground setting and the operator setting could now be chosen from five rotors and in any sequence rather than merely from changing the sequence of three rotors. The new permutations increased by tenfold from the previous ones the Poles had to tackle. Astonishingly, however, in Germany the SS did not switch to the new system but clung to the old, and the Poles could continue to read messages sent between SS units.

For the rest of the communications, though, the Poles were overwhelmed. They would now need sixty bombes, not six, and a tenfold increase in patterns records to read the message traffic. They did not have the resources to deal with such new complexities; moreover, on account of the Danzig Corridor problem, there were rumblings about a German invasion. The solution to continuing the code breaking might be to hand over what they knew to the British and French, who had greater manufacturing and human resources. Accordingly, two Poles from the Biuro Szyfrow, Lt. Col. Gwido Langer and Maj. Maksymilian Ciezki (both of whom had guided the three young mathematics students), set up a meeting with French and British intelligence. They met their British and French counterparts in Paris in January 1939. One of these was Dillwyn "Dilly" Knox, a code breaker from Britain's Room 40 in World War I and a member of a brood of brilliant siblings. One brother was editor of the magazine *Punch* from 1932 to 1949, and another was both a novelist and a bishop. Knox continued code breaking after World War I and had broken commercial Enigma machines that Franco's forces used in the Spanish Civil War. He knew German military branches were using Enigmas enhanced by their own people but believed they could not be broken by mathematical attack. The Poles were under orders at this meeting to be circumspect and not reveal what they had done unless the British and the French divulged that they had done as much or more. The Poles did not detect as much and so did not disclose their principal successes. After a delicious meal, the meeting broke up, and the men resolved to reconnect if there were new developments.

By July there were. Storm clouds over Poland were definitely thickening. The British and the French had pledged to come to Poland's aid against the Germans. The Polish cryptanalysts believed they had information that might well be overrun in the event of a German invasion but also could be of immense value to their French and British allies. Accordingly, Langer wired the British and French that he wanted a second meeting, this time in Warsaw. The meeting was set for July 24. Bertrand, who headed up the French radio intelligence office, and a key cryptanalyst took a train across Germany. Dilly Knox and Alastair Denniston, another veteran of Room 40 and the director of the British Government Code and Cipher School (GC&CS), flew in. With them was a "Commander Humphrey Sandwich," supposedly an admiral interested in radio intelligence. In fact, it was Stewart Menzies, then the deputy chief of MI6, Britain's Secret Intelligence Service (SIS). Soon the men were motored to the village of Pyry six miles outside Warsaw, where the German division of the Biuro Szyfrow had moved to avoid the large numbers of German agents then in Poland. On hand also were Rejewski, Zygalski, and Rózycki. Most of the meeting was conducted in German, the only language common to the three groups.

After a tour of much of the Biuro Szyfrow facility, the Polish hosts took the British and French into an isolated room, then withdrew a sheet covering objects on a table. These were several bombes. The visitors soon understood the devices were made from secret German military Enigma machines and asked where the Poles had got them. "We built them ourselves," Langer answered. Knox and Denniston were speechless. Knox in particular was intrigued; he had been trying to crack the military Enigmas but without success. Specifically he could not figure out the wiring from the keyboard to the contacts facing the first rotor; the possibilities were 26 x 25 x 24 . . . x 2 x 1, or about 400 million million million million. Failing there, he could not determine the wiring of even one rotor. Knox asked how anyone figured out the wiring from the keyboard to the first contacts. Rejewski told him about his guess owing to his recognition of German methodical thinking. Knox was astonished and a bit annoyed with himself for not coming up with the same answer.

To demonstrate the bombes' capabilities, the Poles showed the French and Germans a deciphered message sent only that morning from German SS headquarters. It was astounding. Denniston wanted to call London immediately to have a sketch artist flown over to make drawings of an Enigma and its wirings, but the Poles had already made two spares, one for the French and one for the British. The French and British carried them back to Paris and London, respectively, in diplomatic pouches.

Five weeks later Germany invaded Poland. The three young Polish code breakers fled to Romania. The Biuro Szyfrow had to destroy its equipment and records. But its best secrets had escaped to where they could be put to good use.

A month after seeing the Poles, Denniston was eager to move GC&CS operations out of London and into the house and grounds of Bletchley Park, fifty miles north. Bletchley Park was a late Victorian mansion, sometimes denigrated as an architectural nightmare, on fifty-five acres of pleasant grounds. The mansion had begun life as a simple brick farmhouse but was bought and extravagantly embellished by a London stockbroker who wanted to show society he had arrived. The expanded house blared brick and stone towers, bays, arches, and porticoes, all vying for attention. But the grounds were available for auxiliary buildings, and best of all, Bletchley Park was midway between Oxford and Cambridge, homes of some of the kingdom's most brilliant and irreverent minds. It was also on a main railway line and near major telephone trunk lines that permitted ready access to government offices in Whitehall in London. In 1938 Hugh Sinclair, Menzies' predecessor as head of SIS, bid for the estate, believing the Treasury would come up with the £7,500 offering price. The Treasury did not, so Sinclair bought house and grounds himself and set about making them ready for the SIS and GC&CS.

Bletchley Park (often abbreviated as BP) had significant drawbacks other than its indigestible architecture. It was close to the main highway, and for the time being nearly anyone could penetrate the grounds to the manor house. In the late summer of 1939, when elements of GC&CS began to move in, the telephone exchange was set up in the billiards room, offices were carved out of the library, and furniture was so scarce that people sat among their stacks of paper on the floor. The mansion was never considered adequate to the space needed for any sort of war effort, but the ample grounds soon sprouted unattractive huts set up to house the work.

Denniston had already begun thinking about staffing. In 1937 and 1938, he began discreetly contacting old Room 40 friends, some of whom were now professors at universities. He asked them about brilliant thinkers; being odd was by no means an obstacle. Some he attempted to recruit before the war, others he noted for future recruitment in the event that fighting broke out. Once the war began in September 1939, both men and women were eager to serve, and Denniston worked at swelling the ranks of the GC&CS. He brought in people with odd and specialized interests, not just theoretical mathematicians, but also avid bridge players, crossword puzzle advocates, chess champions, music lovers, experts in medieval German, and people adept at ancient Greek and Latin. Interviews tended to assess whether a potential recruit looked at problems in unusual ways. Denniston used his old-boy network, but he took applicants from any class and social station. He also searched for bright women through the Women's Royal Navy Service (WREN) and Women's Auxiliary Air Force (WAAF).

Once these acmes (to Denniston's eye) were assembled at Bletchley Park, they were, of course, sworn to secrecy. Life was spartan on account of the whole country being on a war footing, so supplies, materials, and money were short. But unlike in the military, there was no concern with rank, no saluting, and few lines of command. Unconventionality was accepted, even encouraged. Dilly Knox promoted fresh and uninhibited ways of looking at problems. For instance, he was noted around BP for the nettlesome question and answer quoted at the beginning of this chapter.

One of the more unusual recruits in this bevy of unusual people was twenty-seven-year-old Alan Turing. The son of a civil servant working in India, he was sent as a boy to school in England, where he was mainly miserable. His writing was illegible, and his papers were covered with inkblots. His math teachers complained that he skipped the elementary rigors and looked to the unusual or arcane in problems. Despite annoying his teachers, he advanced to Cambridge University and began to work on problems of theoretical mathematics and on the nature of mathematics itself. He worked with algorithms and binary code. He wondered about artificial intelligence. But unlike many theoretical mathematicians, Turing had a talent for working with machines. He made them himself using electrical relays of his own manufacture. These early electromechanical devices were aimed at solving problems. Turing spent a few postgraduate years in the United States at Princeton, earning a doctorate and working with some of the world's most brilliant minds, including Albert Einstein and Kurt Gödel.

Back in England, Turing began work at BP with GC&CS the month the war started. There he absentmindedly showed up wearing two different shoes or otherwise rumpled clothing. He chewed his fingernails, and his handwriting was still a mess. Fearing invasion by the Germans, he melted down his silverware, made ingots of it, buried the treasure in BP's woods, then forgot where the burial site was. But he was considered one of the most creative minds in a sea of fruitful thinkers. He studied the Poles' code-breaking work, their methods, and their bombes. He realized that they were right to attack the Enigma machines with the machines themselves, using them to run through thousands of settings until the proper ones were revealed. But he could see, as the Polish mathematicians did, that the Germans' new efforts had put solutions using only the Polish method out of reach.

Turing also believed that the decipherment attack should not be through the six-number indicator setting, which was changed with every message; rather, he and another talented code breaker named Gordon Welchman would attack using the message itself. The notion was that language, especially military messages, used certain words over and over. Turing made different kinds of bombes that searched for such words, and he used the principles of his earlier student-day machines to create ones that now would whirl and spin in search of German-language words. Slowly GC&CS coaxed plaintext out of the enciphered messages. Messages from some of the Wehrmacht services were easier than others. The Luftwaffe operators tended to be lazy in their security, making bombe runs shorter and the messages easier to crack. The German navy held to more difficult procedures and kept Turing's crew frustrated month after month.

Success was sporadic and imperfect, but by the early winter of 1939–40, the British were reading enough German message traffic to be helpful to commanders in the field. Churchill was especially fascinated by the code breaking. He called the process the "Ultra Secret," and soon enough the whole process of breaking the ciphers and getting the messages to the proper commanders was simply called Ultra by the select few who knew about it. Churchill demanded to see the raw transcripts of the German messages, not an analyst's summary of them. He called these messages "my eggs," from the golden eggs laid by the fairy-tale goose.

As welcome as Ultra was, it spawned difficulties. If the British acted too blatantly on a piece of information revealed in a message, the Germans would be tipped off to the fact that their Enigma machine transmissions were being intercepted and read. So the British had to devise ways of preventing this discovery and let on that information was attained in a way other than code breaking. For example, if the British knew by code breaking that a particular convoy would appear at a particular place and time, they would send an airplane overhead that was visible to ships of the convoy. If the convoy was later ambushed, its commanders were likely to believe that the airplane had radioed the convoy's position.

There was also the problem of British commanders understanding the significance of the intelligence given to them and acting on it properly. This development took some time. In early April German naval radio signals were assigned at Bletchley Park to a twenty-year-old Cambridge history student named Harry Hinsley. GC&CS could not read German naval messages at the time, but Hinsley could make certain deductions about German intentions by studying the number of radio messages among ships or from headquarters to ships and where the messages originated. He detected a notable buildup of messages indicating a movement of a sizeable number of ships out of North Sea ports. He concluded that an invasion of Denmark and Norway was imminent. He notified the British Admiralty, which ignored the intelligence, only to be faced with the swift and embarrassing invasion of Danish and Norwegian ports days later. Had the British navy been in proper position, it could have savaged the lightly armed German troop transports.

Less than two months later, Hinsley again gave a warning to the Admiralty. This time he detected movement of ships from the main German naval base at Kiel on the Baltic toward the North Sea. Again the Admiralty ignored the intelligence. But the ships Hensley had detected were the *Gneisenau* and *Scharnhorst*, which steamed up toward Narvik and sank the HMS *Glorious* along with its destroyer escort, causing great loss of life. The lesson at last was learned. The Admiralty suddenly had tremendous respect for Bletchley Park and made a special point of taking telephone calls from Hinsley.

By the time of the invasion of the Low Countries and France, the Bletchley Park code breakers were doing better with the German Luftwaffe and army codes than with the German naval ones; they could decipher many of them. But in the face of concentrated power and swift movement, the French and British could do little to turn the tide even with advance knowledge of some of the Germans' intentions. Lord Gort, leader of the BEF as the German army pressed it back to the English Channel, knew some of the Germans' attack plans and even of the famous panzer halt order of May 24 that gave him time to consolidate his perimeter around Dunkirk. But foreknowledge did not stem the Wehrmacht's overrunning France.

Not all of the code breaking, of course, was an Allied activity. The Germans had their own code breakers, and in the early years they enjoyed some success. The German code breakers—at least half a dozen bureaus were at work on different efforts—were reading some British and French naval codes in the 1930s. Part of the German success against the British and the French during the Norway campaign owed to the Germans reading British naval code, which helped them locate Allied ships and dispatch them with their own. One British commander complained that the only time Britain knew where German ships were was when one of them showed up to sink British ones.[4] The Germans kept their code breaking secret until 1943 when the British, reading German messages, determined that one of their naval codes was broken. They changed it.[5]

But from this point on and although Germany had several code-breaking successes, Britain held the edge. Much had to do with Britain placing all of its code-breaking effort into one place, Bletchley Park, and investing so much by way of money, talent, and machinery into making it work. The Germans, by contrast, had a diversified system, hounded by politics and petty rivalries, as well as a culture that resisted seeing what it did not want to see. And being the aggressor nation, Germany was not so interested in learning its enemy's intentions as was Britain, then on the defensive and absolutely keen on learning where the next blow might fall, the better to thwart it with the limited resources at hand. Finally, the Germans were so confident their Enigma codes were not being broken that they cared less about code breaking in general.

CHAPTER FOUR

JULY

Fire and Wait

"Everyone in the U. S. A. thinks [England] will be
beaten before the end of the month."
—*Ambassador Joseph Kennedy to former prime minister
Neville Chamberlain, July 1, 1940*[1]

July opened with a new map of Europe. From the North Cape above the Artic Circle in Norway to the southern tip of Sicily, from the eastern stretches of Poland to the Atlantic shores of Spain, the lands and peoples were ruled by Nazis or fascists. The small eastern European countries north of Greece were also under Nazi sway. Pétain's French accommodationist government or Italy controlled North Africa from the Atlantic to the Egyptian border. Sweden and Switzerland clung to an endangered and encircled neutrality. Only Britain off the northeast coast held out—Ireland was neutral—and even here fascism had made inroads. Until the war started and it was banned, the British Union of Fascists, founded in 1932, had blackshirts who attacked Jews, Communists, and trade unionists. On the other side of Europe, Russia was friendly to Germany and supplying it with war matériel, including petroleum. Britain had no allies; it was fighting fascism and Nazism alone.

Or not quite. It could count on Canada, South Africa, Australia, and New Zealand, though the latter two had to look anxiously toward an encroaching Japan. Britain might also draw on some manpower from India. But politically, if Britain collapsed, its dominions would fall away as antagonists. Many people felt this scenario was exactly what would happen. All across Europe and beyond, millions believed Britain would succumb or capitulate in weeks. Not the least among these doubters was the U.S. ambassador to Britain, Joe Kennedy, who on the first day of the month told cabinet member Neville Chamberlain that Americans expected England's defeat. During May he had been skeptical of the BEF's chances, cabling U.S. secretary of state Cordell Hull that "only a miracle can save the British Expeditionary Force from being wiped out or . . . surrender." A few weeks later, he followed with a cable that included his opinion: "If the Germans come over here and successfully bomb in a major manner . . . the strong feelings of fighting [to the] death will stop then and there."[2]

Indeed, in countries large and small, people saw the German triumph over France as one of modernism over the corrupt, inefficient, and broken model of government-by-Parliament, universal suffrage, and a free press. Germany and Italy, after all, seemed to work while France did not, and Britain, once so mighty, was clawing for its life. Many in the educated class felt democracies were quarrelsome and ineffective, a feeling running even stronger among the lower-middle and working classes, whose members suffered economically. And in faraway India, Mohandas Gandhi wrote in a newspaper in late June that Germans of the future would see Hitler as "a genius, a brave man, a matchless organizer." Eton-educated Sultan Muhammed Shah, Aga Khan III, a leader of Muslims in India, said he would toast with champagne the day Hitler entered Windsor Castle.[3] The German führer and the Italian Duce had good reason to think that the world was moving their way.

As July opened, however, Churchill's mind crackled with schemes to turn the military tide. Two operations in particular occupied him. One was Operation Susan, a planned attack of twenty-five thousand British, French, and Polish soldiers on French Morocco, the objectives being to give a French-speaking location to the fledgling Free French movement, secure Casablanca as a British base, and deny this coast of Africa to the Germans. The troops would land at small ports, presumably after significant bombardment, then march on Casablanca. The operation particularly suited the way Churchill saw the war going: small but effective cuts at the Nazi-Vichy body of Europe, the sum total of which would eventually topple the intolerant regimes. But the British military chiefs balked at the scheme as taking too many resources from Britain when both it and Ireland were under threat of invasion. Churchill chided them for their caution, but the chiefs held firm. Operation Susan died aborning.[4]

The other plan, which concerned the French fleet, was greater and more painful to contemplate. Twice Churchill had been first lord of the Admiralty, and his strategic thinking ran naturally to oceans, ships, and sea power. The French fleet was the fourth most powerful in the world after those of Britain, the United States, and Japan.[5] Wedded to the Italian Navy, the French fleet could control the Mediterranean and expel the British. In the Atlantic it could choke Britain of the supplies the island nation required for life. In the channel alongside the German navy, it could assist the invasion of England. To Churchill's thinking, if the Germans or Italians took the French fleet, the blow to Britain would be mortal.

The French had repeatedly told the British that they would never allow their warships to fall to the Germans or Italians and that they would scuttle or blow them up first. Churchill and his advisers had little doubt in the sincerity of their statements, but they had to wonder whether, because the ships were under German and Italian supervision, German and Italian raiding parties could not overwhelm the French skeleton crews and seize the vessels. And notwithstanding the language in the armistice document that the Germans would never attempt to put the French ships to their own use, the Czechoslovakia annexation, the unprovoked invasion of Poland, and the seizure of five neutral countries showed that Adolf Hitler's word on matters of international power was worthless.

The French fleet was scattered. Two battleships; four light cruisers; eight destroyers; the world's largest submarine, the *Surcouf*; and some two hundred smaller vessels had steamed to the English harbors of Plymouth and Portsmouth. In Alexandria, Egypt, were one battleship, four modern cruisers, and smaller ships. In Algiers, Algeria, were seven cruisers. Farther to the east near Oran, Algeria, at the military base called Mers-el-Kébir, lolled two battleships, several light cruisers, destroyers, smaller craft, and two of the finest ships in the French navy—the *Dunkerque* and the *Strasbourg*. These new battle cruisers were specifically built to be superior to the German battle cruisers *Gneisenau* and *Scharnhorst*, which had been so deadly in June off the coast of Norway. [6] In Martinique, West Indies, were an aircraft carrier and two light cruisers. Other important French maritime elements were anchored at Toulon, the great French naval base east of Marseilles.

Much to be feared were the largest and newest ships in the French fleet, though each was not yet quite complete. These were the *Jean Bart,* which had escaped Saint-Nazaire in Brittany for Casablanca, and the *Richelieu,* farther down the west African coast at the port of Dakar, French West Africa. The *Jean Bart* did not yet have its guns, and the *Richelieu,* comparable to the incomplete German *Bismarck,* had its guns but was not entirely fitted out.[7] Adm. Dudley Pound, the First Sea Lord and Britain's highest-ranking seaman, believed the *Richelieu* "the most powerful battleship afloat in the world today."[8]

On July 1 Churchill warned the British navy to prepare Operation Catapult—the seizure, neutralization, or destruction of the French navy's ships. On July 3 all actions were to occur simultaneously so that ships in one port could not tip off others. But Toulon was on the French mainland and tactically out of reach. In addition the British lacked the resources to challenge the *Jean Bart* in Casablanca and the *Richelieu* in Dakar while acting elsewhere; therefore, these two giants would have to wait. Operation Catapult was aimed mainly at the English ports Alexandria, and Mers-el-Kébir. English shore batteries and British ships covered the French ships in the English ports and at Alexandria, a British naval base with a sizable British naval force was already present.

Mers-el-Kébir posed a greater challenge. In a fight, shore batteries could assist the French ships, and no British ships controlled the harbor. Accordingly, the British Admiralty, on Churchill's orders, commanded Adm. James Somerville, with his powerful Task Force H at Gibraltar, to steam through the night of July 2–3 west and south across the Mediterranean to Mers-el-Kébir, blockade the harbor, and present the British options to the French vessels. Somerville was appalled. The French were allies, or had been until the week before, and Somerville himself had taken great pride in helping load one hundred thousand French soldiers off the quays and beaches of Dunkirk. Somerville had with him in Gibraltar Capt. Cedric Holland, who had recently been the British naval attaché in Paris and was a personal friend of some French commanders of the ships in Mers-el-Kébir harbor. Holland, too, was appalled at the thought of a naval battle with the French.

But the terms from the Admiralty in London were stark and clear. Somerville was to present to Vice Adm. Marcel-Bruno Gensoul the following communication:

It is impossible for us, your comrades up to now, to allow your fine ships to fall into the power of the German or Italian enemy. We are determined to fight on to the end, and if we win, as we think we shall, we shall never forget that France was our Ally, that our interests are the same as hers, and that our common enemy is Germany. Should we conquer, we solemnly declare that we shall restore the greatness and territory of France. For this purpose, we must make sure that the best ships of the French Navy are not used against us by the common foe. In these circumstances, His Majesty's Government have instructed me to demand that the French Fleet now at Mers-el-Kébir and Oran shall act in accordance with one of the following alternatives:

Sail with us and continue to fight for victory against the Germans and Italians.

Sail with reduced crews under our control to a British port. The reduced crews will be repatriated at the earliest moment.

If either of these courses is adopted by you, we will restore your ships to France at the conclusion of the war or pay full compensation if they are damaged meanwhile.

Alternatively, if you feel bound to stipulate that your ships should not be used against the Germans or Italians unless these break the Armistice, then sail them with us with reduced crews to some French port in the West Indies . . . where they can be demilitarised to our satisfaction, or perhaps be entrusted to the United States and remain safe until the end of the war . . .

If you refuse these fair offers, I must, with profound regret, require you to sink your ships within six hours.

Finally, failing the above, I have the orders of His Majesty's Government to use whatever force may be necessary to prevent your ships from falling into German or Italian hands.[9]

Somerville signaled London: "After talk with Holland and others, Vice-Admiral 'Force H' [Somerville] is impressed with their view that the use of force should be avoided at all costs. Holland considers offensive action on our part would alienate all French wherever they are."[10]

Several hours later, about 6:30 p.m. on July 2, Churchill requested the Admiralty in London signal back: "Firm intention of H. M. G. [His Majesty's Government] that if French will not accept any of your alternatives they are to be destroyed."

Just before midnight, and with Force H—its battleships, cruisers, destroyers, and one aircraft carrier—steaming in darkness down upon Mers-el-Kébir, Churchill sent to Somerville the following message: "You are charged with one of the most disagreeable and difficult tasks that a British Admiral has ever been faced with, but we have complete confidence in you and rely on you to carry it out relentlessly."[11]

Somerville sent Captain Holland ahead of the main force in the destroyer HMS *Foxhound*, which arrived at Mers-el-Kébir about 6:30 in the morning. Holland was a friend of Vice Admiral Gensoul, and they had spent many happy hours together when Holland was stationed in Paris. Holland's task was to present Somerville's terms to Gensoul. But Gensoul, in his flagship *Dunkerque*, did not like the look of Holland's request for an audience at all and liked it even less when the main British fleet appeared on the horizon. He refused to see Holland and ordered the *Foxhound* out of the harbor. Holland debarked from the *Foxhound*, told it to retire, and took a launch to Gensoul's battleship. The *Foxhound* laid mines as it departed to the outer harbor.

Gensoul's last instructions from the Minister of Marine Admiral Darlan had come in late June: "Demobilized ships are to stay French, under French flag. . . . Secret precautions for sabotage are to be made in order that any enemy or ex-ally seizing a vessel by force may not be able to make use of it. . . . In no case obey the orders of a foreign admiralty."[12] Two days later Darlan had cabled: "To respond to outside interests would lead our territory into becoming a German province. [The French worried that being too accommodating to the British would be seen as breaching the armistice and would provoke punitive measures by the Germans.] Our former allies are not to be listened to."[13]

Gensoul still refused to see Holland personally but did allow the written terms to be presented. Then he cabled the Ministry of Marine: "An English force . . . has sent me an ultimatum: 'Sink your ships; six-hour time limit, or we will constrain you or do so by force.' My reply was: 'French ships will answer force with force.'"[14] This rendition of the British terms was, of course, grossly inadequate because it did not mention the non-violent options. Gensoul also conveyed to Holland: "In no case, anytime, anywhere, any way . . . will the French ships fall intact into the hands of the Germans or the Italians. Given the form and substance of the veritable ultimatum which has been sent to Admiral Gensoul, the French ships will defend themselves with force."[15]

Unfortunately for everyone, Darlan could not be reached. The new French government was moving from Bordeaux to the city of Vichy, from which it would take its name. Rear Adm. Maurice Le Luc took Gensoul's message and responded by signaling French naval forces in Toulon and Algiers to steam in reinforcement to Mers-el-Kébir. British intelligence detected and decoded the message. Thus the Admiralty in London grew worried, as did Churchill, whom the Admiralty kept informed.

Noon arrived. Gensoul sent a second message to the ministry: "Initial English ultimatum was: Either rally to the English fleet or to destroy the ships within five hours to prevent their falling into German or Italian hands. Have replied: 1) The latter eventuality is not to be envisaged. 2) Shall defend myself with force at the first cannon shot, which will have a result diametrically opposed to that desired by the British Government."[16] Somerville demanded an answer; Gensoul sued for more time. The French Admiralty signaled Gensoul not to demobilize and that reinforcements were on the way. The British decoded this message also.

Gensoul ultimately agreed to see his friend Holland, but with the deadline approaching, the French, though their most powerful ships were berthed stern to the sea so that most of their big guns could not fire at the British, prepared for action. Gensoul told Holland he had to obey his orders.

The British Admiralty signaled Somerville: "Settle matters quickly or you will have reinforcements to deal with." Somerville, in fact, was in a tight spot. French ships from Toulon and Algiers could box him in, and the Italian Navy, possibly with submarines, might discover his location and show up as well. Somerville signaled Gensoul: "If none of the British proposals are acceptable by 17:30 BST [British Summer Time], it will be necessary to sink your ships." It was almost that time. Gensoul showed the message to Holland then walked out of the room. Holland took a launch back to the *Foxhound*, saluted by officers on both the *Dunkerque* and the *Bretagne*.

With the *Foxhound* safely away, Somerville still waited, scanning the French fleet for a white flag, but the only banner was the Tricolor. Just a little before six o'clock, he gave the order he never wanted to make: "Open fire." The British battle line 17,500 yards away roared in response, and shells began to rain down on the French fleet. The French fired back in return, but tethered as they were, they never had a chance. The *Bretagne* was hit in her magazine, exploded, and sank in two minutes, taking down 977 French sailors. The *Dunkerque* was damaged and beached. One other battleship was damaged, but the battle cruiser *Strasbourg* escaped in the smoke and haze. When Somerville heard that the *Strasbourg* was fleeing, he sent torpedo planes from his aircraft carrier *Ark Royal* in pursuit to sink her. They tried repeatedly but failed, and the *Strasbourg* reached Toulon. Three cruisers in Algiers also made it across the Mediterranean to Toulon.

Churchill had sent one last appeal at 6:26 p.m.: "French ships must comply with our terms or sink themselves or be sunk by you before dark."[17] But the deed was already done.

Nor was this all of Operation Catapult. In Plymouth and Portsmouth, the British seized all the French ships bloodlessly except for one British and one French sailor killed in a scuffle. In Alexandria, as at Mers-el-Kébir, two friends—Adm. Andrew Cunningham of the British fleet and Adm. René Godfroy of the French fleet—were pitted against each other in unnatural contention. Negotiations began at dawn, and the two friends worked out a solution: Godfroy would scuttle his ships the next day. But then Godfroy heard of the devastating attack at Mers-el-Kébir and told Cunningham he would attempt to fight his way out of the harbor. Cunningham then broadcast the British terms to all officers and men of the French fleet. This message seemed to have an effect. Negotiations continued over several more days and ended nonviolently after Godfroy consulted his captains and agreed to neutralize the ships by surrendering vital gun-firing parts.

The next day, July 4, the House of Commons met, and Churchill reported on the actions in the English ports, Mers-el-Kébir and Alexandria, where negotiations were still under way. This devastating attack on Britain's best ally of mere days before was hard news to give the Commons, and the members sat in silence. Churchill ended the report by saying he left the judgment of his actions to the Parliament: "I leave it also to the nation, and I leave it to the United States. I leave it to the world and to history."[18]

But Churchill's oration to the members of Parliament was not over. He moved on to the subject of the possibility of imminent invasion. He admitted the country was in a period "of extreme danger" but also of "splendid hope, when every virtue of our race will be tested, and all that we have and are will be freely staked. . . . It is the supreme hour to which we have been called."

Churchill then asked that the members renew their support for his administration.

> The action we have already taken should be, in itself, sufficient to dispose once and for all of the lies and rumours which have been so industriously spread by German propaganda and Fifth Column activities that we have the slightest intention of entering into negotiations in any form and through any channel with the German or Italian Governments. We shall, on the contrary, prosecute the war with the utmost vigour by all the means that are open to us until the righteous purposes for which we entered upon it have been fulfilled.[19]

Churchill finished and took his seat. Then he was astonished. The members rose to their feet, cheering and waving papers for a long time. To this point the members of the Conservative Party, though Churchill's own, had treated him somewhat with more reserve than had the members of the Labour Party. But here was none of that; they cheered mightily. Churchill was moved to tears. A member of the government, Harold Nicolson, reported in his diary: "The House is at first saddened by this odious attack but is fortified by Winston's speech. The grand finale ends in an ovation, with Winston sitting there with the tears pouring down his cheeks."[20]

Pétain's government was furious over the attack at Mers-el-Kébir. On July 5 it severed diplomatic ties with Great Britain. It also sent warplanes from Morocco to bomb Gibraltar in retaliation for the naval attack, but the planes did little damage.

Operation Catapult, however, had yet more to play out as the much-feared *Jean Bart* and *Richelieu* were still on the loose. On July 8, negotiations having failed, the British aircraft carrier *Hermes* attacked the *Richelieu* cruising outside Dakar. A swift motorboat with depth charges took after the huge ship. A plane from the *Hermes* torpedoed the French battleship and damaged its drive shafts, so the captain repaired to the harbor. The *Richelieu* would be out of commission for at least a while. The British left the *Jean Bart* in Casablanca alone; without its guns, it was for the time being toothless.

The bloody bombardment at Mers-el-Kébir shocked the world. All talk of the previous two months was of the invincible German war machine. All Allied countermeasures had been failures or feeble. Suddenly Britain roared, a contemporary Francis Drake against the Spanish Armada or James Wolfe at the walls of Quebec. As Churchill wrote later:

> Here was this Britain which so many had counted down and out, which strangers had supposed to be quivering on the brink of sur-render to the mighty power arrayed against her, striking ruthlessly at her dearest friends of yesterday and securing for a while to herself the undisputed command of the sea. It was made plain that the British War Cabinet feared nothing and would stop at nothing.[21]

The Mers-el-Kébir shock waves had one of their strongest effects in Washington, D.C. Advisers around President Roosevelt, and the president himself, could see that a cornered and threatened Britain still had the determination to fight. Those who wondered whether sending old navy destroyers and other arms to Britain might only see the Germans seize them within weeks or months were more guarded with their thoughts, and those who advocated supporting Britain pressed their positions.[22] The shock waves were also metaphorically felt in Spain, which had seen the British fleet sail out of Gibraltar and which was cheek-by-jowl with North Africa. Spanish newspapers howled at the audacity of the British, but most Spaniards, as well as Franco himself, were impressed by British resolve.[23]

Still the cost of Operation Catapult was high. It drove Pétain's French government closer to the Germans. It infuriated many in the French North African community. It spurred many French ships to the safety of Toulon, where the British did not want them because they were that much closer to the Germans. More time, less miscommunication, less pride, and less ad-herence to written words in favor of a broader view of the conflict between the democracies and fascism may have settled the French fleet crisis with-out the bombardment. But Hitler's word could not in the least be trusted, and if Britain could not rule the seas, its case was hopeless.

Hitler, in any event, believed he still had Britain in a much-desired po-sition, from which it could only emerge with an agreement in Germany's favor. As far back as his writing of *Mein Kampf* in the 1920s, Hitler had showed less prevalence for conquering Britain than for working with it. In his book Hitler had written that the only two European powers with which Germany could ally were Britain and Italy.[24] He generally admired the British and considered them part of his cherished Aryan race. Now in the summer of 1940, Hitler expected to broker a peace with Britain. Seemingly, once he was assured of the return of Germany's African and Pacific colonies it had lost in 1919, the führer was ready to offer generous terms and said as much to General Jodl as France fell: "Britain can get a separate peace any time after restitution of the colonies." Hitler believed Britain would allow Germany a free hand on the continent and was prepared to allow Britain a free hand in controlling its overseas colonies.[25] Together they would enjoy dividing much of the world between them.

Through the first part of July, Hitler waited for Britain to signal its willingness to talk. Indeed, on the first of the month, he had told Italy's ambassador to Germany that he "could not conceive of anyone in England still seriously believing in victory."[26] While waiting Hitler enjoyed a measure of good cheer. On July 6 he returned to Berlin for the first time since launching the attack against the Low Countries and France. There he would celebrate, and of many Nazi rallies, this one was a standout. Flowers everywhere lined the route from the train station to the Wilhelmplatz in front of the Reich Chancellery, where some people had waited six hours to view the returning conqueror. Nazi flags flapped and crackled. Hundreds of thousands of Germans cheered him when he appeared on his balcony. The enthusiasm was thunderous. Here was a man who was a success, and the electricity could be felt beyond Berlin. All across the Reich, opposition shriveled while workers in war plants hoped to trade their coveralls for army uniforms. The Germans were eager to see Britain quickly put out of the way.

But Hitler had a problem: if Britain did not negotiate soon, Germany had no plan to conquer it. Normally so thorough in their planning, the German military leaders were focused on achieving control of the landmass of Europe, which they now just about had. They and Hitler assumed that if they controlled the continent, Britain would have to acquiesce to some kind of deal. Evidently they paid too little attention to centuries of European history. As Churchill had noted in some of his historical writing, Britain had fought against any nation that threatened hegemony on the continent: Spain in the sixteenth century, France in the seventeenth and eighteenth centuries, and Germany and Austria in 1914–18. Hitler in *Mein Kampf* took note of this precedent but theorized in his book that with the collapse of the German and Austro-Hungarian empires in 1918, Britain would see France as the dominant and thus dangerous power in continental Europe (indeed, some in Britain had felt this way in the early years after World War I). Hitler then theorized that Britain, not threatened by Germany, would accept its friendship as a means of controlling France.[27] Three conditions, of course, changed this assumption utterly: by the late 1930s, Germany had become equal to or greater than France (as it turned out, greater owing to internal weaknesses in French political life); Germany's Nazi government was illegitimate and odious to a freedom-loving people; and Germany had not only savaged its own country but also nine others, which it still occupied. Britain would be no ready ally of Germany's, at least not without a fight.

Oddly there did obtrude into these twilight days after the fall of France whispered talk among German agents of a stunning culmination to any German-British agreement: place Edward VIII back on the throne as a man acquiescent to the Nazi New Order in Europe. Edward had been king for ten months in 1936 upon the death of his father, George V. He wished to marry his twice-divorced American mistress, Wallis Simpson, but could find no way to do so and secure for her what both Simpson and Edward thought was a suitable title. Rather than face a disgruntled empire, Edward had abdicated the throne in favor of his younger brother, who became George VI, and married Simpson. Churchill, a friend of Edward's, generally supported him and his positions during the agony leading up to the abdication. In 1937 Hitler had invited the married couple, now titled the Duke and Duchess of Windsor, to visit Germany. They did, dining with Hitler and other highly placed Nazis, and later had favorable things to say about the regime in Germany. Since the abdication they had lived in Paris, but they fled for Madrid during the invasion. By early July they were in Lisbon, enjoying the hospitality of a man who had pro-German sentiments. Throughout the month, the Windsors' status remained a prickly issue for Churchill and for George VI.

Through these early days of July, while Hitler hoped Britain would come to terms, he had to face the possibility that it would not. Accordingly, he and his commanders saw three ways of bringing Britain to heel. First, Germany could starve it with a blockade and submarine warfare that deprived it of food and supplies from North America and the colonies. Second, it could bomb its cities until its people overthrew the Churchill government. Finally, it could land the Wehrmacht in England, overrunning the country with its panzers and infantry divisions. A combination of these factors, of course, could work as well.

Germany had already taken a large step in the sea blockade strategy by taking control of the French Atlantic coast. From there its submarines could haunt the western approaches to Britain, torpedoing the slow merchantmen as they churned the waves from Canada. It could also send its powerful battleships and battle cruisers out to blast merchantmen with huge guns. The German battle cruisers *Gneisenau* and *Scharnhorst* had already proven their power on British warships, and the larger *Bismarck* and *Tirpitz* were almost complete. Moreover, the Luftwaffe's airplanes could bomb wharves, warehouses, and ships as they neared land. Starving Britain was a distinct possibility.

Of course the most direct and surest means of bending Britain to the New Nazi Order in Europe was to overrun it. Hitler on July 2 ordered his armed forces to develop a plan, code-named Sea Lion, for invading England. The generals got right to work. The army was confident of success, mainly seeing the operation through the lens of advancement once they reached English soil. Even British military experts thought along the same lines: the British army, as it existed after Dunkirk, was so bereft of supplies and weapons that resisting a swelling beachhead of Wehrmacht soldiers and panzers would be difficult if not hopeless.

But first the troops had to get there, and that was the Germans' nettlesome problem. The Wehrmacht was excellent at river crossings, but the English Channel was twenty miles across at the narrowest point. And the German plan was ambitious: transport 250,000 men across the channel from east of Dover for two hundred miles along most of England's south coast.[28] This feat would require more than 1,700 barges, 1,000 light craft, almost 500 tugboats, and 150 large transports. The German navy worried that not only would it have difficulty assembling and sheltering from bombing all these craft, but it would have a great deal of trouble defending them from British ships once the operation began.[29] The German navy's plans called for laying mines in the sea east and west of the landings to thwart the Royal Navy, which was very likely to descend in great strength from Scapa Flow in Scotland and other points to challenge the invasion fleet. Along with the mines, the German navy would set itself east and west to guard the army crossing the water. In addition the Luftwaffe would have to use its vast fleet of airplanes to drive off British naval and air attacks. This point was critical: the commander of the German navy, Adm. Erich Raeder, firmly believed that the landings could not succeed unless there was no significant interference from RAF planes intending to bomb and strafe the German ships. In any event, the British reckoned, the Germans would likely need time to prepare and assemble the requisite shipping and to shoot down as many RAF planes as possible so that the German army and navy would not be troubled from the air when the landings began.

The other potential hammer of conquest was a bombing campaign, which would make the Churchill government sue for peace or stimulate the British citizenry into overthrowing the Churchill government for one more accommodating to German demands. Coupled with a propaganda barrage meant to sow defeatism among the people, bombing was believed by many militarists to be a weapon that would hastily bring a country to its knees. Bombing got its real start in World War I when planes targeted supply depots, assembly areas, and to a small extent factories and cities. Beginning in 1915 the Germans had sent both bombing blimps and winged aircraft against English cities. But it was an upstart Italian military officer, Gen. Giulio Douhet, who envisioned aerial bombing's potential then set it in writing. In his 1921 treatise *Il dominio dell'aria* (*Command of the Air*), Douhet drew lessons from World War I, in particular that wars were wars of whole nations, not mere military units of young men. Wars were won or lost by the industrial capacity and will of the citizenry; in fact, there could be little distinction anymore between soldier and civilian. Douhet submitted that warfare had utterly changed on account of aircraft. These could, at the outbreak of a war, fly to an enemy city and quickly blast it with explosives or infest it with poison gas or even biological weapons. Wars would be won not at front lines, where soldiers met soldiers, but where a nation's people were killed in droves. Douhet also wrote that a country's defenses could not stop enough bombers from wreaking this terrible destruction. "Normal life would be impossible in this constant nightmare of imminent death and destruction," he wrote, and to "put an end to horror and suffering, the people themselves ... would rise up and demand an end to the war—this before their army and navy had time to mobilize at all!"[30] Douhet saw war as total war, and the adversary who was quickest to level cities would be the winner.

Douhet's book attracted much attention and sent chills through all nations, not the least of which was Britain, which traditionally thought of itself as protected by the ships that commanded the seas around it. Airplanes, of course, recognized no such obstacles as narrow seas; a 1935 bomber could reach London from Paris in sixty minutes. Accordingly, the power of air forces grew. Air force commanders needled their superiors about establishing air forces on an equal footing with an army or navy. In this effort they were in some places successful, though army and navy officials often chided their winged warrior brethren as being carpet-bombing baby killers.

By June 1940 celebrated bombing attacks already increased the anxiety of both military planners and civilians. The German and Italian bombing of Guernica in April 1937 during the Spanish Civil War had leveled more than half the Basque town. Spanish Republicans said that thousands were killed, though the number was likely closer to three hundred. Nevertheless, the Guernica bombing worked, and Nationalist troops marched into the town the following day. Pablo Picasso reflected the terror of the day with his famous painting, and the name of the town entered more than one language as exemplifying the horror of bombing innocent townspeople.

The Luftwaffe's bombing of Warsaw on September 25, 1939, used four hundred bombers and destroyed a tenth of the city's buildings, damaging another 40 percent. Thousands died.[31] And when the Dutch in Rotterdam slowed Wehrmacht panzers in May 1940, Hitler had ordered the city bombed into submission. More than six hundred acres were destroyed, twenty-five thousand homes leveled, seventy-eight thousand Dutch left homeless, and eight hundred killed. Again, in this war, the bombing worked; the people's will to resist cracked.[32]

It was in this atmosphere that Churchill made a broadcast to the nation on Sunday evening, July 14. It was Bastille Day, and he gave first mention to France and to reasons why the British fleet had attacked the ships of the French fleet. He reaffirmed his conviction that France would again rise among the nations and "stand forward as the champion of the freedom and rights of man" and asked the citizens of both countries to move on to common purpose. In his grumbling baritone, he talked of the threatened invasion and of the British resolve to defend their island. He reminded his listeners abroad as well as at home that "we are fighting by ourselves alone, but we are not fighting for ourselves alone." As was his wont, he wished to steel his fellow citizens to the hardship ahead:

> Be the ordeal [of invasion] sharp or long, or both, we shall seek no terms, we shall tolerate no parley; we may show mercy—we shall ask for none. . . . We shall defend every village, every town, and every city. . . . We would rather see London laid in ruins and ashes than that it should be tamely and abjectly enslaved. . . . We are prepared to proceed to all extremities. . . .

Last, and with a nod to the United States, he wanted anyone who might hear or later read his broadcast to remember that it was their struggle also: "All depends now on the whole life-strength of the British race in every part of the world and of all our associated peoples and of all our well-wishers in every land, doing their utmost night and day, giving all, daring all, enduring all—to the utmost—to the end."[33]

Hitler, still waiting and hoping for Britain to recognize it was beaten, found nothing to like in Churchill's broadcast. To him much of what Churchill said was bombast—he had a considerably low opinion of Churchill—and he understood that Britain was also holding out hope for greater aid from the United States, whose weapon-making machinery at the moment was modest though bound to increase. He also understood that Britain held a thin hope that the Soviet Union, with its tremendous manpower and impressive industry, could be converted into an ally. But cultivating significant aid from the United States and working to recruit the Soviet Union—both of which were distinct possibilities for Britain—would take time. The quicker he could knock Britain out of the war, the better.

On July 16 Hitler issued a more formal directive about the invasion of England:

Since England, despite her militarily hopeless situation, still shows no sign of willingness to come to terms, I have decided to prepare a landing operation against England, and if necessary to carry it out. The aim of this operation is to eliminate the English homeland as a base for the carrying on of the war against Germany, and, if it should become necessary, to occupy it completely.[34]

A close look at the wording "if necessary to carry it out" reveals some hesitation. Still Hitler had to bring Britain to heel one way or another. On July 19 he took the path of least resistance. He made a speech to the Reichstag assembled in the capital's Kroll Opera House. With a giant Nazi eagle behind him, huge Nazi flags to his left and right, and his military men in new medals arrayed alongside him, he spoke for more than two hours. He recounted his version of the war, its causes and conquests. He praised his military leaders and promoted twelve of them to the honored position of field marshal. He particularly praised Göring and raised him to the lofty position of Reich marshal. He expounded upon Germany's powerful position after its military victories. As if to impart to the British that they could not expect any help from Russia, he also commented on Germany's good relations with the Soviets.

But if any part of his strategy was to pry a gap between the British populace and their leader, he likely took the wrong tack. He mocked Churchill as "that practiced liar," "an inciter and agitator," and " a blood-covered dilettante" who would flee to Canada to continue the war, leaving the British people behind.[35] "I do realize that this struggle," he said, "if it continues, can end only with the complete annihilation of one or the other of the two adversaries. Mr. Churchill may believe this will be Germany. I know that it will be Britain."[36] Then the German dictator came to the crux of his speech.

In this hour, I feel it to be my duty before my own conscience to appeal once more to reason and common sense in Great Britain as much as elsewhere. I consider myself in a position to make this appeal since I am not the vanquished begging favors, but the victor speaking in the name of reason. I see no reason why this war must go on.[37]

To Hitler's appeal the British press and the British Broadcasting Company (BBC) responded immediately that Britain would not negotiate. But it fell to the cabinet's foreign secretary, Lord Halifax, to give a formal reply. By radio broadcast on July 22, Halifax said Britain would not "capitulate to [Hitler's] will." He added, "We never wanted the war; certainly no one here wants the war to go on for a day longer than is necessary. But we shall not stop fighting till freedom for ourselves and others is secure."[38]

Britain then braced itself for what the whole world expected: an onslaught by whatever Hitler could hurl at the nation across the channel. As noted, Britain's army on the island was virtually without weapons, and it would take some time for the factories in Britain, Canada, and the United States to rearm the divisions. But the navy was intact, and the RAF had barely enough fighter squadrons it believed adequate for fighting off the Luftwaffe. As Churchill recognized later,[39] the quick collapse of France in a way worked to Britain's advantage. If, after Dunkirk, the Germans had been slower in their attacks or the French more successful with its defense north of Paris, then the French would have continued to supplicate for British arms, including precious RAF fighter squadrons meant for the defense of Britain. The Germans might have ground down what was left of Britain's army, whittled its reserve of aircraft, and all the while made preparations for landings across the channel. As it was, when the French collapsed, the Germans had no plans for a cross-channel attack, and Britain still had strength in its fighter arm.

The world waited. The king of Sweden asked whether Britain might want to use Sweden as an intermediary for talks. But Britain declined, noting in the reply: "[His Majesty's Government's] intention to prosecute the war against Germany by every means in their power until Hitlerism is finally broken and the world relieved from the curse which a wicked man has brought upon it has been strengthened to such a point that they would rather all perish in the common ruin than fail or falter in their duty."[40]

Britain, especially southern England, braced for invasion. The government quickly organized what was at first called the Local Defense Volunteers, later the Home Guard, which was meant to be a huge civilian defense force. More than a million citizens signed up. Shepherds, soldiers from the old war, and industrial workers flocked to the ranks. Titled aristocrats joined, though they risked taking orders from their own butlers or chauffeurs, temporarily their superiors in the Home Guard on account of having once been ranked sergeants in the army. Home Guard volunteers drilled with broomsticks rather than rifles, as these precious items for the time were reserved only for soldiers. They removed road signs so invaders would become confused in the hodgepodge of fields and lanes of southern England. They painted over railroad station names. They learned how to man crossroads with their hunting pieces or even pitch forks. Some Home Guardsmen were given roller skates, the better to move quickly through cities. They learned how to disable tanks with crowbars thrust into the treads and sabotage a car by pouring sugar into the gas tank. They rigged pipes to flood roads with gasoline they would set alight in an invasion. They held bottling parties, where they prepared Molotov cocktails in old wine bottles. People everywhere arranged blackout curtains or covers so light would not escape from their windows at night and thus guide bombers. They fitted their car headlamps with blackout blinkers, and they painted train windows to hold in light.

People were told to immobilize their cars when they were not using them by removing the distributor's rotor, then carrying it with them (a car was useless without its rotor). Car radios were banned because they could be converted to transmitters. Everyone had to carry an identity card and show it rapidly when asked.

Farmers placed barbed wire, old tractors, and abandoned cars in fields to foil paratroopers and gliders. They dug tank traps and set up concrete "dragon's teeth" that could stop tanks. People were instructed that in case of invasion they were not to flee or clog roads, as had been the case in France and had slowed military units from reaching critical points; rather, folks were asked to stay at home. And fight. "You can always take one with you," Churchill chided someone asking about defense in the event the Germans landed.

A great fear attended the possibility of gas attack. Aircraft could drop gas bombs, so gas masks were distributed to all children and adults. Everyone carried one. There were also detector pads on street poles to sense poison gas.[41] Tens of thousands of children were evacuated from the larger cities. Many were gladly put on ships that would sail them to Canada, where welcoming families took them in. (Churchill did not like this program; he thought it tainted with defeatism.) Londoners practiced air raid drills. The government built public air raid shelters. Sandbags went up outside stores. Proprietors thought it good for business if shoppers inside felt they would not be showered with glass in the event of a blast in the street, and people indeed favored shops with sandbags in front. Higher-up windows were boarded over or crisscrossed with masking tape to restrain shards in the case of an explosion.[42]

British officials were under few illusions. One estimate by the Imperial Defense Committee estimated that in a determined air attack by Germans, six hundred thousand British would be killed and more than a million wounded. And that calculation did not include an invasion by land. The fall of France, however, seemed to rally the nation. Southern England had not been invaded for nine hundred years, and people were determined to make any attempt in this year a failure. George Orwell wrote at the time: "There are moments when the whole nation suddenly swings together and does the same thing, like a herd of cattle facing a wolf. This was such a moment."[43] Churchill remarked later in his memoir: "This was a time when it was equally good to live or die."[44]

People worked around the clock. Posters and pamphlets reminded them that being idle could cost a soldier, sailor, or pilot his life. Most summer holidays were cancelled, and people worked seven days a week. Workers in the aircraft and armaments industries pressed themselves hardest; some dropped at their lathes, revived themselves, and began again. Recycling was a priority in order to save materials. Women even brought in their aluminum cookware for conversion into airplanes.[45]

The military was making its own preparations. Churchill approved the use of poison gas against Germans landing on British beaches; thus, canisters were made and stored. The army also experimented with petroleum pipelines extending from the beaches to a ways offshore. They planned to pump oil out among invasion craft then set it aflame with flare pistols. Making a comment at the time about authorizing the petroleum scheme, Churchill said, "I have no scruples, except not to do anything dishonorable."[46] British engineers also built floating forts. These gun platforms on huge hollow concrete cylinders were towed out into the sea or an estuary and sunk up to the level of the guns. A number of them were placed outside Liverpool and others in the Thames River estuary. They not only stood to repel invaders, but they were also helpful in tracking aircraft with radar.[47]

Gas balloons that looked like blimps began to rise over London and other cities. More than a thousand were ready in July. The balloons were tethered to the ground with steel cables, which would obstruct air attacks. When a number of the balloons were in place, airplanes could not fly at or below their level or they would collide with the cables. Because the balloons could rise to five thousand feet, aircraft would have to fly higher, effectively thwarting the German Stuka dive-bombers. These aircraft had boiled up terror in Poland and France with their crescendo whines as they dived down with bombs on their bellies. The balloons would thwart level bombers as well, for being forced to fly at higher altitudes, the bombers were more likely to suffer haze and clouds and be less accurate in their bomb runs.[48] In addition the British deployed several thousand antiaircraft guns among the cities and around the important factories, such as those making the RAF fighter engines and bodies. Britain also placed searchlights near the antiaircraft guns in areas where planners thought German bombers would come by night. But what they had in guns and searchlights was far short of what they had planned for or wanted to have when the onslaught came.[49]

It was good that the British were preparing. On July 10 Göring started his Luftwaffe on raids and attacks to test the RAF for what he knew would be the immense battle to come unless the British capitulated swiftly. On that day seventy bombers attacked shipping docks in southern Wales. "Granpa Tiger" Jones, who had shot down forty enemy planes during eight months in World War I, took off after the bombers in an unarmed target tug. A hundred yards from one of the bombers, he fired his Very pistol, which shot flares, and was pleased enough to see the pilot jerk the plane away from the flash of light. All of the German bombers returned to their bases safely after delivering a good deal of damage to Swansea and Falmouth docks.

Another cadre attacked a convoy of ships in the English Channel near Dover. The point was less to damage the ships than to draw out some RAF fighters and then pounce on them with twenty Messerschmitt Me-110 fighters and twenty Me-109 fighters coming in behind. The German bombers attacking the convoy did draw up a squadron of RAF Hurricane fighters, and the result was a dogfight above the streets of Dover. Scant damage was done to the convoy, but one British pilot was killed when he dived too close to one of the bombers and struck it. Hurricanes shot down several other German bombers.[50]

Through the remainder of July, Göring had the Luftwaffe attempt to close the channel to British shipping, which used the waterway as a convenient passage to and from the Thames estuary and docks of London. But it mainly wanted to weaken the RAF Fighter Command for a later phase that was meant to finish it off all together. When the Luftwaffe spotted a convoy in the channel, it sent out Stuka dive-bombers to try to sink the ships. This assault would draw out RAF Hurricanes and Spitfires to attack the Stukas, but the Stukas were guarded by high-flying German fighters that would dive down on the British planes. Swirling dogfights would then ensue over the channel, generally observed by the French and the Germans on the French shore and by the British near the Cliffs of Dover. White vapor trails from the planes' engines twisted across the sky with an occasional plane spewing smoke and spiraling toward the waves.

The Germans had reason for optimism. Since May 10 the RAF had lost 950 aircraft, or about half of its frontline force. Most seriously, these losses included 386 Hurricane and 67 Spitfire fighters. The RAF was already seriously weakened. But the Luftwaffe too was bloodied. It had lost about 1,300 aircraft during the Battle of France, or about one-third its strength at the beginning of May.[51] But German factories were turning out new planes and the pilot training schools new pilots. The rush was on to get as many ready as fast as possible.

On July 19, the day of Hitler's Reichstag peace offer speech, the day's aerial fighting was of no succor to the British. Nine RAF Defiants, a new fighter airplane with high hopes from their makers, set out midday to patrol around the channel port of Folkestone. They were set upon by two groups of Me-109 German fighters. The Defiants were an odd sort of fighter, for instead of having wing guns operated by the pilot, they had a single turret gun behind the pilot's cockpit that was operated by an independent gunner. The Germans shot one after another into the sea. Of nine Defiants sent aloft, six went down in flames, and a seventh scurried to base so damaged it never flew again. A squadron of Hurricanes saved the surviving two.

The next day went better for the RAF. Two dozen Hurricanes and Spitfires shot down a group of Stukas dive-bombing a convoy in the channel.

The RAF pilots also flew out of the low sun to surprise a group of Me-109s. In the dogfight that ensued, RAF fighters shot down four Me-109s but lost two of their own. [52]

Again and again, Göring sent over groups of bombers and fighters only to meet with mere handfuls of Hurricanes and Spitfires. Göring and his men concluded that owing to the fights over France, RAF Fighter Command's fighter force numbered only a fraction of that of the Luftwaffe. Actually, this assumption was far from the case. The head of Fighter Command, Air Chief Marshal Dowding, was husbanding his resources, risking only as many Hurricanes and Spitfires at a time as he dared, sensing a more forceful offensive coming later. If the Germans came to the wrong conclusion, so much the better. Dowding well understood that his main task was to keep Fighter Command alive into the autumn, when a seaborne invasion would be impractical. He more or less had to hold the Luftwaffe at bay rather than defeat or overwhelm its forces. Göring's was the harder job—that is, whittling Fighter Command until it became toothless.[53]

Through July, Göring made progress. From July 10 to the end of the month, Göring's planes shot down 69 RAF fighters. They also sank 4 Royal Navy destroyers, 2 large ships, and 18 coastal vessels. But their own losses were significant: in this same period they lost 155 fighters and bombers to RAF pilots.[54] Indeed, the RAF was getting better at what the Germans were calling the *Kanalkampf*, or "channel struggle." The British fighters learned they should not fly in tight formation; instead, they flew rather loosely, the way the Luftwaffe pilots had learned to do during the Spanish Civil War. The looser formation gave the pilots more flexibility and allowed them to concentrate more on possible German formations in the vicinity than on keeping their wingtips close. The British also learned they should withdraw the Defiant fighters from daylight battles and convert them to night fighters. And they came to believe, owing to Ultra intercepts and the husbanded numbers of planes the Germans were sending up, that the real test was yet to come. Dowding watched and waited, and he rationed his Hurricanes and Spitfires sparingly.

On July 31 Churchill cabled Roosevelt. He had not done so for six weeks, since June 15 or before the fall of France. This lengthy time was one of serious anxiety in Britain. In part, Churchill's dearth of personal appeals had to do with American politics—the Democratic Convention that nominated Roosevelt to a third term was held in mid-July, and the prime minister shrank from seeming to interfere during an anxious time for the president—yet he also did not want to make so many entreaties that one diluted another. After all these weeks of silence, however, Churchill's cable took a desperate tone.

> It has now become most urgent for you to let us have the destroyers . . .
> for which we have asked. . . . We could not keep up the present rate of
> casualties for long, and if we cannot get a substantial reinforcement,
> the whole fate of the war may be decided by this minor and easily
> remediable factor. . . . Mr. President, with great respect I must tell you
> that in the long history of the world, this is a thing to do now.[55]

That same day Hitler gathered his major military leaders at his Bavarian Alps residence, the Berghof, near Berchtesgaden. Up in the clean, cool air of the pristine mountains, the Nazis led a major planning and strategy session. Admiral Raeder of the Kriegsmarine made the first presentation. The naval chief again stressed that an invasion of England could not succeed without local air superiority, which had not yet been achieved. Stressing other difficulties, Raeder suggested that a date for the invasion would be better set in the spring. Hitler did not contest this perspective but remarked that renewed and larger Luftwaffe attacks would be telling; if Göring's planes could achieve air superiority, the Germans would invade in the middle or latter part of September. Raeder was then dismissed, and Hitler ruminated with his generals.

The führer told them he believed Britain was relying on two prospective allies: Russia and the United States. He was beginning to feel that if he could smash Russia, Britain could then only look for salvation to the United States. On the one hand, doing so looked like weak succor. For the time being, the United States would very likely be distracted by Japan's belligerence in the Pacific; moreover, within the United States was a powerful isolationist element working to keep it out of the European war. The nation was not yet close to having the army or the armaments production it would need to save Britain; indeed, the U.S. Army was only about a third the size of what Belgium had put into the field in May. Further, it had only about 150 fighter aircraft.[56] On the other hand, Britain seemed to be making inroads in American public opinion, and the industrial potential of the United States was enormous. When the United States mobilized its manpower and industrial capacity for war, it might then weigh in against Germany. Therefore, time was not on Germany's side, Hitler said; the sooner it knocked Britain out of the war by defeating its prospective ally Russia, the better. Hitler told his generals that if it could not happen in a lightning stroke in the autumn, it would be a season's campaign once good weather resumed in the spring.

To the attendant German generals, Hitler's confidence about success in Russia seemed well founded. Stalin had executed the cream of the Red Army's officer corps in the purges of 1937–39. Moreover, the Russians had done poorly against the underequipped Finns in their brief Winter War of November 1939–March 1940. And if the Wehrmacht could overrun France with its immense and respected army in only a few weeks, it was very likely to slice readily through the Soviets, who, according to Nazi doctrine, were an inferior people anyway. So with Russia smashed, Britain would have no hope of getting aid from that country and scant help any time soon from the United States. It would have to face coming to terms or be crushed.

The führer told his generals an invasion of Russia might commence in May 1941.

CHAPTER FIVE

RADAR, RADIO WAVES, AND THE RACE FOR AIR SUPERIORITY

"Unless science can find some way to come to the rescue,
any war within the next ten years is bound to be lost."
—*A. P. Rowe, British Air Ministry, 1934*[1]

All other things being equal, if two air forces set against each other in a battle of attrition, the larger one would eventually win. In July 1940 the Luftwaffe could put twice as many planes into the air as RAF Fighter Command had fighter aircraft. Although half the German planes were bombers, in a battle of attrition, the RAF looked to be the loser.

Most of the aircraft on either side were developed using mid-1930s technology and now were in mass production. Some models were better than others, and each air force had its superior types. Overall, the planes on the opposing sides were fairly evenly matched. With equal losses, the RAF would lose air superiority over its island.

Britain, however, did have a number of advantages. For one, if a pilot bailed out over Britain and landed uninjured, he could promptly rejoin the fight, but Germans who bailed out over Britain became prisoners of war and were lost entirely to the German cause. In addition, the British fighter aircraft could remain aloft for an hour or more at a time whereas the German planes, requiring time to travel to and from their destinations, could only remain over southern England for twenty to thirty minutes. These two advantages might work to lessen the RAF's odds against the Germans, but technology in one form was working against the British.

The problem was the speed of the aircraft. Once over the channel, German fighters and bombers could reach their targets in minutes. If they wanted to bomb London, they would need little time to fly from the sea to what was then the largest city in the world. On a clear day, observers along the English coast could telephone a warning to RAF airfields, but the RAF fighters would need at least two minutes just to get off the ground. Moreover, they would need ten to fifteen minutes to climb to the necessary height of twenty thousand feet from which they could attack the enemy bombers. The remedy to this problem was to have squadrons of RAF fighters constantly patrolling the skies over southern England, with each assigned to a sector and looking for invading bombers. But given the manpower and fuel required, flying around in circles to merely keep a watchful eye was out of the question. The area of greatest threat—the portion of southern England from the channel north to London—was 250 miles long and 150 miles wide. Squadron patrols would require too many pilots and too much fuel while engaging too few enemy aircraft. The RAF fighters would be used highly inefficiently. In that situation, the likelihood of Fighter Command holding the Luftwaffe at bay was poor indeed. Britain would need still more advantages. Luckily, strategists in the mid-1930s had foreseen this requirement.

In the early 1930s, much strategic thinking about airpower revolved around the mounting strength of bombers. Planners thought these aircraft were developing so swiftly and in such numbers that in a future war, fleets of them would obliterate industrial complexes and even whole cities. As noted, they believed that wars could be won after air fleets destroyed the enemy's infrastructure and broke the will of the civilian population. Stanley Baldwin, who served as Britain's prime minister three times during the 1920s and 1930s, echoed this thinking when he gave a dreary speech to the House of Commons in late 1932, intoning, "The bomber will always get through."[2] In a sense, this belief was a mantra for peace: the prospect of mutual destruction by bombers would prevent future wars.

But Baldwin's admission also recognized that Britain was no longer an island; indeed, in minutes enemies could span its surrounding North Sea, Celtic Sea, and English Channel to wreak havoc on its people. Britain's successful barrier to invasion for a thousand years was suddenly of little consequence. Britain decided to build bombers in the wan hope that such aircraft would be a deterrent to a future war and to build fighters with which to defend itself against bombers. As money was scarce during the Depression years, the fighters would be few, especially compared to the numbers of aircraft acquired by the burgeoning Nazi Germany across the North Sea.

If, as some people suspected, Germany would conduct an air war against Britain and with superior numbers, then under conditions as military planners understood, British fighters would eventually dwindle due to attrition. Constant patrolling would speed the attrition by wearying the pilots and depleting fuel supplies. Moreover, since British fighters would have to regularly descend to refuel, they could be caught on the ground or at low altitudes by arriving German planes.

But if fighter coordinators could know where invaders were, they could tell pilots directly where to go. Pilots would not have to waste fuel or time in wearisome searches. They would be efficient, flying to their enemy targets, shooting at them through their hour in the air, and returning to their airfields. And so long as the fighter coordinators knew when and from what direction the enemy planes were coming, the British planes would not be caught at low altitude or on the ground. But how could the planners accomplish this state of readiness?

A quick first answer was to use observers on the ground. But weather over England is often cloudy, and when observers spotted bombers, there would likely be too little time to alert fighters then get them up to the proper altitude and location before the bombers could bomb their targets. In all, British fighters would need about twenty to thirty minutes' lead time to properly position themselves to attack.

Another idea was sound detection. But sound travels at about 750 miles per hour, or only three times faster than the incoming airplanes themselves. In the time it took a sound wave from an airplane engine to travel across the channel, the airplane would have flown a third of the way across. Again this type of detection was not fast enough. The British needed a way to spy enemy planes while they were still thirty minutes away, over the coasts of France and Belgium.

In August 1934, physicist and Oxford professor of experimental philosophy Frederick Lindemann, a friend of Winston Churchill's, wrote a letter to the London *Times* and publicly declared:

That there is at present no means of preventing hostile bombers from depositing their loads of explosives, incendiary materials, gases, or bacteria upon their objectives I believe to be true; that no method can be devised to safeguard great centres of population from such a fate appears to me to be profoundly improbable . . . To adopt a defeatist attitude in the face of such a threat is inexcusable. . . .[3]

At the same time, a civil servant named A. P. Rowe at the Air Ministry was mulling the bomber problem. He decided to research all he could find on aerial defense. Afterward he wrote a memo to his boss, Director of Scientific Research H. E. Wimperis, that bluntly said science had to find a way to defend against the bomber threat within the decade or Britain could expect to lose the next war.

Unlike countless other government memos, this one received attention. Wimperis wrote his own boss, Secretary of State for Air Charles Vane-Tempest-Stewart, Lord Londonderry, and to Hugh Dowding, the former World War I fighter pilot who at the time was in charge of RAF research and development, about setting up a committee to look into the problem. With a stroke of genius or courage or both, Rowe suggested that the Air Ministry itself might not have the necessary brainpower to do the job and should bring in outsiders. Both Londonderry and Dowding were unconventional thinkers and so out of the mainstream, in fact, that they were somewhat ignored by the bureaucrats around them. Londonderry and Dowding took Rowe's and Wimperis's suggestions and set up the committee. They appointed Wimperis and Rowe and turned the chairmanship over to a respected outside scientist, another World War I flier named Henry Tizard.

The Tizard Committee, as it was often called (though the official name was the Committee for the Scientific Survey of Air Defense), immediately enlisted a brilliant forty-two-year-old Scot by the name of Robert Watson-Watt.[4] Then the superintendent of radio research at the National Physical Laboratory, Watson-Watt looked into the scientific merit of using radio waves as a defense against high-flying intruder bombers. In those days fiction writers were much enamored of "death rays," or invisible energy beams that could stun or kill. Their Buck Rogers–like characters boasted pistol-style ray guns that almost silently subdued enemies, and radio genius Guglielmo Marconi was rumored to be developing one for Mussolini.

The committee doubted there could be much truth to these fantasies but asked Watson-Watt to look into them.

Watson-Watt did not believe in the feasibility of death rays either but scribbled a message to his subordinate Arnold "Skip" Wilkins. Specifically, he asked Wilkins to calculate the amount of radio frequency power needed to raise the temperature of eight pints of water from 98 degrees Fahrenheit to 105 degrees Fahrenheit at a distance of five kilometers and at a height of one kilometer.

Wilkins was not fooled by the obtuseness of the inquiry. A pilot flying at three thousand feet has eight pints of blood, nearly pure water, and if the pilot's temperature rose to 105 degrees Fahrenheit, he would lapse into delirium and lose control of his plane.

Wilkins replied that the amount of energy needed for such radiation, or death rays, was much too enormous to consider. He added that a 1932 report by British Post Office engineers indicated that their radio waves showed a disturbance when airplanes flew nearby. In fact the airplanes re-radiated the radio signals, and this physical property might be a means of rapidly detecting aircraft at a distance.

Scientists for years had known that metal objects such as ships or airplanes interfered with radio waves. Technically what happened was that when an electromagnetic wave—a carrier of energy—struck a metal object, it stimulated the electron clouds in the metal's atoms. Thus stimulated, the electron clouds emitted a new wave as they returned to an unstimulated state. Generally, these "echoes," or interference, were thought to be a nuisance. But some scientists had made the detection connection. In the 1920s two radio researchers at the Anacostia Naval Air Station in Washington, D.C., had noticed radio-wave interference when a ship passed, and suggested a shore-to-shore warning system by placing a transmitter and receiver on opposite sides of a harbor entrance. Thus the radio gear would detect ships entering at night or under foggy conditions. Nothing came of the harbor entrance scheme, though by the 1930s the Americans, Japanese, and Germans were all working on radio wave detection systems. But the British, perhaps because they had suffered the air raids from blimps and bombers in World War I, were more defensive-minded than the others and were more determined to research how radio waves could identify the location and bearing of aircraft. Radio waves overcame the defects of ground observation and sound detection. They traveled at the speed of light, so if they could detect an airplane 150 miles away, they would do so practically instantaneously.

Wilkins and Watson-Watt calculated. They believed that the best radio wave for detecting a metal bomber of about a seventy-five-foot wingspan was one of about the same length, or a wavelength of seventy-five feet. Moreover, in terms of power and reception, such radio waves could be relatively easily transmitted and their echoes, or re-radiated waves, could be detected on equipment that could be built.

They reported their finding at the committee's first meeting in January 1935. Rowe checked the math; Wimperis checked the math. Indeed it seemed possible.

Wimperis asked Watson-Watt for more information, and the Scot scientist within weeks presented the committee with a paper called "Detection and Location of Aircraft by Radio Means." Now the committee had something to work on, and a reasonable amount of money was given to Watson-Watt to continue his research.

The Scot began work at once. His idea was to create a short pulse— about 0.0002 seconds (and later trimmed to an even shorter duration)—of a radio wave and then determine if a re-radiated wave was generated. The time between the pulse and any echo wave would determine the distance of the object that created the re-radiated wave. Watson-Watt called this system radio direction finding (RDF). Later in the war the British term was changed to conform to the American acronym, radio detection and ranging (radar).[5] To this point he did not so much attempt to determine height as focus on location and bearing.

Watson-Watt established an experimental station on an isolated spit of land near the town of Orford on the North Sea sixty-five miles from London. He and his crew began building transmitters and receivers. The receivers were to capture both the original pulse and the echoes and display them on a cathode ray tube. By summer Watson-Watt's team of radio engineers were reading echoes from aircraft. But there was much work yet to be done. They had to figure ways of not being fooled by commercial radio waves and to counter efforts should an enemy detect the radar pulses and send out their own "jamming" pulses on this wavelength. By the autumn of 1935, the committee had decided to build a line of transmitters and receivers from Southampton on the channel east past Dover and up the coast to Scotland. The sites would be called Chain Home (CH) stations. (When locals grumbled, the Air Ministry promised to build the towers so as not to "gravely interfere with grouse shooting.") Thus, a curtain of radio waves would pulse outward from half the coast of Britain so that no aircraft could approach from these directions without detection.

To help solve the problem of determining the altitude of an intruding aircraft, receivers were placed at different heights on the CH towers. The difference in the strength of a signal received from an upper and lower receiver would indicate the height of the approaching intruder. Such altitude determination was crude at best.

Direction was another problem, but Watson-Watt developed an elegant solution. He had pairs of receivers placed at right angles to each other. A plane flying directly at one would produce a strong signal in it but a low signal in the other; however, if flying at an angle midway within the right angle formed by the two receivers, it would produce a signal of equal strength in both. Analyzing the signal strength between the two echo receptions would thus give a rough idea of the aircraft's direction. The strength of the echo wave also was an indicator of the size of the plane formation, should there be more than one plane. Nevertheless, accuracy was elusive. Seventy-five miles out, the RDF could only judge that a plane or planes would be in an area of fifteen square miles and at an altitude range spanning two thousand feet. During training, fighters sent out to intercept often could not find practice intruders.

Moreover the RDF was meant only to look outward, across the seas; detecting the position of airplanes over the landmass of Britain was a complication readily dismissed. Once planes passed from the channel or North Sea over the CH stations, they went off the cathode ray tubes because the beams were blocked in that direction. Tracking the planes passed to members of the Royal Observer Corps, mainly civilian volunteers who set up on hills, in church steeples, or atop tall buildings. These men and women were equipped with binoculars, aircraft identification illustrations, and simple instruments meant to determine the planes' altitude and bearing. They would telephone their findings to Fighter Command group and sector stations. More than thirty thousand Observer Corps men and women served in 1940.[6]

Dowding could see the great advantage of RDF and the Observer Corps from the first. When he took over Fighter Command in July 1936, he continued to champion the work and urged its advancement.

It was a close call. The radar effort might have been squashed early on, even at the hand of Winston Churchill via his good friend and science adviser Lindemann. Since Lindemann's letter to the *Times*, the Oxford professor had developed his own ideas about dealing with bombers. RDF was not the way, he believed. Detecting them with heat sensors would be better, and the way to counter them was developing either aerial mines that floated down on the aircraft from above or steel cables that would foul their propellers. Had Churchill been appointed prime minister in the late 1930s rather than in 1940, Lindemann may have had more power and thereby scuttled radar in favor of his other schemes.

As it was, though, by the time of the Munich crisis in September 1938, many CH towers had been built, and five were already operating twenty-four hours a day. Accuracy was still a problem, but operators could detect airplanes taking off in Belgium and France 150 miles away. A blind spot was below three thousand feet; planes flying this close to the ground could not be detected with the regular radio waves. Thus, a shorter radio wave was needed and new towers built—they were—but these stations could detect planes only about 50 miles away.

Engineers also had to work on communication and coordination, which was just as vital to the defensive effort as detecting the intruder planes themselves. They faced problems of determining whether two CH stations were detecting the same or different groups of aircraft and how to resolve any differences in their estimates of location, bearing, and altitude. Then they had to figure out how to assemble the information, route it up the chain of command, evaluate it correctly, and send it to the RAF commanders, who would then order specific fighter squadrons into the air.

They accomplished it in part by deeply burying telephone lines from each CH station and Observer Corps site to the headquarters of Fighter Command at Bentley Priory northwest of downtown London. Here the RDF's and Observer Corps' results were analyzed and coordinated in an underground filter room. When the bearings and approximate size of German plane groups were understood, the information was sent to an underground operations room, where personnel would organize and synthesize the information. At the center of the room was a table-high, fifteen-foot-diameter horizontal map of southern England and the nearby coast of the continent. When groups of enemy aircraft were detected, their number and location were placed on the map by a red marker; black markers noted positions of RAF squadrons. Women's Auxiliary Air Force staff, outfitted with headphones with wires attached for receiving information on the planes' locations, used casino croupiers' rakes to push and pull the markers around the map as the plane groups moved. Watson-Watt and Dowding believed that mainly women should operate the radar scopes at CH stations and the telephones and the filter rooms at group and sector locations around the country. Men, of course, would be in short supply, and both leaders thought women were more precise than men would be in these roles. Women would not give commands to pilots in the air, however; that job was reserved for those pilots who were not flying missions at the time.

Perched in a mezzanine viewing area above the rake-wielding WAAFs and the large map of southern England were senior Fighter Command officers who could look down on the map and see the movements of the battle. They decided which of three RAF fighter groups to alert: 10 Group, which roughly covered southwest England; 11 Group, southeast England to just north of London; and 12 Group, north of the other two to Liverpool. The three groups themselves had similar operations rooms with large map tables and people to move markers. The groups decided which of their several sectors to alert, sending orders to the Sector Control stations. These sectors, in turn, alerted the airfields, whose personnel decided which squadrons to "scramble" and slash into a group of invading aircraft. Operations rooms also had lighted vertical boards showing the status of squadrons: released (not available), available (airborne in twenty minutes), readiness (airborne in five minutes), standby (pilots in the cockpits), airborne and moving into position, enemy sighted, ordered to land, and landed and refueling or rearming.[7]

Once the fighters were in the air, controllers at the airfields told them their headings and desired altitude. For example, "vector 180" meant head due south, and "angel 15" meant level off at fifteen thousand feet. The fighters were to follow the controllers' instructions until they had enemy aircraft in sight. Then they were on their own.

Henry Tizard and Hugh Dowding championed the new technology with the passion of men who sensed the conflict of survival was drawing nigh. Through the late 1930s, the RAF continued to test the system with mock air raids. Group commanders learned to immediately obey any telephoned command for whatsoever number of squadrons to be scrambled, and fighter pilots learned to accept radioed directions.

However, there was yet another problem to address: the RAF planes gave the same echo that enemy planes would. Engineers solved this difficulty by installing in each RAF plane a receiver/transmitter called the Identification Friend or Foe (IFF). It would detect pulses sent by the CH stations and send back a response signal whose echo on the cathode ray tubes looked larger than those from enemy planes. Engineers began to fit IFF boxes into British planes in 1939. They were, of course, highly secret. Their general code name was Parrot, and any RAF pilot who forgot to activate his device once in his aircraft was reminded to "squawk your parrot."

The RDF, of course, was also very top secret. The British had no intention of letting the Germans learn how RAF fighters could spot invaders 150 miles away and then hone in on them with fighter aircraft. But no one could miss the 350-foot spindly towers rising along the southern and eastern coasts of Britain. Moreover, Germany was well versed in electromagnetic radiation waves, as it was a German, Heinrich Hertz, who in the 1880s discovered radio waves as well as their characteristic of "echoing" off metal. The Germans suspected the towers were associated with radio wave transmission and perhaps with detection. In 1938, in order to learn more, they equipped a lighter-than-air zeppelin with radio gear; sent it up and down in international waters off Suffolk's Bawdsey Manor, then the center for radio research after the Orford site had been outgrown; the point was to listen in on the Bawdsey Manor towers' transmissions and determine their purpose. But the zeppelin crew heard nothing—their radio receivers were faulty. The Germans tried again in the summer of 1939, but again the zeppelin crew heard nothing; this time the British RDF was in need of repair and not functioning. At the time German radar could detect planes at fifty miles, and German engineers had only a scant notion that the British could detect their planes at three times the distance. The Germans thought more of using radar for their navy because they were thinking in terms of offense and attack and not of defense against airplanes. They did not appreciate how rapidly the British developed their detection capabilities or how effectively they had learned to put it to use.

Even after the war began, however, the RDF and CH station system had kinks to be worked out. On September 6, just three days after Britain declared war on Germany and with King George VI alongside Dowding in the operations room of Bentley Priory, a report of enemy planes came in, so a section station sent up a squadron. Then a second blip showed on the cathode ray screens, and another squadron was sent aloft, only to have yet another blip appear. Soon all the squadrons in the sector were aloft and the screens were filled with blips. Two fighters were shot down in the melee, and when the RAF fighters had to descend for refueling, the blips on the screen disappeared. An investigation later in the day showed that no German planes had invaded British space; instead, all the blips represented British aircraft, including the two planes that were shot down, killing one of the pilots. The problem that day was that the RDF signals had not been properly blocked on the transmitters' land side. Since the cathode ray screens could not tell the difference between echo waves coming from forward positions or behind, cathode ray tube readers believed the blips were emanating from over the sea. The more RAF planes took to the air, the more blips appeared on the screen. Technicians quickly ensured this kind of trouble would not be repeated.[8]

Across the waves of the North Sea, the Germans were laboring to harness electromagnetic radiation to the service of airplanes as well as ships. But as noted they tended to think in terms of offense rather than defense. What they wanted was a way to navigate their bombers to the proper targets under any condition, including cloudy days or at night over a blacked-out countryside. For nighttime flying there was navigation by the stars; indeed, it was how the British bombers charted their courses. But the Germans, believing they could do better, worked on a variation of an airfield bad-weather and nighttime landing system. The method depended on radio wave impulses narrowed into a beam lined up with the end of runways and named for the company that made the equipment, Lorenz.

Radio waves spread out from their point of emanation similar to ripples from a stone thrown into a pond. To create a directed beam, the Lorenz airplane landing system first blocked the radio waves from emanating back toward the runway so that the waves went out only toward where planes would fly in for a landing. Using the characteristics of wave interference, the system used three transmitters—a central one and ones set out to either side. The central transmitter emanated a standard and continuous wave. The one on the right transmitted the same wave but was turned off at regular intervals, creating a kind of "dash" sound in an auditory receiver. The one on the left was on when the one on the right was off and turned off when its counterpart was turned on, so that the left transmitter gave a kind of "dot" sound in an auditory receiver.

When a plane approaching the runway was too far to the left, the pilot would hear a stronger dot sound and move to the right. If he was too far to the right, he would hear a stronger dash signal and move more to the left. When he was exactly aligned in the center, the dots and the dashes would meld into a continuous hum, and the pilot would know that he was on the proper course for touching down on the runway.

For radio navigational bombing the Germans then used two beams emanating from two different locations. If the transmitters for such beams were far apart and the signal beams adjusted to point properly, they would intersect over a target. Bombers would fly along one beam, correcting their heading all the while by avoiding the dots on one side and the dashes on the other. Eventually the planes would enter the region of the second beam, but being far off to the second beam's side, their operators would hear either a strong dash or strong dot. Eventually the stronger of the second beam's dots or dashes would weaken as the planes approached the center of the second beam. When the second beam's dots or dashes dissolved into a continuous hum, the planes were where the two beams intersected. They would then drop their bombs.

The system required stronger transmitters than the ones used at the ends of airport runways and two receivers in each bomber, each more sensitive than ones hitherto known. The German technicians put their minds to it and came up with a reasonable working system by 1940. They called it *Knickebein* (crooked leg).

The British, using star navigation for night bombing, had little inkling of Knickebein until November 1939 when the naval attaché at the British Embassy in Oslo found a seven-page typewritten letter (in German) in his mail from a "well-wishing German scientist." The package, which came

to be known as the Oslo Report, contained notes about German technological advances. It included secret and fantastic weapons systems, such
as long-range rockets; jet-powered, remote control gliders; proximity fuses
for naval torpedoes; proximity fuses for artillery shells; and radio beams to
guide bombers to targets.[9] The package soon made its way to British intelligence officials, who did not give it much credibility. They thought, that no
single person would have so much information, that the weapons systems
seemed too implausible, that the package seemed too good to be true, and
that one of its pieces of information—an estimate of the production of new
Junkers Ju-88 bombers—was exaggerated tenfold. Indeed, the British intelligence officials suspected the package was a German plant to put them off
the scent. Some officials who had copies destroyed them.

But a twenty-eight-year-old British scientist in the Air Ministry and
science adviser to MI6, Reginald V. Jones, thought the grasp of technology
exhibited by the Oslo Report's author rang true. He decided to devote some
of his time to studying the weapons. Jones, with a doctorate in physics from
Oxford, had been a student of Lindemann's for a time, and in 1940 he was
the only person in the Air Ministry working on scientific intelligence. He
well understood that in its eagerness to develop a defensive radar system,
the Air Ministry had generally ignored offensive measures to take against
German radar or other radio wave technologies. For months through the
Phony War, Jones worked virtually alone and with nothing to show that
the Germans might well be developing some of the systems sketched in
the Oslo Report.

Come spring, however, two captured Luftwaffe fliers were found to be
carrying scraps of paper inscribed with the word "Knickebein." About the
same time, a prisoner was overheard to mention Knickebein as if it might
be a bomb-dropping technology. And two prisoners who had revealed
nothing about Knickebein during their interrogation were later overheard
saying to one another that the British would never find Knickebein in their
crashed airplanes. But these instances were tenuous clues and not much
else. Then in June, Enigma cryptanalysts deciphered a message that read,
"Knickebein, Cleves, is adjusted to position 53^0 $24'$ north and 1^0 west."[10]
The cryptanalysts did not understand it, but Jones did: the Germans were
transmitting from Cleves, a town in Germany, a beam that crossed a point
near Derby in the Midlands, where Rolls-Royce made Merlin engines for

RAF fighter aircraft. Jones recalled that two Luftwaffe airmen had said investigators would not be able to find "Knickebein" in the aircraft. He asked an engineer who had been examining downed German bombers if there was anything unusual about the Lorenz receivers used for foul-weather landings. The engineer replied that indeed the Lorenz equipment was more sensitive than it had to be for aligning with a runway in low-visibility conditions.

Jones became convinced that the Germans had surpassed the British and overcome technical difficulties to create beams that projected hundreds of kilometers, not the thirty or so kilometers for runway landings. When he brought this idea to Lindemann, the professor balked, though he thought it merited further examination. In Lindemann's view, such beams would need to be of very short wavelengths, which would not follow the curve of the earth; instead, they would move in a straight line from the transmitters and shortly into outer space. Lindemann was right, but he forgot that an airplane could fly thousands of feet in the air and detect a short-wave radio wave not detectable on the surface of the earth below.

In mid-June Jones received an invitation to a meeting on the twenty-first at 10 Downing Street. A practical joker himself, Jones thought it was a colleague's ruse, but he went anyway, arriving late. Churchill was in a conference room full of science advisers, and when Jones walked in, Churchill gave him the floor. Recovering from his shock, Jones explained to Churchill and the men around the table the circumstantial evidence of the German bombing system. This news indeed was disquieting because the British had been relying on their normal bad weather and the difficulties of bombing in a blacked-out country at night to limit the enemy's bombing runs to clear days or to times when British fighters could best interfere. If the Germans could bomb accurately in foul weather and at night, Britain would be in dire straits. Officials gave Knickebein the code name Headache.

Churchill was impressed with Jones's explanation and ordered flights to see if German directional beams could be detected. The RAF put up a plane with special radio equipment, and it did find a beam, one that was four hundred to five hundred yards wide over the Midlands.[11] Now what could the British do? Officials decided not to jam the signals directly, for doing so would have tipped the Germans to the fact that the British had direct knowledge of the beams. Instead they engaged in an operation—

code-named, of course, Aspirin—in which they broadcast stronger dash beams alongside the real ones. This deception would cause German fliers to overcorrect away from the real dashes and send their bombs askew. If the Germans figured their bombings were inaccurate, they would likely blame faulty transmission or receiving equipment.

Thus at the end of July, as the Germans were stepping up their bombing efforts, the British were more alert to German advances in radio wave warfare and took some countermeasures. The bombings they suffered were quite enough without adding ones that would be going astray to cattle pastures.[12]

CHAPTER SIX

AUGUST

The Mailed Fist

"Tomorrow, the first of August, is the opening day of
the most critical month in history. If the British are standing
upright on September 1, I will say there is a good chance
of beating the Boches, no matter what may be
happening elsewhere."
—*Maj. Gen. Raymond Lee, U. S. military attaché,
U.S. Embassy, London*[1]

All through late July, Hermann Göring's Luftwaffe had attacked shipping in the channel, both to cripple Britain's lifeline and to draw up and then shoot down RAF fighters. The progress reports Göring received were good. Throughout July his pilots indicated that significant numbers of Hurricanes and Spitfires were destroyed, and the Luftwaffe chief passed along the welcome news to Adolf Hitler.

Accordingly, the day after his July 31 strategy session with his military leaders at the Berghof in the Alps, Hitler allowed Göring an expansion of the air battle by issuing Directive no. 17. It read in part:

In order to establish the conditions necessary for the final conquest of England, I intend to continue the air and naval war against the English homeland more intensively than heretofore. To this end, I issue the following orders: 1) The German Air Force is to overcome the British Air Force with all means at its disposal and as soon as possible.[2]

Directive no. 17 tasked the Luftwaffe with the effort to "destroy the RAF and Britain's air defenses, once and for all, by attacks not only against flying formations, but also against airfields and . . . aircraft industry." Then the harbors along the southern coast would be bombed into ruins, except those to be used by the invading Wehrmacht. Destroying the RAF and making other preparations for Operation Sea Lion—the invasion of Britain—were to be completed by September 15, but Hitler would decide whether to launch the invasion after analyzing the results of the air war one to two weeks after this newest and intense phase had begun. Directive no. 17 also forbade terror bombing of cities unless Hitler personally ordered it.[3] The Luftwaffe's expanded assignment could begin on or after August 6.

Thus Directive no. 17 set the stage for what the German High Command called *Adlerangriff,* or "Eagle Attack," with its first day of the offensive to be called *Adlertag,* or "Eagle Day." In order to crush the RAF, principally Fighter Command, Göring laid out in broad strokes an offensive beginning sometime after August 5 that for five days would attack targets up to a hundred kilometers from London, to be followed by three days of attacks up to fifty kilometers from London, and followed by five days of attacks up to the city's outskirts. With these attacks Göring expected the Luftwaffe to need only about two weeks to win air superiority over southern England, the key prerequisite to a seaborne invasion.

Göring had reasons to be optimistic. In the battles over France, his Luftwaffe had done well against the Hurricanes and Spitfires, especially against the Hurricanes, which the Germans shot down in encouraging numbers. But Göring was unaware of some of the reasons for his pilots' success. Over France the British did not have the advantage of RDF. Their fighters did not know when and from what direction the German planes were coming. So a significant portion of Hurricane and Spitfire losses were owed to being surprised in the air or being destroyed on the ground. Moreover, without RDF, the pilots had to patrol and used their planes far less efficiently.

In addition Göring believed his aircraft were superior to those of the RAF. On July 16 a Luftwaffe intelligence report claimed that one of its major fighters, the Me-110, was better than the RAF Hurricane and in some ways than the Spitfire, and that the Luftwaffe's premier fighter, the Me-

109, dominated both types of British fighter. The ordeal of validating these notions was about to come. Not only would the pilots be tested in this coming battle for air superiority over southern England, so would the planes themselves.

The same day that Hitler ordered Directive no. 17, August 1, President Roosevelt was visited by members of the Century Group, which was so named for a private club where they met in New York City. Comprising a handful of powerful private citizens intent on helping Britain, the Century Group pressed the idea that destroyers could be given to Britain in exchange for the use of military bases in the Western Hemisphere, notably in the Caribbean and off the coast of Canada. They also posed the notion that in exchange for the destroyers, the British would promise that in the event of a German conquest the Royal Navy would sail its fleet to America or scuttle it.

The next day, August 2, Roosevelt met with his cabinet and discussed the idea, which was politically sensitive—even more so in this election year—owing to the neutrality laws and to isolationists both among the public and in Congress. Roosevelt was especially keen that Republican presidential nominee Wendell Willkie not make sending old destroyers to Britain an election issue. But the cabinet approved the idea, and with the support of the Century Group, back-channel negotiations on a destroyer-for-bases deal between the British and the Americans began in earnest.

In addition the White House reached out to the Willkie campaign, revealed what it was working on, and asked that Willkie not make a campaign issue about the arrangement. Willkie agreed not to attack Roosevelt for his inclination of helping Britain, but he declined to make any promises about not coming out publicly for sending destroyers to Britain. Indeed, doing so would likely vex many of the isolationists in the Republican camp.

Meanwhile, Philip Kerr, Lord Lothian, Britain's ambassador to the United States, worked with officials in both governments on how a bases-for-destroyers arrangement might be made. Churchill did not like the proposed promise, in the event of Britain succumbing to the Germans, of sending the British fleet to Canada or to the United States as a condition for receiving the destroyers. Through Lothian, he tried to reassure the Americans that he was pledged never to allow the British fleet to fall to the Germans; however, he could not speak for a government that might succeed his own and that might bargain away the fleet in order to receive easier armistice terms. In any event the prime minister thought that if this condition were included in the negotiations about the destroyers, it might look as if Britain felt it was facing defeat, and he did not want to encourage that line of thinking.

Other efforts at cooperation between Britain and the United States were in the offing. By the middle of August, aides had paved the way for a meeting between Roosevelt and Canadian prime minister Mackenzie King in Ogdensburg, New York, on the Saint Lawrence River north of the Adirondack Mountains. Roosevelt was to be in the area, watching First Army maneuvers at the military camp nearby (bereft of modern weapons, army units used trucks with protruding telephone poles to act for tanks).[4] The meeting led to an agreement later in the month to set up a Joint Defense Board by which Canada and the United States would collaborate on defense in the hemisphere, including the sharing of military installations. For the United States, this accord was a notable step away from isolationism.

HURRICANES, SPITFIRES, MESSERSCHMITTS, AND MORE

Into the early 1930s, the British were building airplane fighters that were biplanes with open cockpits. The argument for biplanes was that the two wings could be wired together, each thus drawing strength from the other. But improvements in metals and design techniques were showing that single-wing planes could make good fighters. In addition the wings could be made to support the weight and recoil of machine guns, which could thus be outside the radius of the propeller and fire continuously. (In biplanes the machine guns were attached to the fuselage, generally in front of the pilot, and had to conform to the rhythm of the propeller in order to fire bullets through the propeller's sweep.) Freer, more rapid fire from the machine guns was seen to be increasingly important because by the mid-1930s it was thought, and was likely, that if a fighter had a bomber in its gun sights for only one to two seconds, it would need six—eight would be better— guns firing a thousand rounds a minute to bring it down. In addition, for the pilot's added protection, the cockpit could be covered with a sliding or tilting canopy.

All of these proposed changes caused considerable debate in the Air Ministry. The men with the power to approve aircraft design had been combat pilots only twenty years before and defended the notion that pilots had to carry hammers to free jammed bullets in the breeches of their guns. This action would, of course, be impossible if the guns were in the wings.[5] Their arguments were countered by the fact that the Browning machine guns were more reliable than the earlier models.

Conceived in 1933 principally by an aeronautical engineer named Sidney Camm at the Hawker Aircraft Company, the first Hurricanes were flying in 1936, showing a top speed of 315 miles per hour at 16,000 feet. They were powered by a 12-cylinder, liquid-cooled Rolls-Royce engine given the name Merlin. Although the wings were of stressed metal, much of the fuselage of the Hurricanes was fabric, and the propellers were made of wood. The planes' operational ceiling was 34,000 feet, and they could climb from the ground to 20,000 feet in 8 minutes.[6]

Since 1935, Britain had been trying its best to strengthen its fighter arm or at least catch up to Germany's. Factories worked furiously. Even so, when war was thought to be imminent during the Munich crisis in the autumn of 1938, only five of the twenty-nine fighter squadrons in Britain had Hurricanes.[7] In fact, Hugh Dowding, the head of RAF Fighter Command, advised Prime Minister Chamberlain during the Munich crisis to develop a peaceable solution because Dowding feared the nation did not yet have a sufficient fighter force to defend itself.[8]

The story of the Spitfire's development has its own peculiarity. The Supermarine Aviation Works made racing seaplanes. Vickers took over the company in 1928 and wanted to develop aircraft for the RAF. Although only in his thirties, Reginald J. Mitchell, a designer for Supermarine, had been diagnosed with cancer and in 1933 underwent an operation, which was not particularly successful. He traveled to Germany during his recovery and was unsettled by the Nazis' fervor. When he returned to Britain in 1934, he resolved to refuse additional treatment for the cancer and plunged into the work of creating an airplane that could stop German bombers.[9] It resulted in the Spitfire, and work began on it a year after efforts began on the Hurricane. Like the Hurricane, the Spitfire's design was powered by the Rolls-Royce Merlin engine, but the plane had an all-metal body. The first Spitfire took to the air in 1936, about four months after the Hurricane's debut. The government's first order was for 310 of them.

The Spitfire was slightly faster than the Hurricane, reaching 370 miles per hour by the outbreak of the war. It also could turn sharply. But many pilots preferred the better forward view of the Hurricane and its closely set machine guns in the wings rather than the widely spaced ones of the Spitfire. Moreover, the Hurricane could endure more damage than the Spitfire, and it was easier to maintain.

The Hurricanes and Spitfires during the Battle of France used 87-octane fuel, but back in Britain the engineers upgraded them to 100 octane. Doing so increased their performance, especially their rates of climb. German fighter pilots flying over the channel or Britain noticed this improvement, to their dismay, and wondered at the reason. Only when an RAF fighter had been forced down in France and its fuel analyzed did they understand why the British fighters were quicker than they had been only weeks before. The fuel that saved many a Fighter Command pilot in a dogfight was supplied by U.S. refineries.[10]

The basic unit of RAF Fighter Command was the squadron, of which there were about forty-four ready in mid-July 1940.[11] Each squadron was meant to have twelve aircraft and eighteen pilots. A sector station might serve three to four squadrons at any one time, and a forward or subordinate airfield would have fewer, with the squadrons being assigned as required for the battle and for a squadron's rest and refitting. Collectively, the squadrons at a sector station were called wings, but normally they did not fly as a group; rather, squadrons were scrambled individually. If a squadron needed to be reinforced, normally another one was called from a different airfield. Generally squadrons did not fly as units either but split into A and B flights of six fighters each that were often identified by a color—red, green, or blue, for example. The leader of a flight was called by color and title, for example, Red Leader. Other planes in a flight would have numbers—Red 1, Red 2, and so on.[12]

When squadrons were scrambled, their sector stations told them where to go by compass bearing—"Vector two-seventy," for instance—and height, with the word "angel" standing for altitude. So a typical command would be "Vector ninety, angel twelve." The fighters wanted to gain their height (taking about ten minutes) and position themselves against the sun before attacking enemy plane formations. Barring technical difficulties that could arise, the British pilots were in continual contact with their sector stations about developments and changes. The German ground crews, however, had neither any way of knowing where the RAF planes were nor any way to exercise general control of the German planes once they took off.[13]

In Germany the Me-109 was also a product of the mid-1930s. Designed to be the Luftwaffe's frontline production fighter, its prototype first flew in 1935. Its Daimler-Benz engine was similar to the Rolls-Royce Merlin, except that it had fuel injection and a supercharger, both of which improved its performance. It was faster than a Hurricane and somewhat slower than a Spitfire, though it could climb faster. Owing in part to the supercharger, it also had a higher ceiling than that of either British plane, thirty-six thousand feet. Given this was two thousand feet higher than the Spitfire's top ceiling, one of the Me-109 pilot's tactics was to fly higher and then pounce down on unsuspecting aircraft. During the Battle of Britain, however, Me-109s mainly fought at lower levels in order to protect the low-flying bombers. This situation prompted one military historian to say, "If the Battle of Britain had been fought at 30,000 feet, the RAF would have lost it."[14] Unlike the Hurricane or Spitfire, the Me-109 was equipped with one or two cannons, whose shells exploded on impact, as well as with machine guns. The cannons had a longer range than machine guns did, allowing the Me-109s to open fire sooner than the RAF fighters could, and the cannon shells were better at piercing armor. The principal disadvantage of the Me-109 was its range. Even flying from northern France, it only held enough fuel for twenty to thirty minutes over southern England and ten minutes over London if it were to get back to base.[15]

In part to make up for the Me-109's range problem, the Germans developed a two-engine, two-person fighter—the Me-110. The plane had a gunner facing to the rear, two bulbous engines on its wings, and a twin tail. It also served a dual role: as a fighter-bomber, it first carried two 500-kilogram bombs under the wings; after dropping its bombs, it became a fighter. But at 365 miles per hour (without bombs), it was slower than a Spitfire and, being larger than an Me-109, easier to hit. It never lived up to Göring's promise of becoming the elite machine of the Luftwaffe's fighter force.

Mainly the Luftwaffe would throw at England its waves of bombers. They were meant at first to wreck aircraft factories and lure up the RAF fighters, which the German Me-109s and Me-110s were meant to destroy, thus gaining the air superiority the German army and navy would need for a successful invasion. Principal among the bombers was the Dornier 17, developed in the early 1930s as a fast mail-carrying airplane and only later converted to bomber duty. British fliers dubbed the Dornier 17 the "flying pencil," owing to its long and slender body when seen from the side. Its nose was nearly all Plexiglas. It carried a crew of four and a bomb load of about two thousand pounds, which with the proper crew and conditions it could deliver with exceptional accuracy. But its top speed was only about 265 miles per hour; it had no chance of outrunning the British fighters.

The other workhorse of the Luftwaffe bomber fleet was the Heinkel 111H. Also developed in the early 1930s, it was successful in the Spanish Civil War but was nearing obsolescence. A twin-engine bomber, the He-111 could carry two and a half times the bomb load of the Dornier 17, or fifty-five hundred pounds, but it was also a bit slower. It had six machine guns, including one unmanned gun that shot directly out the rear in hopes of a lucky hit on a pursuing fighter, and one 20mm cannon, but it could never adequately defend itself against the charges of Hurricanes and Spitfires.

In addition to these bombers were the Junkers 87s, also known as Ju-87s or Stukas. Designed by Hermann Pohlmann and modeled after an American Curtiss Helldiver at German aircraft designer and pilot Ernst Udet's urging, it was successful in the Spanish Civil War and again in Poland against both ships at sea and massed troops on land. The Stuka also proved the bane of French troops, supply masters, and commanders during the Battle of France. A Stuka could consistently place a bomb within forty yards of a target, but its slow dive—only 150 miles per hour—allowed the far speedier Hurricanes and Spitfires to run it down as the Stuka moved against a target.

These three principal German bombers were not developed for subduing the likes of Britain by blasting industrial targets and cities, but more for supporting ground troops. Yet what they lacked in individual striking power, they made up for in numbers in the summer of 1940. The Luftwaffe could put more than a thousand of them into the battle.[16] In all, Göring's air force could launch about 1,100 long-range bombers—mostly the Dornier 17s and He-111s, and more than 300 Stukas. For fighters, it had 800 Me-109s and 150 Me-110s.[17]

Against this lineup, Britain's Fighter Command could put up about 350 Hurricanes and 250 Spitfires, plus 60 or so obsolete or otherwise unworthy fighters. The Germans had cause for optimism. They knew the RAF had suffered heavily during Dunkirk and the Battle for France. At Dunkirk alone the British lost 106 fighters and 75 pilots.[18] German intelligence reports said the British aircraft factories and pilot training schools could not possibly match these rates of loss. The German pilots looked ahead to Adlerangriff with confidence. Keep shooting down the Hurricanes and Spitfires day after day, they were told, and soon there would be none left.

THE ANTAGONISTS

It was Hugh Dowding's job to keep the Hurricanes and Spitfires flying and attacking, day after day, until the Germans saw the futility of their efforts. Born in 1882, Dowding began his military career in the artillery but took flying lessons just before World War I. He became a pilot during the first part of the war, commanding a squadron of planes and later a wing, or group of squadrons. He specialized in radio communications that allowed airplanes to be artillery spotters. For the last two years of the war, he was a trainer and at thirty-five years old became a brigadier general. He moved up steadily and by the early 1930s was in a position to push hard for technological developments. Referring to the windows in Al Capone's car, he once supposedly said when government bureaucrats wanted to save money, "I do not see why the gangsters of Chicago should be able to have bulletproof glass when our pilots cannot."[19] He championed the metal monoplanes over the wooden biplanes as the future fighters. He pushed hard for the Hurricane and the Spitfire, and as noted in chapter 5, he supported Watson-Watt's radio direction finding system from its early stages.

Dowding was absolutely dedicated to the need for a fighter shield to protect Britain. He fought officials and politicians, including Churchill, to hold back fighter squadrons from the fight in France and keep them for what he felt was certain would be a decisive battle for air superiority over Britain. Lord Halifax quoted him as saying at the time France dropped out of the war, "I went on my knees and thanked God," presumably because he would receive no more appeals to send his fighters across the channel and see them whittled away in a losing cause. A championship skier, a spiritualist, a vegetarian, and a member of both the Fairy Investigation Society and the Ghost Club, Dowding also believed he communicated with his long-dead first wife. He also maintained that God had intervened to save the British army at Dunkirk and that God would pull Britain out of this battle with Germany.[20] Some found Dowding prickly—his nickname from youth was Stuffy—and he was due to retire first in 1939, then in March 1940. Three times his duties were extended because his superiors felt he was the right man to lead Fighter Command during the coming battle.

Dowding's two principal lieutenants were Trafford Leigh-Mallory, who commanded 12 Group, and Keith Park, who commanded 11 Group. Unfortunately, the two men resented each other bitterly. Leigh-Mallory had flown in World War I, but for army coordination and not in fighters. Perhaps to compensate for his lack of fighter experience, he quite forcefully championed fighter pilots. Although intelligent and athletic, he seemed always overshadowed by the renown of his brother, George Mallory, Britain's most famous mountain climber, who died in 1924 within a few hundred yards of Mount Everest's summit.

Park was a New Zealander, a fighter ace from World War I. Small and wiry compared to the large and husky Leigh-Mallory, Park was also the more nimble and clever fighter to Leigh-Mallory's defeat-by-mass philosophy. Leigh-Mallory's 12 Group was thought to be the one that would take the brunt of the fighting on account of its being closest to German airfields, but when France fell, the Luftwaffe happily moved into French and Belgian bases closer to southeastern England. Park was thus in charge of the most important Fighter Command group. Soon enough the two men would clash about fighter tactics as well as nursing their other enmities. Leigh-Mallory wanted massed formations of fighters to battle the waves of German planes; meanwhile, Park was more in league with Dowding and wanted to send Hurricanes and Spitfires up in small packs so they could sting the Germans and slip away to fight again.[21]

Dowding's counterpart across the channel was Hermann Göring, head of and chief strategist for the Luftwaffe. By July 19 Göring was also Reichsmarschall, the highest-ranking military figure in Nazi Germany after Hitler. An early Nazi and a longtime ally of Hitler's—he had been shot while at Hitler's side in the 1923 Beer Hall Putsch—Göring held tremendous power in both political and military affairs. An athletic and skilled pilot, he had shot down twenty-two Allied airplanes in World War I and received

Germany's highest award for valor, the Pour le Mérite, also known as the Blue Max. Vain—he adored all the medals he won and wore them ostentatiously—ruthless, corrupt, and prone to both morphine addiction (first developed while recovering from his 1923 wound) and overeating, Göring nonetheless had a great deal of energy when it came to promoting his Luftwaffe and Nazism.[22]

Göring had little doubt which side would win in the coming struggle. Arguably he commanded the largest and best air force in the world. He and his fellow high Luftwaffe officers and Nazis stressed how invincible the Luftwaffe was, and they took pains to convince others. Charles Lindbergh, who had been escorted to Luftwaffe airfields in 1938, told U.S. ambassador Kennedy that year, "I feel certain that German air strength is greater than that of all other European countries combined. . . . Germany now has the means of destroying London, Paris and Prague if she wishes to do so. England and France together have not enough modern war planes for effective defense or counterattack."[23] Germany's quick defeat of the Polish air force and destruction by incendiary and explosive bombs of large portions of both Warsaw and Rotterdam emphasized Lindbergh's point.

Facing this huge and tested army of the air were the fighter pilots of the RAF. Almost all were younger than twenty-five years of age, some only nineteen. Many of the regular RAF pilots were older, even thought of as "over the hill" (though many of the aces turned out to be in their thirties). About a quarter of the pilots were really weekend fliers who came out of the Auxiliary Air Force (AAF). Others moved from what were called University Air Squadrons into the AAF or served in the Volunteer Reserve and were then called up. Many pilots came from Canada or Australia by way of what were called short service commissions, by which they transferred from their own country's air forces to the RAF.[24] By one estimate only about two hundred of the twenty-four hundred British pilots who fought at some time in the Battle of Britain enjoyed what they call a public school education and Americans call a private school one. Most did not speak with a university accent and came from ordinary backgrounds; they were bank clerks, factory workers, shop assistants, even young doctors. AAF 601 Squadron from London had a reputation as being the squadron of wealthy gentlemen pilots, but as the battle progressed and losses were filled with men of more humble origins, 601 Squadron became as homogenized as any other. Some of the pilots were officers and some were sergeants. In accordance with the British class system, they were meant to be segregated, but this system was often not practical. Rank was meant to separate them; however, the "band of brothers" spirit tended to bond them.[25]

The RAF fighter pilots were by no means all British. Roughly 600 came from other countries. Besides the 87 Canadians and 21 Australians, there were 100 New Zealanders and 21 South Africans. Seven Americans also served as pilots. Renowned for their ferocity were 135 Polish and 85 Czech pilots. These men had lost their homes and loved ones to the Nazis, so they were most eager to strike back. Particularly adept at shooting down German planes was a Czech sergeant named Josef Frantisek.[26]

Celebrated among the British pilots in 1940 was thirty-year-old Douglas Bader. He joined the RAF in 1928, but three years later while performing a roll upside down too close to the ground, one wing tip caught the turf and the plane crashed. Discharged for medical reasons after losing both legs below the knee, he reapplied for duty when the war broke out, knowing that the RAF was desperate for pilots. Told to sit out the war, he persuaded a commanding officer to go aloft in a companion plane while he, with his artificial legs, flew another. Bader made the man agree that the RAF would take him back if Bader could outfly him. The two men went aloft, and Bader outflew him.[27] He became an outspoken leader in Leigh-Mallory's 12 Group,[28] and eventually he was credited with shooting down twenty-two German planes.

BATTLE IN THE SKIES, SEAS, AND AFRICA

Enigma intercepts tipped British planners that, as they expected, the Germans' next offensive would be a massive air attack against England to clear the way for a landing on the southern shores. On August 8 Dowding sent an order of the day to his Fighter Command: "The Battle of Britain is about to begin. Members of the Royal Air Force, the fate of generations lies in your hands."[29] But already Dowding's young pilots were hard pressed. By this time they were already flying three or even four sorties a day, each up to ninety minutes long. (One aircraft on one raid makes a sortie, thus one aircraft making two separate raids makes two sorties.) The dogfights with German fighters might have only lasted ten to fifteen minutes, but they were intense and draining.[30] The strain was mounting.

The day of Dowding's order was a tough one for the RAF. The Luftwaffe spotted a convoy steaming near the Straits of Dover and attacked with scores of bombers and fighters. The RAF responded, and a large battle ensued over the straits. The German planes sank seven of the convoy's twenty ships and damaged six more. In all that day, the British pilots shot down thirty-one German planes but lost twenty of their own.[31] August 8 was not as bad as it could have been, though, for Göring had wanted it to be the Adlertag, the first day of Adlerangriff, his offensive to destroy Fighter Command. Conditions were not right, however; he rescheduled the big offensive for August 10, then delayed it again on account of weather reports to August 13. Göring set aside the day before, the twelfth, for massing attacks against what he thought might be helping Fighter Command in its struggles with his airplanes: the CH stations with those gangly radio towers. He'd smash RAF airfields, too, so the fighters could not land, take off, or be repaired.

Meanwhile, Churchill and his advisers were increasingly anxious about the Mediterranean and Africa. In June and July, Italian forces made incursions into Sudan and Kenya from their bases in Eritrea. Britain had only slight forces in these countries to offer resistance. On August 5 the Italians attacked British Somaliland on the Gulf of Aden with a good prospect of overrunning it in short order. Moreover, Britain held Egypt with only 50,000 men facing an Italian army of 215,000 just to the west in Libya.[32] If the Italians attacked eastward and overran Egypt, not only would Britain lose its quickest communication with India and Asia through the Suez Canal, but Italy and the Axis powers would also have close access to Saudi Arabia's oil fields. Accordingly, Churchill's administration proposed sending substantial army resources to Egypt—including more than 150 tanks (almost half of the best tanks on the British mainland) and 50 antitank guns, plus antiaircraft guns, field guns, and small arms—all at a time when the British feared they would be facing German infantry and panzers in Kent, Sussex, and Hampshire. Churchill was so anxious about losing Egypt that he wanted to risk sending the tanks and other military supplies, if not the bulk of the soldiers, through the Mediterranean—where they might face the gauntlet of Italian aerial and naval attack—rather than have them spend another three weeks steaming around the Cape of Good Hope.

In this respect, Churchill wanted to include the tanks in Operation Hats, the effort to bring supplies and antiaircraft equipment to Malta just west of the strategic Strait of Sicily as well as to reinforce the British fleet operating out of Alexandria, Egypt. The Alexandria naval squadron was to receive the new aircraft carrier *Illustrious* as well as the reconditioned battleship *Valiant* and two cruisers. These warships would bolster the operation's chances of success, but the British admirals still feared risking the tanks on a dash past Italy. Churchill was flummoxed by Adm. Dudley Pound, the First Sea Lord, and Gen. Archibald Wavell, the commander in Egypt, when both argued for the route around the Cape of Good Hope. Operation Hats was scheduled to begin at the end of August.

In addition, although Operation Susan had been scrubbed, the British continued to anxiously look at the French colonies in western Africa, which were under the Vichy government's control. The British feared that German agents were already at work preparing the colonies' ports and airfields for their U-boats and Luftwaffe planes, respectively. From this western bulge of Africa, German submarines and planes could range with greater ease over the Atlantic and make a quick leap to the South American coast. Moreover, they would severely menace Britain's Atlantic shipping route to South Africa, India, and Asia, which was also its longer but safer route to Egypt. Accordingly, in early August the British worked with Charles de Gaulle, who had been condemned to death in absentia by the Vichy government,[33] and his Free French to organize an expedition to win the colonies for the Free French movement. The ships and sailors would be British, but the twenty-five hundred soldiers who went ashore would be Free French. Operation Susan had meant to target Casablanca, but it was postponed owing to limited resources plus a sense that French sentiment there was too strongly oriented to the Vichy government.

British planners now looked farther south, to French West Africa and its principal port of Dakar. They understood that their effort against Dakar risked a declaration of war from Vichy France, but they thought it was worth the risk, considering the prospective benefit. Through early August the British worked on the plan, code-named Menace. It called for appearing off Dakar, which had significant shore batteries and the battleship *Richelieu,* and announcing that the Free French had come with assistance to ward off German aggression and to ask for permission to take control. British ships would bombard any resistance until the Free French could land and secure the city.

Adlerangriff

On August 12, before the Adlertag on the thirteenth, German planes were meant to bomb the RDF towers as well as the shacks alongside them. The Germans were not certain how the towers worked, but they strongly suspected that the towers somehow alerted the Hurricanes and Spitfires of the location of approaching Luftwaffe planes. Destroying the towers and their sheds would deprive the RAF fighters of early warning and save the German bombers from attack on their way to blasting aircraft factories, ports, and other vital targets. The Luftwaffe would also go after Fighter Command airfields, for cratered runways and destroyed repair sheds would prevent the Hurricanes and Spitfires from flying.

On the morning of the twelfth, under the command of Capt. Walter Rubensdörffer, flights of Me-110 fighters loaded with bombs under their wings moved southwest along the channel, then turned abruptly and, flying low over the waves in order to elude the RDF, swooped in over four CH stations. Neither RAF fighters in the air nor antiaircraft guns on the ground contested Rubensdörffer's planes, which made accurate drops of their bombs. The explosives blasted the RDF sheds apart and split electrical cables, which writhed in the air. At the Rye CH Station near Dover, all the sheds were destroyed or severely damaged. Destruction at other CH stations was also severe, and both male and female operators were killed. The bombing was disciplined and fairly accurate, and postattack reports sent to Luftwaffe fleet commander Albert Kesselring indicated that the attack was 75 percent successful. In the afternoon Kesselring launched convoy attacks to see if the RDF was still functioning. His planes were unmet, so he concluded that the British along this part of the coast were now blind. Indeed, the CH stations had been disrupted, but crews had them operational again in a few hours. The RDF towers themselves suffered only slight damage because they were, after all, mainly air. The struts that reached high into the sky were visible from afar, but when the bombs hit the ground near the base of the towers, the blasts merely passed between the struts without knocking the towers over.[34]

Around midday a hundred new twin-engine Ju-88 medium bombers set off to attack naval facilities in Portsmouth and Portland, Supermarine Spitfire factories near Southampton, and a major CH station at Ventnor south of Southampton on the Isle of Wight. In the confusion of trying to repair the bombed CH stations, the British RDF operators failed to anticipate or detect this large raid on southern England. But some Observer Corps members did and gave warning. Molested only by antiaircraft fire on shore and from ships, the Germans got their bombs away and did a great deal of damage to the Ventnor station before fifty Hurricanes and Spitfires arrived to bedevil them.

Later in the day, the Luftwaffe attacked three 11 Group forward fighter airfields: Lympne, Hawkinge, and Manston. Around 5:30 p.m., German bombers arrived at Lympne at the same moment as the RAF inspector general, who was intent on seeing that the airfield was shipshape. The German bombers ruined it, though the inspector general escaped, and men from the British Army were ordered to fill the crater holes and deal with unexploded bombs. Manston was hit equally hard. At Hawkinge twelve Spitfires were taking off just as the German bombers appeared. Eleven roared into the sky, but the engine of the twelfth stalled when a bomb blast reversed the spin of its propeller. Me-109s attacked the slowly rising Spitfires, but owing to the fact that they had never encountered Spitfires flying so slowly, all overshot and made no hits.

By the end of the day, the RAF claimed it had shot down 62 German planes, though the total was really 26. This kind of exaggeration was common on both sides and understandable: pilots often had only a second or two to shoot before their target turned in haste; more than one pilot shot at a plane, and then each took credit when he saw it smoking; and some planes that had suffered hits and began smoking actually returned to their home bases. Up to this point in the struggle over the channel and England, the Luftwaffe had lost 286 airplanes, the RAF Fighter Command 148.[35]

Göring's attempt to blast the coastal CH stations was intense and caused considerable damage, but so many men and women worked through the night that all the airfields and CH stations were operational the next morning. The exception was the major CH station at Ventnor, which required days to get it fully functional again.

Göring ordered Adlertag for the thirteenth. The massive attack was meant to destroy British airfields and aircraft factories and draw so many RAF fighters into the air that a great many of them would be shot down. Göring had sent a message to all units, which was decrypted and read by Ultra: "Operation Eagle. Within a short period you will wipe the British air force from the sky. Heil Hitler."[36] Göring boasted he would get the job done in a matter of days, well ahead of schedule for an Operation Sea Lion attack in mid-September. But the clearing weather that the Luftwaffe expected did not arrive at dawn, and Göring postponed the major attacks from morning to afternoon. One fleet of seventy-four Dorniers did not get the message, however. The aircraft formed up over France and, with their fighter escort of Me-110s, headed for two airfields—Eastchurch and Sheerness—east of London. A radio signal to the fighters called them back, but again the bombers missed the message. They noted the absent fighters but flew on among the clouds. Having been detected by the repaired CH stations, they were set upon by three squadrons of Hurricanes and Spitfires. Without the Me-110 fighters' harassment, the British shot down five of the Dorniers and damaged another six, or 15 percent of the whole force. Nevertheless the Dorniers bombed the two airfields and claimed many planes on the ground. In fact, they had destroyed only one Spitfire, and as it turned out the airfields were only of minor importance to Fighter Command.

The Germans' real blow fell in the afternoon. Hundreds of German planes massed over France and the channel, then turned toward England. Three hundred alone headed for the vicinity of Southampton, aiming for the port's docks as well as nearby airfields. Two squadrons of Hurricanes circled up to meet them, outnumbered more than ten to one. The bombers devastated central Southampton, though without damaging the nearby Spitfire factory, but the Hurricanes also took their own toll.

More formations of German planes, looking from the ground like wave after wave of black silhouettes, droned over southern and eastern England. At one RAF field, four hundred bombs hit the runways alone. Some of the worst damage came at Detling airfield, where the runway was wrecked and sixty-eight people died. Being a Coastal Command airfield, not a Fighter Command one, the damage did not materially affect the RAF's capacity to keep up the fight. And in other places, German formations could not locate their targets, while yet others were scattered by squadrons of RAF fighters.

Göring's Adlertag, however, was still not over. That night the Luftwaffe heavily damaged an aircraft factory in Belfast, Northern Ireland, and bombed a Spitfire factory in Birmingham. In all, on August 13 the Germans made nearly fifteen hundred sorties. Again, and as usual on both sides, the Germans exaggerated the damage they had caused both in the air and on the ground. Indeed, considering the destruction at Detling, they had reason to feel they made some headway. In truth, they knew they had fallen short of their goals and could not deny that they had lost forty-five airplanes. The RAF lost thirteen that day, a serious misfortune but fewer than the twenty-two of the day before and the thirty-two on the eleventh.[37]

On the fourteenth the weather was not as good and the German offensive less intense. The Luftwaffe mounted attacks on Hastings along the channel and again on Southampton. In these attacks the Germans lost thirty-one airplanes while the RAF lost eight fighters. That night saw little German bomber activity, and prospects for the morning were clear weather. Dowding suspected a large assault, and Ultra intercepts confirmed his suspicions.[38] Dowding, in fact, received the gist of most of Göring's orders during the August battles, often the day they were issued. The messages did not contain targets—the Luftwaffe pilots got them only at preflight briefings—but Dowding could discern Göring's overall strategy, a general notion of the Luftwaffe's losses, the efficiency of its aircraft replacement operation, and the magnitude of an effort for any coming day, all exceptionally valuable information when husbanding RAF forces and keeping them fighting day after day.[39] This day Dowding kept forces i n the Midlands to harass attacks he expected there and did what he could, moving other squadrons around, to fight against bombers from the south.

Indeed, as Dowding suspected, August 15 was a desperate day. Göring, displeased with the results of Tuesday's and Wednesday's, uncoordinated attacks, proclaimed August 15 as the actual Adlertag, and ordered a massive offensive. Meanwhile, British technicians and engineers worked furiously to put the damaged CH stations back into action. At Ventnor, which suffered the worst damage of the August 12 raids, the technicians started transmitting signals even though they could not immediately receive any, hoping the Germans would believe their attempts at knocking out the CH stations were futile.

Part of Göring's plan for his new Adlertag was, as Dowding had learned from the Ultra intercepts, to fly hundreds of planes across the North Sea from Norway and Denmark to attack the industrial Midlands and northern Britain. They would not have fighter escorts except for some Me-110s because of the distance they would have to fly and return, but Göring believed they wouldn't need many. To his mind, Fighter Command was just about finished, and its little opposition to the massive bombing would show the British people just how defenseless their island was and, indeed, how hopeless their position.

The morning of the fifteenth was cloudy, but by midday the weather cleared. Suddenly RDF operators saw blips multiplying on their cathode ray tubes. Astonished, they had never seen so many before, and they imagined the sky must have filled with planes. Out went the information to Bentley Priory, then to the groups and sector stations, and up went the Hurricanes and Spitfires.

In the north Dowding had safeguarded his resources well. Although he had shifted squadrons around the country, he had retained enough at airfields north of London to fall upon the massed bombers droning in from the east. What few Me-110s were flying escort were no match for the Hurricanes and Spitfires. Four squadrons from 13 Group fell upon the German bombers, which soon didn't have much of a chance. The British planes shot down sixteen Heinkels and six Ju-88 bombers and destroyed seven Me-110s. In all, the British fighter pilots eliminated more than 20 percent of the Luftwaffe planes sent across the North Sea that day. Dowding's efforts to protect Britain's flank paid double dividends: the RAF did severe damage to an entire fleet of Luftwaffe planes, and a whole section of the country could look to the sky and see that it was being robustly defended.

Meanwhile, in the south, the fighting was tougher because the German bombers had the protection of Me-109s. There the Luftwaffe planes arrived by the hundreds. Göring would send more than a thousand planes on almost eighteen hundred sorties before the day was over. Bomber groups blasted aircraft factories in Kent, but the factories were making RAF bombers, not fighters. The Germans flew back to France, and there was a lull of several hours.

Then RDF screens showed that they were rising again over the French coast, coming by the hundreds. Fighter Command put up more planes than

they ever had before—150 from 14 squadrons—to tangle with these formations. As hundreds of bombers attacked airfields, the RAF could not deal
with the German formations, which dropped their explosive loads unmo-
lested and droned back toward the channel in good order. Smaller groups
of German planes flew in at wave-top and then treetop level to avoid RDF
detection and unleashed their bombs on RAF airfields. They did terrible
damage to Martlesham airfield near the Suffolk coast in this way. In all, it
was the Luftwaffe's biggest assault so far and, in fact, the largest air assault
in history with its tremendous show of power and numerical strength. But
still Dowding stuck to his strategy of sending up small groups of fighters to contest the attackers. He would husband his resources, keep Fighter
Command alive, and deny German intelligence a chance of determining
just how many fighters it had left.

Churchill made a special trip in the afternoon to the Bentley Priory
Fighter Command headquarters and watched the commanders there handle the battle. He was much impressed with Dowding's generalship. After
he returned to his residence at 10 Downing Street, Churchill telephoned
Neville Chamberlain, who was recovering from a cancer operation, to tell
him the Germans had suffered heavily. Chamberlain, scorned for his gull-
ibility at Munich, was also the prime minister who had ushered in the
Hurricanes and Spitfires. He was touched that Churchill thought enough
to call him.

At the end of the day, Göring boasted to Hitler that the Luftwaffe had
done its job, destroying the twelve most vital airfields and having shot
down more than a hundred planes. Göring was misled, however; the toll
was bloody but not that bad. In truth, the RAF lost thirty-four planes that
day—their most costly day so far—but the Luftwaffe suffered at least seventy-five planes destroyed. Dowding took heart that the aircraft factories
were making Hurricanes and Spitfires about as fast as the Germans were
destroying them—twice as fast, in fact, as Göring believed—but he worried about the airfield damage. Without runways, mechanics' sheds, and
supplies, the RAF was crippled. Most of all, he worried about his pilots
because he was losing them faster than he could replace them. Seventeen
more fighter pilots had been killed and sixteen wounded on August 15.
Fighter Command's only solace was that the Luftwaffe was suffering more.
Of their seventy-five planes shot down on August 15, many had crews of

two, three, and four pilots plus gunners, so the Germans were losing more trained men than were the British.

Moreover, the British ground crews were doing heroic work. Once a fighter landed at an airfield, they madly dashed to get it ready again. At a minimum fuel and ammunition were reloaded, oil checked, radio batteries recharged, and the oxygen bottle changed. Many men servicing the Hurricanes and Spitfires were RAF men, but others were employees of the private manufacturers. If a fighter came in with a damaged engine, it was wheeled to a hanger where Rolls-Royce men pulled out the damaged Merlin engine and installed a fresh one. Employees of the Hawker and Supermarine companies generally worked on the airplane bodies. On call virtually all day, these ground crewmen of the RAF and the Civilian Repair Organisation (CRO) rarely got a meal in their mess halls, and sleep was brief. One CRO unit had a workweek of a hundred hours, and some of the men never left the airfields for all the work they had to do. A fresh-from-the-factory Hurricane or Spitfire might appear at an airfield on Saturday, be damaged in action on Tuesday, and be back in service again that weekend.[40] Even while their airfields were being bombed, the ground crews would still run out to refuel and rearm a Hurricane or Spitfire down on the ground for only as long as the replenishment took. Pilots, zipping off into the sky again, often felt sorrier for the ground crews suffering the German bomb barrages than they did for themselves among the Me-109s.

Ground crewmen were continuously pressed for ingenuity. They cannibalized damaged fighters to gain parts for ones that could fly. At least one crew did not take the time when a tire needed changing to lift the plane on jacks; instead, they got ten men together, tilted the plane, and held it while one man made the replacement.[41] With no time to find a water hose, one ground crewman dowsed a small fire in the wing of a plane by urinating on it. Squadron Leader Henry Hogan recalled later, "My everlasting impression of the Battle was that the organization for replacing aircraft and the supply of equipment was marvelous."[42]

Nor were the ground crews the only ones on a frantic pace. Serving as the telephonists and plotters in the operations rooms, WAAFs also worked as clerks, cooks, drivers, and balloon fabric repairers. They operated the cathode ray tubes in the CH stations' RDF sheds. Here they were cool under fire, astounding quite a number of the male military higher-ups.[43] Not a few died at their posts. WAAFs also ferried planes from airfield to airfield. More than one man was startled to see a pilot hop to the ground, remove the flying helmet, and shake out her hair.[44]

But still Göring did not let up. On August 16 he sent in his planes again by the hundreds and managed almost as many sorties as he had the day before. Again, his principal targets were airfields. Hard hit was Tangmere, near Portsmouth. There, two hangers were destroyed, three were damaged, and seven Hurricanes were smashed on the ground as well as six bombers. North of London two Ju-88s flew to an airfield called Brize Norton, lowered their wheels in hopes of being mistaken for British Blenheim bombers, then dropped sixteen bombs, destroying eleven Hurricanes, more than forty trainer aircraft, and an aircraft maintenance facility before escaping. In one bright spot, the swift work and the deception of broadcasting from Ventnor, despite its inability to receive echo signals, bore fruit. The CH stations were not targets because Göring was convinced that earlier raids had damaged them significantly and because he still did not understand how truly helpful they were to Fighter Command.[45]

Shot down in the fighting this day was American Billy Fiske, a gold medal–winning Olympic bobsled driver in 1928 and again in 1932, when he also had the honor of carrying the American flag during the opening ceremonies. Scion of an American banking family and married to a countess, he was dedicated to the British cause. Burned badly on the hands and face, he nonetheless landed his Hurricane and was hauled out by a ground crew. He was taken to a hospital and treated, but he later died from shock.

That day Churchill went to the operations room of 11 Group at Uxbridge, west of London, and watched as the plotters marked the incoming German formations and the numbers of squadrons sent up to contest them. At one time he and his chief military adviser, Maj. Gen. Hastings Ismay, could see that all the available squadrons were aloft, nothing was held in reserve, and fresh waves of German planes were heading north across the channel. Ismay later wrote that he was "sick with fear." In the evening when the two men were being driven to Churchill's rural residence at Chequers, Churchill told Ismay, "Don't speak to me: I have never been so moved." The prime minister mulled words about how the destinies of so many hung on the actions of so few.[46]

Soldiers of the British Expeditionary Force are led away as prisoners after the shrinking Dunkirk perimeter surrendered. Although most of the army escaped, the BEF abandoned so many of its tanks, heavy guns, and vehicles to the Germans that many people believed Britain would be overrun in short order. *National Archives*

All city dwellers in Britain feared similar devastation to what the Luftwaffe wrought on central Rotterdam after a single raid in May. The British also feared that chemical and biological weapons might be dropped from German planes. *National Archives*

The interior of a Chain Home station, whose radar equipment detected Luftwaffe planes farther away than the Germans had imagined. Women often operated the instruments in such stations all along the south and eastern English coastline. *National Archives*

Winston Churchill worked his oratory both on Parliament's House of Commons and over the microphone to the British people in their homes. This picture shows Churchill in a broadcast studio in 1939. *Library of Congress*

There were several Lord Haw-Haws, but William Joyce proved to be the most prominent. He beamed Nazi propaganda from Germany in an attempt to foment defeatism among the British. *National Archives*

Attracting a crowd, the German-American Bund marched down the streets of New York City in late 1939. It ran summer camps for boys and girls and promoted friendship with the Nazi government. *Library of Congress*

Hitler and Mussolini motoring through Munich in mid-June at the height of their success. Hitler outlined to Mussolini the surrender terms he would present to the French a few days hence. *National Archives*

The British citizens' Home Guard lacked uniforms but not pluck. Here men drill with what rifles they could muster, determined to do their part if the German army invaded. *National Archives*

At Mers-el-Kébir, a French battle cruiser—the *Dunkerque* or the *Strasbourg*—makes way while ships and shells explode around it. The British navy attacked to keep French ships from falling into the Nazis' hands. *Jacques Mulard*

An Enigma machine. In this version, the tops of three rings are barely visible at the rear. At the very front is the stecker panel. Above it are the keys the operator pressed, and beyond them are the letters that were illuminated, to be written down one by one for composing the cipher message. *National Cryptologic Museum*

Hermann Göring trains binoculars on the British coast across the channel from conquered territory in northern France. He believed that his highly trained and superbly equipped Luftwaffe would cow the British within weeks. *Library of Congress*

Hermann Göring examines situation maps with pilots and staff early in the battle against RAF. He would soon bring German airpower's whole strength into the skies over England. *Library of Congress*

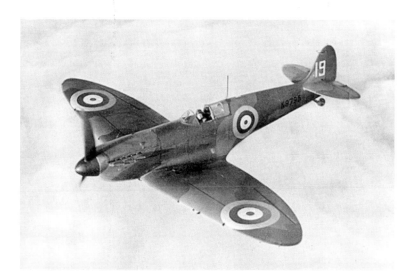

The RAF Supermarine Spitfire was the best fighter airplane the British could send against the Luftwaffe in 1940, but there were fewer of them than the Hawker Hurricanes. *Royal Air Force*

Hugh Dowding led RAF Fighter Command during the critical months of 1940. Although critics thought him unstable and antagonists fiercely challenged his strategy, Dowding sustained airpower over southern England long enough to dispirit Hitler's invasion plan. *Library of Congress*

In September in an eastern suburb of London, children sit outside their wrecked home, destroyed the night before during a bombing raid. *National Archives*

Londoners bed down for the night in a subway tunnel to wait out the Luftwaffe's nighttime bombing raids. *National Archives*

Indeed, August 16, just as the day before, was a desperate battle, but the ferocity raged mainly before late afternoon. By then clouds were thickening. The Germans could not find their targets and wandered about. Hurricanes and Spitfires could not find the Germans and wandered as well. By nightfall the German bombers struck targets outside London, along the Bristol Channel, and in East Anglia. In all that day, forty-five German planes were destroyed for twenty-one British.

On Saturday, August 17, Göring slacked off despite clear weather; only occasional German planes stirred over England. The British made good use of the time, filling in bomb craters on runways, repairing telephone cables from damaged CH stations, setting up mess tents where kitchens had been destroyed, shoring up blasted hangers, and repairing damaged aircraft. In France and Belgium, Luftwaffe mechanics worked on their planes as well, and the pilots took what they believed was a much-needed rest.

But on Sunday the eighteenth, the Luftwaffe struck again, hard. They pummeled eight airfields. Low-flying Dorniers surprised Kenley airfield south of London. Swooping in, unbothered by fighters, the Dorniers destroyed ten hangers as well as half a dozen Hurricanes and some bombers caught on the ground. At Kenley, ground crews fought back with a novel weapon called Parachute and Cable, or PAC. A rocket launched a five-hundred-foot cable, which at the top of its trajectory opened a parachute so that the cable made a slow descent. If an airplane wing hit the cable, a parachute at the other end would open, burdening the plane with the deadly drag of two parachutes on its wing. One Dornier so encumbered dipped its wing and shed its burden, but PACs brought down two other bombers.[47] Still, damage at Kenley was so bad and communications so fouled that crews moved the operations center to a nearby shop in town. The disruption at Kenley was a significant blow, but again the Luftwaffe intelligence was faulty, for only three of the eight airfields they attacked served fighter squadrons.

Another major target was Biggin Hill, an important fighter base south of London. Like Kenley, two waves of Dorniers hit it. PAC cables were used here too, and when fighters fell upon the Dorniers, they shot down seven out of nine in one section. The fighters' opportune arrival made the German bombers release their bombs in haste, and the damage was less severe here than at Kenley.

In the afternoon more than a hundred bombers protected by fifty Me-109s headed toward airfields and the Poling CH Station east of Portsmouth. Fighter Command put up every squadron in the region. German formations that did not encounter RAF fighters before they dropped their bombs did much damage to the airfields, while those that were attacked by fighters before their bomb runs scattered or were less accurate. The airfields did not belong to RAF Fighter Command, and the damages did not crimp the fighter effort; but the important Poling CH station was heavily bombed and put out of action.

Still the fighting of August 18 was not over. The days being long at this latitude and time of year, there were three hours of daylight left at 5:00 p.m., and Group Commander Keith Park felt certain the Luftwaffe would be back for another attack. They did return, this time aiming for Fighter Command airfields east and north of London. Many of the pilots had already been up twice, but Park put them in the air again. In all, shot down that day were seventy-one Luftwaffe planes and twenty-seven RAF aircraft, concluding for both air forces the second worst day of the battle after August 15.

Where there was dogfighting, pilots inevitably floated down by parachute or brought their damaged planes down in fields. One pilot, having hastily run to his plane, was not in proper uniform. When he landed by parachute, dirty and bloody, he was taken to a nearby golf club, where life was more or less normal. Here some members complained that the airplane droning disturbed their putting. Shortly after the disheveled RAF pilot was brought in, one member turned to another and asked, "Who's that scruffy looking chap at the bar? I don't believe he's a member?"[48]

Fighter pilot Peter Simpson received a better reception at another golf club and was given lunch and a brandy. Another pilot landed his plane in a small field and required only fuel and small repairs. A ground crew nearby was called out. When they arrived, they found the young man sitting in an armchair the locals had brought out to the field with two crates of ale and plates of sandwiches. The ground crew said he looked like a king in his court. The flier shared the ale and food with the ground crewmen who repaired his plane and added a bit of fuel. They then restrained the plane while the pilot, back in his cockpit, revved to full throttle for very a short takeoff, and they let the plane go. The flier cleared the fence at the far end of the field, and then, with a flick roll over the villagers and ground crew, he was off to his airfield.[49]

Not all pilots who were forced down or had to bail out were so lucky. Landing in the channel often meant death by drowning or by exposure in the cold water. Sometimes parachutes were on fire even as the pilots jumped and hence were useless. Some RAF pilots were mistaken for Germans. On one occasion Home Guard observers thought two descending Fighter Command pilots were part of a German parachute attack. They opened fire and killed one.

By all measures the tolls of the continual aerial fighting were becoming increasingly fearsome. In the twelve weeks of May 10–July 29, the RAF had lost 173 Hurricanes and 110 Spitfires, a loss of roughly 24 planes a week. From July 30 to August 5, it lost a total of 6 planes. But during the week of August 6–12, it lost 79 Hurricanes, and during the week of August 13–19, the destructive total reached 106. The RAF could take heart that factory workers during that same week produced 54 Hurricanes and 37 Spitfires. But replacing the planes themselves was less of a problem than finding the men to fly them. Since August 8, 91 RAF pilots had been killed and 60 severely wounded, a large percentage of whom were the most senior and experienced fliers.

Day after day they went up to fight. Pilot Harold Bird-Wilson recollected later,

> the solid boredom and the rush of excitement. The scramble, the clear and steady voice of the controller giving us directions and height, the number of enemy aircraft, ever-growing, sometimes into hundreds. We were only twelve Hurricanes. We hoped and prayed that other squadrons had also been scrambled, but we never saw them. We just plowed in, picked our targets and fought. . . . There was no time for tears . . . only sorrow and off into the next scramble.[50]

The training schools could not quickly supply new pilots to make up for killed or injured ones; moreover, the replacements were not nearly as skilled as those whose places they took.[51] Fighter Command began recruiting naval fliers, bomber pilots, and coastal defense plane pilots. In addition, the experienced men were tired, and they had a difficult time convincing themselves they were winning. Dowding ordered that fighter pilots have twenty-four hours off each week.[52]

The Luftwaffe too was reeling from this week in mid-August, a period of the greatest damage and the most attacks and dogfights to date. The Luftwaffe had lost hundreds of planes. So many Stukas and Me-110s had been shot down that Göring decided to take the remainder out of the battle.

Each side was trying to learn and adjust. Now the Hurricanes were mainly sent against bombers and Spitfires against fighters. While the RDF scopes could not distinguish between the two, in good visibility the Observer Corps could, using illustrations that identified enemy planes' silhouettes. Both Hurricane and Spitfire pilots learned not to try to evade the Me-109s by diving or climbing but rather by jerking into as tight a turn as they could manage, turns the Me-109s could not match. For their part the Me-109 pilots learned that they could evade the Hurricanes and Spitfires by plunging into a steep dive. Their fuel-injection Daimler-Benz engines would work fine, but the Rolls-Royce engines had carburetors that could fail to deliver fuel.

The Hurricane and Spitfire pilots worked on a technique of attacking formations of bombers head-on. This way they would avoid the rear gunners and face the bombers' minimal forward firepower. Moreover, in a frontal attack, the bomber pilots were vulnerable and likely terrified to see Hurricanes and Spitfires coming right at them, guns blazing. The trouble with a frontal attack was that the attacker and the defender approached each other at more than five hundred miles an hour, or three hundred yards per second, allowing little room for error. Late in the month, South African Teddy Morris headed into a group of He-111s this way but misjudged the speed and smashed into the nose of one of the bombers. Both planes broke up. Morris found himself still in his seat with parts of both planes all around when he pulled his parachute's rip cord. Later, recovering in the hospital with a broken leg, he was visited by a comrade. Morris complained, "I thought you told me they would break formation if we pressed home for a good frontal attack." "No, Teddy," the other said. "They don't if the pilot is dead. You are supposed to allow for that." "How the hell are you supposed to know he's dead or not?" Teddy asked. "The way you did," was the best the other man could answer.[53]

Despite the losses Göring was determined to continue. Counting up the numbers of planes his pilots said they had destroyed and underestimating the production capacity of the British aircraft factories, he believed Fighter Command was down to 300 planes. After a few more days of intense fighting and at the kill rate his pilots were telling him, the RAF would be down to 150 planes in no time.

But on the nineteenth, it rained, and the weather was cloudy or rainy for the next five days. Göring fumed. He had promised Hitler he would finish off Fighter Command in a matter of days so that all would be ready for Operation Sea Lion in mid-September. Göring had not done so, and time was slipping away. The RAF was repairing its airfields and CH stations, mending its planes, and training new pilots. The German pilots, too, were resting and getting their planes repaired, but time was on the side of the British.

On the twentieth Churchill again addressed the House of Commons. His subject was the progress of the war, nearly a year old. The speech rambled and touched on many aspects of the war, including science, submarines, the occupied countries, comparisons to World War I, and more. He pressed on to the air war. Rolling in his studied cadences, he worked in the thought he had developed in the automobile on the way to Chequers five days previous:

> The gratitude of every home in our Island, in our Empire, and indeed throughout the world, except in the abodes of the guilty, goes out to the British airmen who, undaunted by odds, unwearied in their constant challenge and mortal danger, are turning the tide of the world war by their prowess and by their devotion. Never in the field of human conflict was so much owed by so many to so few.[54]

A very thin red line was defending the democracies, as existed then and down the ages.

Churchill's ringing sentence regarding "so much . . . owed to so few" did not conclude the speech, but it was the one snatched by an anxious public. The pilots soon made fun of it by suggesting Churchill was referring to the pilots' bar bills, but the sentence resonated as a catchphrase for standing up to the Nazis. Posters were made of pictures of pilots, calling them "The Few."

Churchill's August 20 speech actually ended with a reference to the notion of leasing some of the empire's bases in the Atlantic to the Americans as well as transferring American destroyers to the Royal Navy. This action, surmised Churchill, would bind together the two great English-speaking nations. Perhaps to reassure his listeners he said, "For my own part, looking out upon the future, I do not view the process [of binding the two nations] with any misgivings. I would not stop it if I wished; no one can stop it. Like the Mississippi, it just keeps rolling along. Let it roll. Let it roll in full flood."[55] His speech completed and in the car on his way back to 10 Downing Street, Churchill sang "Ole Man River."[56]

As if to give substance to Churchill's thought, three high-level American officers—one a rear admiral and another a major general—at this time debarked in England to begin serious coordination talks between the two countries' armed forces. They were shown military bases and airfields, where the Americans were especially impressed with the speed at which fighter pilots scrambled to get their planes into the air. The tour had another impact: the American brass was able to counter some of the negativity about Britain's chances coming from Ambassador Joe Kennedy.

For three days after the Churchill speech, the weather remained sour and the fighting relatively moderate. Then clear weather returned on August 24, and the Luftwaffe again sent over waves of warplanes. They concentrated on airfields. They bombed the one at Manston north of Dover in five waves until it was obvious to anyone that it could no longer be used. Göring's planes also targeted oil storage tanks, airplane parts factories, and any airfields Göring thought useful. Runways became so cratered that RAF pilots were killed or injured trying to land on them. (Churchill at one point asked about whether crater-appearing canvases could be laid on the runways to fool Luftwaffe bomber pilots.) Hangers, repair sheds, and communications huts were blasted apart. Fighter Command was being seriously crippled. If it could not keep its aircraft fitted and fueled, its sector stations communicating with fighters aloft, and its airfields operational, then the Luftwaffe would win air superiority over southern England and offer Hitler a good chance at a successful invasion.

Part of the problem with defending the airfields owed to a clash between Keith Park of 11 Group and Trafford Leigh-Mallory of 12 Group.

Park's 11 Group across southeast England was bearing the brunt of nearly all the action, and its fields were being blasted when his fighters were airborne, dogfighting. Accordingly, 12 Group fighters were supposed to fly down from the north and cover the 11 Group's airfields while the 11 Group fighters dueled with the Luftwaffe. Doug Bader, a squadron leader of 12 Group, however, had Leigh-Mallory's blessing to try his "Big Wing" idea of massing fighters so they could attack in strength. The problem was that it took so much time for 12 Group squadrons to form up these big wings that when they finally arrived at the 11 Group's airfields to fend off the Luftwaffe bombers, the Germans had already loosed their bombs and fled. Bader and his fighters might catch up and tear into the German formations, but by then the airfields were blasted, smoking, and cratered.

In addition, Göring was escalating night bombing in the hopes of disrupting aircraft factories. Sporadic night bombing had occurred since June, but now Göring intensified it significantly, though London was to be off-limits. More than two hundred bombers attacked targets in the Midlands on the night of August 23 and a hundred the following night. They did considerable damage to an airplane factory north of Bristol on the night of August 22 and to a rubberworks near Birmingham on the night of the twenty-third. The British had little means of defending against such night bombers, as antiaircraft guns were not then guided by RDF. Some slow Blenheim bombers were fitted with a primitive form of radar that could guide them at night to a German plane, but generally they were not effective.

On the night of August 24, against Hitler's clear orders, a hundred bombers loosed their loads over London, mostly on the East End, and set more than seventy fires. One bomb knocked a statue of Milton off its pedestal.[57] For weeks, the citizens of other cities—Plymouth, Southampton, Birmingham, and more—had suffered bombings, but not Londoners. British citizens had wondered why, because before the war they were led to believe London would be the primary target in a war, the mark for a "knockout blow." But to this point Londoners had been spared. Perhaps the bombers on the night of the twenty-fourth were lost, perhaps they mistook the blacked-out city for something else, or perhaps one bomber jettisoned its bombs and scores of other bombers, confused, followed its lead. The cause was clouded in mystery, but the effect was signal and significant: Churchill called for an immediate retaliatory raid on Berlin.

The British bombers went at night. Daytime bombing was out of the question because guardian fighters, essential in daylight, could not accompany the bombers all the way to Berlin. Eighty RAF planes set course for Berlin, but the continent was blacked out, the weather was poor, and their navigation was crude. Only twenty-nine bombers made it to the German capital and could identify their targets. These were armament factories on the north side, but their bombs did no military damage. Some went astray and fell on the center of the city, though no Berliners were killed. William Shirer, the American journalist in Berlin, said the antiaircraft barrages were terrific, but they too were ineffectual. No RAF planes were shot down.[58] The attack, superficial as it was, enraged Hitler. Göring had assured him, as well as the German populace, that the Luftwaffe would keep the British from ever bombing Germany, let alone Berlin.

All through the remaining days of August, the Germans kept bombing the RAF airfields. August 30 was particularly bad at Biggin Hill, where thirty-nine people were killed and twenty-five injured. Nearly every day the fighting was fierce and the toll high, though in numbers the Luftwaffe suffered worse losses: August 26, forty-one Luftwaffe planes to thirty-one RAF aircraft; August 27, nine planes to one; August 28, thirty planes to twenty; August 29, seventeen planes to nine, August 30, thirty-six planes to twenty-six; and August 31, forty-one planes to thirty-nine. These are actual figures, but at the time both Germans and British believed they were destroying far more enemy planes than they actually were.

On the twenty-eighth the Luftwaffe again stepped up bombing by night as well as by day. It sent six hundred sorties against Liverpool and other targets in darkness.[59] Despite the large number of planes involved, the Germans lost very few, and they took note. Bombers again made major bombing attacks on Liverpool on August 29–31, all at night because the city was too far away for the Me-109s to offer protection in daylight. The Germans made another discovery, or thought they did, on the twenty-ninth when British fighters did not meet some of their daylight attacks. Their conclusion—Fighter Command was at last at the breaking point—reflected their wishful thinking.

Actually, though, it was true. The airfields in southern England were so bombed and battered that the RAF had a difficult time putting fighters into the sky. At the end of August, the Germans believed they had shot down 791 British planes during the month while losing 169 of their own, or that Fighter Command had lost half of its force since August 8. Actually Fighter Command had lost about 440 planes in that time, but such was the production of British factories that on August 31 it had 417 Hurricanes and 212 Spitfires operational with more in storage depots. Thus available to the British were more fighters, in fact, than it had had operational in mid-July.[60] The RAF Fighter Command was alive, if barely.

VIBRATIONS EAST AND SOUTH

There were other developments near the end of August. Hungary threatened war with Romania over Transylvania, which Hungary had lost to the latter after World War I. Such a war would have disrupted petroleum shipments from Romania's Ploiesti oil fields to Germany, an intolerable situation to Hitler, and a war between these two Eastern European countries might well have drawn in the Soviets to occupy Romania. On August 28 the situation was so bad that Hitler readied five panzer divisions and three motorized divisions to seize the Ploiesti fields if need be. He sent Joachim von Ribbentrop to Vienna to demand a peaceable settlement, which the German foreign minister got. But the arrangement surrendered so much of Transylvania to Hungary that Romania's king Carol II had to abdicate within two weeks. Taking his place as ruler of the country was a fascist friend of Hitler's, Gen. Ion Antonescu, who set himself up as dictator.[61]

In the Mediterranean the British navy's Operation Hats began smoothly. On August 30 the two British fleets in the Mediterranean met near Malta, and the resupplying ships docked for unloading. The two fleets had encountered little interference from the Italians rather than the bombing attacks they had dreaded. Perhaps the presence of their own planes on the aircraft carrier *Illustrious* had been a sufficient deterrent. After resupplying Malta the two fleets left for their home ports of Gibraltar and Alexandria, each arriving safely several days later. Churchill felt somewhat vindicated in his opinion that shipping the precious army tanks across the Mediterranean rather than around the cape would have succeeded. In any event, owing to Italian procrastination, the tanks were not needed at the front until later. They would arrive in good time.

CHAPTER SEVEN

CRACKING A PEOPLE'S WILL TO FIGHT

"Opposition to Churchill grows. . . . We keep attacking him,
but we spare the English people on psychological grounds."
—*Joseph Goebbels's diary of early July*[1]

Nazi Germany did not have to defeat Britain by rolling the Wehrmacht across Kent and Sussex as it had across the provinces of France. It had other ways. One was to starve Britain into submission by depriving the island of its food and materials. Another was to undermine the will of the British to persist until they threw out the Churchill government for one that would bargain with Hitler's. This war, it turned out, was not just of airplanes, bullets, and bombs, but also of people's minds, hopes, and hearts.

THE MENACE BY SEA

The British isle was dependent on the sea for importing its food and vital materials. Beef from South America, lumber and grain from Canada, mutton from New Zealand, and oil from the Middle East were just a few of its needs. At any given time, more than two thousand merchant ships were at sea fetching supplies, as much as a million tons a week, for Britain. The Germans sent out their battleships and cruisers, as well as disguised freighters with guns large enough to sink merchant vessels, against this fleet of merchantmen. They dispatched their bombers to blast vessels as they neared land and to wreck the docks and other port facilities needed to unload and store the materials the ships delivered. And they unleashed their U-boats, the deadly submarines that had proved so fearsome in World War I. These craft were soon sinking British ships from near ports to far out into the Atlantic.

The Germans also sowed mines by airplane and submarine in British harbors and along the close-in shipping lanes. The newer magnetic mine lay dormant until the steel hull of a ship approached. Once the ship distorted the earth's magnetic field, then the mine would rise toward the metal and explode beneath the keel. A British remedy involved "degaussing" the hulls of steel ships. Using steel cables along the hulls, electric current passed through them and nullified the magnetic nature of the steel; in shallow water, this measure was less effective. The Germans had other kinds of mines, including one that exploded once it detected the sound of a ship's propellers. Every measure, however, was followed by countermeasure and by a measure again in a cycle of attempts to gain the upper hand.

By the spring of 1940, 460 merchant ships had been lost to all these causes. Allied shipping losses rose to more than 600,000 tons in June alone, half owing to submarines. When the war broke out, Germany had only about 45 submarines. This total was far less than the 300 coveted by the chief of the German submarine arm, Rear Adm. Karl Dönitz, who declared that with that many he could bring Britain to its knees. Before the war Hitler had the option of expanding the submarine fleet but decided instead to build a balanced navy of battleships, cruisers, aircraft carriers, and submarines. It would be a while, if ever, before Dönitz would get his 300 vessels. But with the fall of France, the submarine fleet picked up a prize—the Atlantic coast of France. Previously the German U-boats had to sneak out from their base at Kiel, up the North Sea, and around Scotland to reach the Atlantic. With western France under Nazi control, they could use French ports on the Bay of Biscay as bases, saving tremendous amounts of fuel and time in cruising to where they could launch their attacks. They could more readily infiltrate the western approaches to Britain, and they could range farther out into the Atlantic to strike against merchantmen there.

Since World War I, the British and others had been working on ways of detecting submerged submarines. The principal means was emitting a sound underwater and then listening for an echo, for sound travels particularly well through water. Although the source of the word is disputed, the British name for this technique was Asdic while the Americans settled on the name sonar for *so*und *n*avigation and *r*anging). The sound pulse was a kind of "ping." Its echo was similar but subject to interpretation, and an operator needed long hours of training before becoming proficient. The pings could echo off steel wrecks on the seabed, rocks, or even boundaries between currents of different temperature. Two other defects of Asdic were that it generally could not detect a submarine farther than a mile away or one that was very close, within about three hundred yards. The submariners were well aware of Asdic and began to limit their time underwater, because Asdic could not detect a submarine on the surface. They also preferred to attack during moonless hours at night.

GOEBBELS TWEAKS THE AIRWAVES

German radio propaganda against the West began early in the war and concentrated its efforts on France. Owing to the Nazi-Soviet Nonaggression Pact of August 1939, the Communist Party in France could no longer rail against the Germans; therefore, it redirected its ire against the French government, which responded by outlawing the party in September 1939. Nazi propaganda chief Joseph Goebbels's ministry then set up radio broadcasts as if they were from French Communist leaders, advocating—as indeed the suppressed French Communists did also—resistance to conscription and overtime at armaments factories. It beamed to the French audiences the notion that France could never hold up to German might and that Britain was only using France as a lackey for its own imperialist agenda. Once the fighting started in May, the radio broadcasts did their best to foment panic among the French and instill the notion that their cause was hopeless. Broadcasts said the government had fled the country, that cholera had broken out in Paris, and that the water was poisoned. Goebbels was quite pleased with these radio efforts and thought they had a great deal to do with the collapse of France.[2]

With France in the German orbit, Goebbels turned his attention to Britain. His radio people set up bogus broadcasting stations that listeners were meant to think originated in Britain. One was called the New British Broadcasting Station (NBBS). Its broadcasts opened with popular British songs, and as did those of the BBC, they ended with a rendition of "God

Save the King." At first the NBBS reported events as the BBC would have, but it later worked in reports that were detrimental to the British cause. It professed to be run by British citizens bent on speaking the truth—namely, that the Churchill government was under Jewish control and that it was responsible for the war. NBBS broadcasts urged their British listeners to oppose their government and side with Germany. The announcers themselves were British; one was even Oxford educated.

Another station purported to be broadcast from Scotland and promoted the notion of Scottish independence. A similar one intended to make its listeners believe it was coming from Wales and promoted Welsh independence. Still another, called Workers' Challenge, meant to foment social revolution among the laboring class. Typically this broadcast of about fifteen minutes a day began, "Here is Workers' Challenge calling, the movement for revolutionary action against the bosses and warmongers." It might then exhort, "Down with Churchill! Up with the workers' Britain!" Workers' Challenge broadcasts used foul language, because the Germans and exiled British fascists believed British workers liked to swear. In fact, though the broadcasts generated some interest, the novelty soon wore off.[3]

Yet another radio station set itself up as the Christian Peace Movement. It broadcast homilies laden with biblical passages chosen to polish its own purposes. By turns it urged its listeners to "judge not" (the Nazis' deeds, of course) but rather set their tasks to being good Christians and working for peace. A POW from the Dunkirk campaign was the principal announcer of the Christian Peace Movement broadcasts, having been released from prison camp for the work. The hope was that the radio shows would rally the pacifist currents so prevalent in the mid-1930s. Indeed this broadcast gained more traction than the separatist or worker-rebellion ones did.

Goebbels also recruited immigrant British fascists to make broadcasts. One of the most noted propagandists was a man with a not-quite upper-class accent whom the British audience soon labeled Lord Haw-Haw. His broadcasts from Hamburg began "Germany calling." No one in Britain at the time knew who he was. Later he was revealed to be William Joyce, a fascist and an anti-Semite who was politically active in the mid-1930s as a member of the British Union of Fascists (BUF) and had fled to Germany the month before the war broke out. Goebbels was generally delighted with the man and in January 1940 wrote in his diary: "Our English-language broadcasts are stirring things up in London. Our speaker has the nickname Lord Haw-Haw over there. Everyone is talking about him, and that is important for us. In London they are planning to put up a counter-speaker. We could not ask for anything better."[4]

By March Lord Haw-Haw's broadcasts were heard in America. Soon Haw-Haw was broadcasting to America three times a week, and the press there was taking notice. Goebbels was delighted and called the man a worldwide celebrity.[5] Few British listeners tuned in Lord Haw-Haw broadcasts for their political content; rather, they did so for information not otherwise available in Britain, notably the fate of aircraft crews that did not return from bombing missions. A British investigation during the war found that during the winter of 1939–40, three in six British citizens listened to Lord Haw-Haw's broadcasts regularly, two in six occasionally. Once Germany invaded ~~Britain~~ *France* on May 10, the size of the audience fell off to about 13 percent of the country.

Other German broadcasts featured popular songs but with anti-Churchill, pro-peace, and anti-Jewish lyrics. They crooned to soldiers that the government was merely selling out to rich Americans and that they were dying for a losing cause. Goebbels also broadcast jazz to America, slipping in pro-German, anti-British lyrics. The Germans did not yet use anti-Soviet tunes on account of Russia being an ally.

Not merely content with radio broadcasts, Goebbels's propaganda organization also dropped materials from airplanes. It scattered translations of Hitler's July 19 speech in hopes that British citizens would accept the führer's logic for ending the war. Other aerial distributions included a picture of cigar-chomping Churchill, in bowler hat and pin-striped suit, toting a Thompson submachine gun. The photo was real—albeit doctored to eliminate other people—and meant to reveal the prime minister as a gangster. "Save at least your families from the horrors of war!" the leaflets admonished.

The propaganda at least worked on Goebbels. Once the bombs began falling on the British capital in earnest, he noted in his diary: "Shattering descriptions from London. An inferno on an appalling scale . . . Slight signs of failing morale can be detected . . . We are returning our radio message . . . to focus on creating alarm and panic. We are putting on the big squeeze."[6]

Britain could not let these efforts of distortion go unanswered. They countered with an Anti-Lie Bureau and placed it under the Ministry of Information. The Anti-Lie Bureau's mission was to squelch rumors that came through the German radio broadcasts. Unfortunately the Anti-Lie Bureau lost credibility when debunking stories from German transmissions that were true. One was of a woman who thought her neighborhood in London was too perilous and moved out. The Anti-Lie Bureau said it was false, but the populace found out otherwise. The story had come from an item in the London *Times*.[7]

FASCISM IN BRITAIN

Truth be told, Goebbels was not entirely deceiving himself when he believed his broadcasts and leaflets could find nodding heads in Britain. Knots of fascists had arisen in the early 1920s owing to a mixture of admiration for Mussolini's movement in Italy and anxiety over communism. Fascist factions rose and fell through the 1920s and into the early '30s when the BUF represented most fascist thought in the nation.

The most prominent of the British fascists was Oswald Mosley. The eldest son of a baronet, he entered the Royal Military Academy at Sandhurst—the same college Churchill attended twenty years previously—but was soon expelled for attacks on another student. He nonetheless became an officer in World War I, serving in the infantry and Royal Flying Corps before becoming injured in an airplane crash. He was elected a member of Parliament at age twenty-one, switching from the Conservative to the Labour Party and then becoming an Independent. His first marriage, in 1920 to the daughter of a lord, was attended by King George V and Queen Mary. In 1931 he became enamored of Italian fascism and in 1932 worked to unite British fascists in the new BUF. Some members of the party were "blackshirts," a paramilitary clique that confronted Jewish and Communist groups. At one point, the BUF claimed fifty thousand members and the support of two newspapers. One, the *Daily Mail*—owned by noted German sympathizer Lord Rothermere—ran the editorial "Hurray for the Blackshirts" in January 1934 that praised Mosley for his common sense. Rothermere after the war was also revealed to have written Hitler a congratulatory letter for annexing Czechoslovakia and urged him to occupy Romania.

When Mosley's first wife died, he married one of his mistresses, Diana, who was formerly married to an heir of the Guinness brewery fortune and one of the infamous Mitford sisters.[8] This marriage, in 1936, took place secretly in Joseph Goebbels's home in Berlin, and Hitler was one of the guests. That October Mosley and BUF members clashed with opponents in the East End of London, a rumble thereafter known as the Battle of Cable Street. By then support for the BUF was falling off, notably because of the violence that attended some of its marches, meetings, and rallies.

Mosley's view in the 1930s was that Britain was in decline, which had been hastened by World War I. He wanted to restore Britain's prominence and put himself forward as the man to do it. Democracy would be discarded, and he, as a strong leader, would take its place. He spurred his movement with a series of books, the first in 1932 called *The Greater Britain*, followed in 1936 with *Fascism: One Hundred Questions Asked and Answered*, and in 1938 with *Tomorrow We Live*.[9]

As war approached Mosley continued to voice German-related views, and beginning in September 1939, Mosley was a leading voice in the call for a negotiated settlement. He continued to lobby this position until May 1940 when the authorities imprisoned both Mosley and Diana, though in pleasant enough quarters. In addition, the government interned more than seven hundred avowed fascists and banned the BUF.

The British internment policy squelched Mosley's supporters, but it did not end the talk of at least exploring a brokered peace with Hitler. Prominent among people of this inclination were the respected military strategist Basil Liddell Hart, Maj. Gen J. F. C. Fuller, powerful politician R. A. B. "Rab" Butler, and pacifist Charles Roden Buxton. Another who thought talks and accommodation might be the best policy was the World War I leader David Lloyd George. The former prime minister had called Hitler the George Washington of Germany and even in the autumn of 1940 singled the German dictator out as "among the greatest leaders of men in history." In June dozens of members of Parliament supported Lloyd George to head a peace plank.[10]

The Churchill government put people in cafés and pubs to eavesdrop on ordinary conversations then report back to Home Intelligence on the mood of the people. Support seemed softest among people of the working class, some of whom felt there would be little distinction working under a pro-German Britain as an anti-German one. "[Hitler] won't hurt us," ran one conversation, "it's the bosses he's after." But in general the mood supported the Churchill government. One poll showed 85 percent of men and 65 percent of women favored continuing the fight against Germany.

Once serious land bombing began in mid-August, Home Intelligence found a strengthening of resolve, even a flush of exhilaration and defiance. Although Europeans for two decades had been subjected to the most dire predictions of the devastation that could be wreaked by bombers, Home Intelligence found the morale of people in heavily hit areas "excellent." People seemed content to erect their air raid shelters, help their neighbors, read the fliers and publications about how to prepare for bombing attacks, and handle the stress.[11]

ANTI-BRITISH FLAVORS IN AMERICA

The United States, too, had its nodules of ultra right-wingers in the late 1930s. If not widely supported, these isolationist, pro-German, and anti-Semitic groups nonetheless made noise and headlines. The German-American Bund, known until 1936 as the Friends of the New Germany, was founded by two men involved in the 1923 Beer Hall Putsch and had since taken American citizenship. Bund members at first wore uniforms reminiscent of the SS, then switched to ones more resembling those of the U.S. veterans group American Legion. Led by Fritz Kuhn of Detroit and with much of its support coming from German immigrants or Americans of German ancestry, the Bund claimed close to ten thousand members and cooperation with 125 organizations. It promoted cultural and economic ties to Germany, and it ran Camp Siegfried and Camp Nordlnd in New Jersey and New York, respectively, for boys and girls in the summer. The Bund flag, which it flew alongside the American flag, displayed a swastika, and at Bund rallies members excoriated both communism and international Jewry. Bund literature called President Roosevelt "Rosenfeld" and the New Deal the "Jew Deal." It published propaganda magazines and brochures, organized rallies and marches, and sometimes clashed with those who showed up to oppose them. Some in Berlin thought the organization an embarrassment and wanted to cut off aid, but a congressional investigation in 1939 found ties between the Bund and Hitler's government.[12]

This organization was a small movement, however. The isolationists composed a far larger group and gave President Roosevelt greater pause. These people could trace their sentiment back to George Washington's farewell address, in which the first president urged his country to avoid entanglements in Europe. Isolationists found new energy in the 1920s when many were repelled by what they believed had been either a conspiratorial or wrongheaded intervention in World War I.

One of the isolationists' leading lights was also one of the nation's greatest heroes: Charles Lindbergh. In April he addressed the country by radio when France was being overrun: "The only reason that we are in danger of becoming involved in this war is because there are powerful elements in America who desire us to take part. They represent a small minority of the American people, but they control much of the machinery of influence and propaganda."[13] His mail ran twenty to one supporting his views. In August Lindbergh spoke to forty thousand cheering listeners at Soldier Field in Chicago. He advocated a strong defense for America while staying out of entanglements in the European war. He said that America should contemplate a Europe dominated by Germany and that inevitably cooperation with Germany need not be considered impossible.

In October 1940 Lindbergh's wife Anne published *The Wave of the Future: A Confession of Faith,* a small book of conflicting thought in which she deplored Nazi and Stalinist "barbarisms." But she also noted, "It is futile to get into a hopeless 'crusade' to 'save' civilization . . . there is no fighting the wave of the future any more than as a child you could fight against the gigantic roller that loomed up ahead of you suddenly." The book quickly became the best-selling nonfiction book in the country. DeWitt Wallace of *Reader's Digest* ran *The Wave of the Future* in condensed form and called it "*the* article of the year." The book was widely condemned as well. Some store owners sent it back to its publisher, and customers boycotted it.[14]

Coalescing much of the isolationist sentiment in the summer and fall of 1940 was the America First Committee. Officially formed in early September to counter the freshly minted Committee to Defend America by Aiding the Allies—also known as the White Committee after Kansas publisher William White—the leading lights of the America First Committee were several Yale undergraduate and law students. Soon the committee gained strength by enfolding pacifist groups, along with one of their leaders, Norman Thomas, who had run for president six times as a socialist. America First attracted a good deal of publicity and financial support. Prominent politicians stood up for it. The chairman of Sears, Roebuck was a founding member, as was Alice Longworth, daughter of president Theodore Roosevelt. Charles Lindbergh soon became its principal celebrity. It organized petitions to President Roosevelt and Congress. America First was splintered almost from the first, there being within it pacifists, anti-interventionists, anti-Semites, people who loathed Nazism, and people who were willing to see a negotiated settlement between Britain and Germany.[15] America First said it would accept no Nazis or Communists and would not take contributions from Nazi-leaning organizations, though likely it was in part supported by money from Germany.[16] But this denial did not stop critics from tarring the group with pro-German, pro-Nazi sentiments.

BRITISH SUBTERFUGE IN THE UNITED STATES

Some of the America First critics took inspiration from a man working undercover in America for the British government, William Stephenson. Born in Winnipeg, Manitoba, to parents too poor to keep him, Stephenson took the name of the foster family that raised him. As a teenager he volunteered for the Canadian army at the outbreak of World War I and, once he arrived in Britain, learned how to fly. He became a daring and decorated fighter ace credited with shooting down more than twenty enemy planes, winning the Distinguished Flying Cross and the Military Cross. He was finally shot down accidentally by a French plane and became a German prisoner of war for five months.

After the war Stephenson studied radio communications. He developed radio equipment in Britain and is said to have been the first person to transmit a photograph by radio waves in 1922. Improving radio equipment and dealing in phonographs, cars, and airplanes, he made a fortune before he was thirty. He even won a European lightweight boxing title.[17] Having gained a reputation as a visionary and adept scientist, he was noticed in the 1930s by Winston Churchill and his cadre of professors who were interested in new technologies. Stephenson's telecommunications equipment business sometimes took him to Germany, where he visited factories and took note of where he thought the Germans were secretly producing arms. He passed this information to Churchill, who used some of it in his addresses to Parliament about the rising Nazi menace.

At the outbreak of the war, Stephenson learned about Enigma and helped the deciphering effort at Bletchley Park. He promoted the idea that the Americans should be apprised of this work so that they might apply their own brainpower and industrial capacity to breaking more codes more quickly. He soon acted as a kind of information messenger between Churchill and Roosevelt. In June 1940 Churchill made him a secret agent for running British intelligence operations in America. Stephenson thereupon quickly established British Security Coordination (BSC), which by the end of the month had set up offices in New York's Rockefeller Center. Stephenson's charge was "to do all that was not being done and could not be done by overt means to ensure sufficient aid for Britain and eventually to bring America into the war." [18]

Stephenson worked at countering the efforts of agents who meant to lure American businessmen to mutually rewarding arrangements with Germany. The Germans' pitch—Germany would triumph and control the continent, so it was best for American businessmen to play ball—had its appeal. In late June at least one agent made this point at a party he threw for prominent American businessmen in New York's Waldorf Astoria Hotel. The organizer of this celebration of German victories on the continent, Dr. Gerhard Westrick, promised American industrialists monopolies in Germany if they would pledge not to join rearmament programs in the United States. Stephenson notified his friends in the press that Westrick was less a trade representative than an agent who ultimately reported to SS leader Reinhard Heydrich. The State Department expelled him from the country.

Stephenson surreptitiously worked to help Wendell Willkie win the Republican Party's nomination in July. He also fed pro-British information to widely read newspaper columnists Walter Winchell and Drew Pearson. Winchell especially tended to the British line and passed along BSC-invented stories of nefarious German schemes, to his readers.[19] The BSC took on many projects: work to inject pro-British information into American comic strips and surreptitiously underwrite pro-British radio broadcasts, secretly establish and pay for various anti-Nazi groups in America, endeavor to defeat the reelection of isolationist Congressmen and undermine isolationist meetings, and monitor and harass America First.[20] The BSC also worked to disrupt German businesses in South America, recruiting Nelson Rockefeller for some of this effort. When J. Edgar Hoover of the Federal Bureau of Investigation (FBI) cast a skeptical eye on the BSC's operations, Roosevelt ordered him to be cooperative.[21]

There was yet more to Stephenson's efforts. Roosevelt wanted another set of eyes and ears in the British Isles than those of Amb. Joseph Kennedy. For years Kennedy, an Irish-Catholic with an anti-British bias, had been telling Roosevelt that Britain could not stand up to a war with Germany. In July Roosevelt sent William "Bill" Donovan, an acquaintance from law school and a World War I Medal of Honor winner, as a personal representative on a fact-finding mission to London. Donovan was also an acquaintance of Stephenson, who was eager that Donovan get the right message while in Britain. Stephenson cabled his contacts in London: "The American government is debating two alternative courses of action. One would keep Britain in the war with supplies now desperately needed. Other is to give Britain up for lost. Donovan is President's most trusted personal advisor . . . and I urge you to bare your breast to him."[22]

The telegram and the fact-finding tour bore fruit. Ambassador Kennedy was upset that this visit was organized and conducted out of channels, but British government and military officials were more than happy to show Donovan how they were holding up and let him in on secrets no foreigner had yet been told. King George VI walked Donovan around Buckingham Palace. The RAF drove him to airfields and not only showed him how swiftly the pilots got into the air but also how RDF guided them directly to invading Luftwaffe formations. Donovan was introduced to the head of the MI6, Stewart Menzies, and the two men struck up a friendship. And Donovan was given a good deal of information about the Enigma code-breaking effort.

In short, Donovan was sold on the British capacity for staying in the fight, and when he returned to Washington on August 4, he spent two days with Roosevelt on the presidential yacht *Potomac*. There he gave the president a much different story than the one coming from Ambassador Kennedy. Donovan reported that British morale was good, the nation seemed determined to hang on despite the Luftwaffe's attacks, and it had a good chance of prevailing. Donovan also urged Roosevelt to accede to

Churchill's repeated request for the fifty World War I destroyers. Finally, he warned the president that America's best defense was Britain holding the line in Europe.

Roosevelt, already inclined toward helping Britain, was receptive to Donovan's message. Indeed, despite whatever efforts German propaganda was attempting in America or Britain, the Germans' actions themselves negated all their propaganda endeavors. Overrunning neutral countries and bombing cities from Portsmouth to Liverpool likely were doing more than anything else to stiffen British resolve and sway American opinion to support Great Britain.

CHAPTER EIGHT

SEPTEMBER

From under the Rubble

"Suddenly we were gaping upwards. The brilliant sky
was criss-crossed from horizon to horizon by innumerable
vapour-trails. The sight was a completely novel one. We
watched, fascinated, and all work stopped. The little silver
stars sparkling as the heads of the vapour trails turned east.
This display looked so insubstantial and harmless, even
beautiful. Then, with a dull roar which made the ground
across London shake as one stood upon it, the first
sticks of bombs hit the docks."
—*Anonymous soldier outside London*[1]

In late August the notion of bargaining for fifty U.S. World War I destroyers in exchange for naval or air bases in the Atlantic or Caribbean began to gel. Churchill was desperate for the ships, old as they were, and Roosevelt and his cabinet felt the transfer was necessary. The naval and air bases were in Newfoundland, Bermuda, the Bahamas, Jamaica, Trinidad, and a few other British Caribbean possessions. Roosevelt was reassured that Wendell Willkie would not make a campaign issue of it, so that anxiety was behind him. He worried that Congress would vote it down, but he had his advisers working on a way to complete the deal via executive action rather than congressional law. And he was apprehensive about the public's perception, wanting the public to feel the country had gotten the best of the bargain. For his part, Churchill did not want to see any quid pro quos;

therefore, rather than make a deal, he preferred that Britain make a gift of the bases and the United States make a gift of the destroyers. For one, he did not want his countrymen to compare values of the exchange because Britain was giving away a portion of its empire for fifty obsolete ships.

There were other problems. Roosevelt believed Congress and the electorate would be more receptive to the exchange if in the bargain the British pledged to send its fleet to America or to scuttle it if England were overrun. Churchill opposed making any such pledge. He felt that at such an anxious time the British people might interpret it as the government showing a lack of confidence in its forces' ability to defend the island. Further, there was the fear that should the war's circumstances worsen, America might demand the fleet even before Britain were to succumb.

In the end they compromised, and in the formal documents some of the bases were exchanged for some of the destroyers. Thus Roosevelt could say there was a deal while Churchill could say that there was a coincidental exchange of gifts. Still Roosevelt worried he might be impeached for what he was doing. When he explained the destroyers and bases action to reporters on a train returning from Tennessee, where he had dedicated a Tennessee Valley Authority dam and the Great Smoky Mountains National Park, he likened the deal to Thomas Jefferson's Louisiana Purchase. In that instance, Roosevelt reminded the press, Jefferson had in mind national security issues—just as Roosevelt did with the naval bases—and feared (according to Roosevelt) that going to Congress would mean crippling delays. Roosevelt exaggerated Jefferson's concerns for national security, but it served Roosevelt's purpose in putting the best possible light on the exchange for an American public leery of foreign entanglements.

Indeed the *St. Louis Post-Dispatch* called the transfer an "act of war" in full-page advertisements it bought in major newspapers, describing Roosevelt as a "dictator" and the transfer as tantamount to a military "alliance with Great Britain."[2] But U.S. citizens on the whole welcomed the bases as a security measure and the reinforcement to Britain as reasonable policy. Roosevelt was not impeached, Willkie did not make an issue of the transfers, and most of Congress went along with the deal. Officials signed the documents on September 2 and lost no time getting the destroyers reassigned. Four days afterward the first six American warships were turned over to British sailors at Halifax, Nova Scotia, the eager British having arrived the same day as the first destroyers. American sailors crammed the ships with foods that the war-rationed British sailors might appreciate: hams, fruit juice, clams, and more. The British would have to change the ships' names as well. Eventually the scheme was to name the destroyers after British towns that were also town names found in the United States: *Chesterfield, Chelsea,* and so on.[3]

As September opened the British had no respite from the air battles over the green and patchwork fields of southern England. The first days of September were fine and clear, with touches of puffy clouds. The Luftwaffe planes arrived in waves just as they had for the previous two weeks and more. On the first day of the month, they hit Biggin Hill again and other airfields. That night they kept up their attacks on Liverpool, as well as on Bristol, South Wales, and cities of the Midlands. And on this day, for the first time since the air war had begun over England, the RAF lost more planes than it destroyed, fifteen aircraft to the Luftwaffe's fourteen. It was an ill omen indeed.

On the next day, September 2, the Germans again hit Biggin Hill as well as the airfields at Detling and Lympne. They bombed the airfield at Hornchurch twice and at Eastchurch three times. Thirty-one RAF planes were destroyed and ten pilots killed while thirty-five Luftwaffe planes were shot down. At night bombers blasted Liverpool, Sheffield, and Manchester. There was little if any defense against them. Fighters found them mainly by luck, and antiaircraft fire was generally ineffective.

In the week of August 27–September 2, Fighter Command had lost ninety-six Hurricanes and forty-eight Spitfires, the highest number of losses since the Battle of Britain had begun. It had two hundred serviceable Spitfires left and four hundred Hurricanes. Worse, 20 percent of Fighter Command's squadron commanders and 33 percent of the flight commanders had been killed or wounded.[4] Newly trained pilots were available to fill the cockpits, but they had no combat experience; indeed some arrived never having fired their guns while flying. The daily fighting was showing that the neophytes were shot down at a significantly higher rate than the experienced pilots were. Moreover, the experienced men were sometimes flying three and four sorties a day, and the strain was wearing them out. Some developed tics and shakes, some fell asleep in their cockpits as soon as they landed, and others lugged themselves away from their planes to cots or chairs and fell asleep immediately. Dowding was forced to move squadrons from the north and west into the beleaguered south, but they had to relocate without some of their ground crews, which affected morale. Fighter Command was teetering.

On September 3 the Luftwaffe again attacked airfields and, despite having bombers as part of their attacking fleet, saw an even split of lost planes, sixteen for sixteen. On this day too and despite—or perhaps on account of—seeing firsthand what bombing could do, Churchill remained convinced that Britain's chance of winning the war was with its bomber fleet. He wrote his staff:

> We must therefore develop the power to carry an ever-increasing vol-
> ume of explosives to Germany, so as to pulverize the entire indus-
> try and scientific structure on which the war effort and economic life
> of the enemy depend. . . . In no other way at present visible can we
> hope to overcome the immense military power of Germany and to
> nullify the further German victories which may be apprehended as
> the weight of their force is brought to bear upon African or Oriental
> theatres.[5]

On the fourth, more Luftwaffe bombing attacks occurred at the air-fields by day and on aircraft factory, industrial, or shipping targets by night. A Vickers factory in Brooklands southwest of London was one of the worst hit. Perhaps aiming for the Hawker factory that made Hurricanes—or not recognizing it because it was cleverly camouflaged—the Nazi bombers hit the Vickers machine shops, killing eighty-seven people and wounding four hundred more. Total aircraft scores for the day were twenty-five Luftwaffe planes and seventeen RAF ones destroyed.

In a visit to towns near Dover during these days, Churchill overheard a small restaurant owner lament how his establishment and home had been destroyed. On the train back to London, Churchill wrote his chancellor of the Exchequer that the national government should compensate people for destroyed homes and businesses and that they should be paid immediately and in full. His notion was that all of Britain's citizens should share in the loss of the most unfortunate. The chancellor was concerned that this commitment was very open-ended, but Churchill held firm and a kind of insurance scheme went forward that dispensed aid to people who lost property in the bombings.

Churchill continued to urge bombings of Berlin, and they were carried out whenever possible. British bombers flew at night to avoid German fighters, and they had to fly five times farther than did the German bombers. The British bombers were meant to target industrial and military targets, but owing to crude navigation, obstruction by clouds, and antiaircraft fire from below, their aim was generally inaccurate. Nevertheless the British bombs killed some Berliners and made the rest nervous and even skeptical of Germany's prowess. The nightly raids embarrassed Göring, and Hitler worked himself into a fury. Churchill also wanted other German cities bombed. "You must remember," he wrote Air Marshal Richard Peirse, "that these people are never told the truth, and that, wherever the Air Force has not been, they are probably told that the German defences are impregnable."[6]

On September 4 Hitler gave a publicly broadcast speech at the large Sportpalast in Berlin. The audience was mainly women, including nurses and social workers. The führer lashed out at the British bombers: "When the British Air Force drops two or three or four thousand kilograms of bombs, then we will in one night drop 150-, 300- or 400,000 kilograms." He was interrupted by wild applause. "When they declare that they will increase their attacks on our cities, then we will *raze* their cities to the ground. We will stop the handiwork of these night air pirates, so help us God!"

At one point in the speech, he addressed another issue uppermost on the minds of his listeners: "In England they're filled with curiosity and keep asking, 'Why doesn't he come?' Be calm. He's coming! He's coming!"[7]

Furious that the British were bombing Berlin, Hitler made a momentous decision: he relented from his discretion about bombing London. He now said that the largest city in the world was a legitimate target, though for military and commercial points rather than for its residential neighborhoods. He told Göring to get on with it.

Fine weather continued over England on the fifth. By day Biggin Hill and Detling airfields were bombed again and by night oil storage tanks at Thames Haven east of London. The Luftwaffe lost twenty-three planes, shot down for twenty RAF fighters. Decorated Australian fighter ace Lt. Paterson Hughes claimed yet another Me-109, this one flown by Oberleutnant Franz von Werra, who crash-landed south of Maidstone and was made a prisoner.[8] Also on this day, British authorities announced that 1,075 civilians—more than half of them women and children—had been killed and 1,261 seriously wounded in the air attacks of August.[9] On the sixth, another day of fine weather, German planes bombed aircraft factories in Rochester southeast of London and in Weybridge to the southwest, as well as the oil storage facilities again at Thames Haven. And as had been their habit, they bombed RAF airfields.

Indeed Fighter Command was reeling. Between August 6 and September 2, it had lost 410 Hurricanes and Spitfires.[10] The factories helped make up these losses, but in the second half of August, 103 Fighter Command pilots had been killed and 128 badly wounded, or about a quarter of the pilots ready for combat missions in mid-August. As bad, in terms of getting the aircraft aloft, sector stations and smaller airfields were badly damaged, and the whole Fighter Command's communications structure was under dire stress. If this bombing campaign continued, Fighter Command might well collapse.[11]

On Saturday, September 7, again the weather was good, but throughout the morning the RDF scopes were mainly clear. The Hurricane and Spitfire pilots lay in beds, rested in chairs, kicked soccer balls around, or played skittles and waited. Only at around 4:00 p.m. did their operators begin to see images of massed formations of German planes rising over France. They circled, gaining altitude. Beneath them, on the cliffs at Cap Gris Nez, stood Reichsmarschall Hermann Göring himself. He had come, as he said, to take personal command of the air war against Britain and of what he was certain would be its final phase. He was convinced that Fighter Command was down to only several hundred fighters and that the airfields, with their precious runways and facilities, were mainly blasted ruins. Now, with the fresh directive from Hitler, he could bomb the commercial, cultural, financial, governmental, and shipping capital of the country: London. To defend this precious city, Göring reasoned, the RAF would put up all of its remaining Hurricanes and Spitfires, which would be shot down day after day until no appreciable number was left.

Göring watched his planes, waves of hundreds—by one estimate 625 bombers with another 600 fighters stretching twenty miles—drone toward England. It was an awesome sight.

Across the channel the call went out to scramble the squadrons of 11 Group. They took to the air and circled for height. Moving north across the channel, the formations of German planes slipped and slid, hoping to confuse ground controllers of their targets, and for a time they did. When the German planes turned to concentrate, it became clear that unlike the previous weeks, the targets were not going to be airfields; indeed the targets were in London itself. Off-balance at first owing to the change in German concentration, the Hurricanes and Spitfires nevertheless swooped down, picking their targets in the bomber formations. They sent solitary planes down, trailing smoke, only to be set upon themselves by the Me-109s.

The Luftwaffe bombers' main targets were Thames Haven east of the city proper and the docklands of the city's East End. The Woolwich Arsenal, where bombs for the RAF and artillery shells for the army were made, was an early and spectacular target. Smoke and flames boiled up from the hapless buildings. The docks where the supplies for the city arrived by ship were pummeled with bombs. Ships sank, bridges crumbled, and warehouses poured out flames. Gasworks and power stations were also hit. London's poor took the worst of it as whole blocks of dense housing were reduced to rubble. The attack went on for two hours and hundreds of people were killed. The smoke obscured the sun, and miles to the south, it was so thick that Hurricanes and Spitfires poised on their runways could not see far enough ahead to take off. In one London neighborhood called Silvertown, the residents were surrounded by flames and had to be rescued by boats on the river.

But the bombers received some of their due. In their turns toward France and the Lowlands again, they generally had their hardest times, and today was no exception. Bereft of the Me-109s, which could only range over London for less than fifteen minutes, the bombers had no margins protecting their flanks or their approaches, high and low. It was then that the Hurricanes and Spitfires liked to find them, though the Dorniers and Heinkels had already done their worst. The RAF fighters raked them with fire, zipped through them, and turned to come at them again. As the sun sank toward the horizon, planes fell from the sky.

This massive two-hour bombing was not the end of it. As darkness came, new formations of 250 bombers droned toward the East End of London.[12] Guided by the fires ignited by the afternoon's strikes, they couldn't miss. From nine o'clock that night until three o'clock in the morning, wave upon wave of German bombers loosed three hundred tons of large bombs and thirteen thousand smaller incendiary ones meant to start fires. Fighter Command put up night fighters, but these planes as usual had a difficult time getting close enough to get good shots. The antiaircraft fire only brought down one German plane. Despite the fires in the East End acting as guiding beacons, some of the bombs hit other parts of the city. Roads were blocked and train stations blasted. Londoners were shocked. Although Liverpool, Bristol, Sheffield, and other cities had been attacked, Londoners had so far largely been spared. Now that time was past.

As hard as the afternoon and night of September 7 were for Londoners, all across southern England, soldiers, women, and maintenance crews were at work restoring the RAF airfields, splicing vital telephone lines, filling in craters on runways, and fixing fighter repair hangers. No new fires were started near them and no new craters made. The fighters could return to airfields that were in better shape than when they had left them. But the toll this day was nonetheless high: twenty-eight aircraft down and twenty pilots killed or missing. Australian ace Paterson Hughes was shot down and killed by an Me-109. South African Caesar Hull and Australian Dick Reynell, considered two of the best Hurricane pilots in Fighter Command, also lost their lives.[13]

In a meeting with his senior officers that day, Dowding told them that Fighter Command had 348 pilots killed or seriously wounded in the past month. The training programs had only supplied 280 in the same time. "I want you to take away from this meeting the feeling that the situation is extremely grave," he said.[14]

As if September 7 were not bad enough, the war leaders meeting in the underground bunker—known as the Hole in the Ground—beneath the government offices at Whitehall debated whether to send a signal to the army that an invasion was imminent. There were tangible signs. Four German spies had been caught on the September 4 coming ashore by boat along the south coast. Their mission was to report on coastal defenses and military movements. They were picked up within hours and confessed to their mission, adding that an invasion could be expected any day. RAF reconnaissance photographs showed a fresh buildup of barges and other cross-channel craft in ports along the Belgian and French coasts. There were reports of Germans preparing a smoke screen in the channel and of reinforcement airplanes moving up to coastal airfields. In addition, military intelligence had for some time told commanders that the best tide and moon conditions for an invasion ran in the middle of September.

With the sound of bombs for the first time blasting London neighborhoods to their south and east, the military commanders issued the code word Cromwell, meaning an invasion was imminent. The warning was meant for the army only, to place it on high alert, but the barrier between the army and the Home Guard was in places tenuous. By evening word got out, and Home Guard men left their homes with rifles in hand. Some bridges were blown and roadblocks put up. In places the church bells rang, a cacophony meant only for when an invasion had begun.

Morning revealed no invasion. Vexed, Churchill and the chiefs called for measures that would increase readiness by stages rather than Cromwell's on/off absolutes.[15] In London's East End, Cockneys emerged in the daylight to find rows of homes reduced to rubble, streets blocked, and crews working to extract people trapped in piles of concrete and brick. They tried to cope as best they could with the devastation and disruption. The *Daily Telegraph* reported that under the cleared skies, people put their possessions in baby carriages and wheeled them to the untouched tenements of relatives or friends, and mothers prepared food in partly bombed apartments that had no water or gas, borrowing water and lighting small fires. Pubs were set up as domestic quarters for those who had lost their homes. The newspaper said of the people in blasted neighborhoods, "Their morale was astonishing." In one tavern, windowless on account of a bomb blast, neighbors raised money to pay for a Spitfire.[16]

The day, in fact, remained generally calm despite good weather, though there was a raid against coastal areas in Kent. The British could only guess what the Germans were planning. On the one hand, if the invasion was on the way, why bomb London? On the other hand, they knew the Germans had bombed to rubble very large portions of Warsaw and Rotterdam as their troops approached, hoping to terrify the population into surrendering. On the ground Fighter Command worked at rebuilding its southern airfields and resting its pilots. King George journeyed to the East End to view the damage and to try and shore up the residents' spirits. Churchill too visited the East End and talked with the residents of an air raid shelter where a direct hit had killed forty people. "It was good of you to come," they told the prime minister. "We thought you'd come. We can take it. Give it 'em back."[17]

Not all East Enders were as patriotically plucky. Some of the Cockneys in this part of London felt, correctly, that the poor and industrial sections were taking the brunt of the bombing. Communists organized a demonstration against the upper class and marched into the West End's fashionable Savoy Hotel. Police would not throw them out because, without being nuisances, they were considered the hotel's guests. The manager called for tea, but the demonstrators soon left. Government censors wanted to downplay the story, which the newspapers did.

Ranging through the blasted neighborhoods were air raid wardens, generally part-timers wearing army-issue steel helmets stamped ARP (Air Raid Precautions). Many donned a drab, one-piece jumpsuit over their clothing. (Churchill also had one and liked to wear it.) The ARP men and women were meant to scurry to damaged areas, sometimes with a policeman; report back on what was needed—for example, medical teams, firefighters, or excavation teams—and then do whatever work was possible, such as shoveling dirt on the small incendiary bombs, pulling people from debris, and leading people to shelters. Sometimes teenage boys worked as messengers on bicycles; it was important work because telephone lines were often cut and streets too blocked for vehicles.[18]

At this time air raid shelter protection was skimpy at best. Most Londoners stayed in their homes and trusted in luck. Some took to railway tunnels, which would not survive a direct hit, and at least one tunnel quickly became an unsanitary horror. Using stations of the subway (called the Underground or Tube) was at first not permitted. The government distributed free corrugated steel kits that were called Anderson shelters after the home secretary John Anderson. Homeowners were to assemble them with nuts and bolts in their gardens, the more deeply set into the ground the better, but in many neighborhoods nearly every square yard fore or aft of a house was paved. The Anderson shelters became matters of pride for some people, who showed off to their neighbors how tidily they arranged their cots and survival gear. The corrugated steel roofs were curved, offering protection from a falling brick or shrapnel from antiaircraft fire but not from a direct hit or near miss.[19] In the West End, some of the substantial buildings and hotels made their basements into shelters, setting up bunks. A deep bunker for Churchill and important government officials was constructed underground, part of what was called the Number 10 Annex, or the Annex. Plans for evacuating the government from central London were drawn up as a last resort in case bombings made efficient operations at Whitehall impossible.

So the daylight of the eighth passed; the hammer blow came after dark. London again was the main target. Hundreds of bombers, droning in waves, set their sights on the smoldering city, aiming particularly for power stations and railway lines. They could hardly miss. Even under the rules of the blackout, the Thames Estuary was easy to spot. Then the wide river led back to the docks, noted by the river's S turns. Only in completely cloudy conditions was the city obscured.

Air raid sirens wailed through the London streets, and Londoners took to their shelters or made ready. Bomb blasts rocked the air and trembled the ground. Hospitals, rail lines, and warehouses were all hit or set ablaze. Where the fires were in riverside warehouses, fireboats on the river attempted quenching them. The attacks were more or less continuous through the night, giving no respite to firemen or even people hoping for a little rest from the sound of nerve-shattering bomb bursts. At least four hundred civilians were killed this night. Owing to the fact that the raid was in darkness, only fifteen Luftwaffe planes and two British ones were shot down.

Bombers also went the other way. RAF bombers struck at German ports such as Hamburg, Bremen, and Emden. Told that the Luftwaffe's bombing of London was indiscriminate (inaccurate and therefore indiscriminate may have been a better description), the British War Cabinet in retaliation told Bomber Command that its bombers should not return to base with bombs but to find something in Germany on which they could blast them.[20] But Bomber Command night raids, in William Shirer's words, were "pinpricks compared to what the Luftwaffe was doing to Britain's cities."[21] More effective were Bomber Command raids on barges and other potential invasion equipment in the ports of Ostend and Boulogne. But the toll on the command was significant, losing eight RAF bombers.

On September 9 the Luftwaffe was back in daylight. Bombers struck at Southampton. Two hundred bombers headed toward London, but RAF fighters broke up much of the attack, with many planes going down. The Luftwaffe ended up losing twenty-eight for the day against nineteen for the RAF. That night the bombing of London began at 10:00 p.m. and continued through 4:30 a.m. Fires raged around St. Paul's Cathedral, and the Bank of England was hit. The Docklands again were bombed, and a school that sheltered people who had lost their homes took a direct hit. Near the Tower of London, a warehouse storing paraffin wax was set ablaze, sending flames two hundred feet into the air.[22] German bombers also struck Bristol, Liverpool, and cities in the Midlands. In all about four hundred civilians were killed that night.

Meanwhile Fighter Command was rebuilding itself. Keith Park, the commander of 11 Group, changed some of his tactics. Previously stingy about fighters taking on large formations, he now allowed two squadrons to act as a pair. Albert Kesselring, who commanded roughly half the Luftwaffe planes across the channel, noted the difference almost immediately and issued an order allowing his bombers to break off attacks if they were met with concentrations of Hurricanes and Spitfires. His order acknowledged that the RAF fighter force was retaining a strength beyond what either he or Göring had expected.

In addition Park noted that rather than coming in smaller independent raids, the German bombers assembled in two large formations, one about fifteen minutes behind the other. He ordered that fighters not merely attack the first wave but that a good portion of them hold off and attack the second wave as well. Meanwhile Dowding was forced to make changes he loathed and called it his Stabilisation Scheme. He had long made a point of holding squadrons together, for each had an esprit de corps that he encouraged. But some of the squadrons were so depleted that the Fighter Command leader had to transfer experienced pilots out of some squadrons and into others. He also ranked squadrons A, B, and C, with the A squadron being more operationally fit and placed in or near 11 Group. A B squadron could be thrown into the fight only as a reinforcement, whereas a C squadron, which was worn out or depleted, was placed far from the fighting and its pilots broken out to other squadrons.

Edward R. Murrow, a reporter for the Columbia Broadcasting System (CBS), said in his radio broadcast to America for September 9 that he had seen "hundreds of people being evacuated from the East End, all of them calm and quiet. . . . These people are exceedingly brave, tough, and prudent. The East End, where disaster is always just around the corner, seems to take it better than the more fashionable districts in the West End."[23]

A great many Americans began tuning in Murrow's broadcasts. These reports and newspaper stories of the bombardments of English ports and cities aroused sympathy for the British civilians' plight. American opinion began to turn away from strict isolationism toward supporting increased aid for Britain.

September 10 was a day of poor weather, but the Germans nonetheless sent bombers against London, Liverpool, and South Wales. RAF Bomber Command raided Eindhoven, Holland, blasting an airfield and destroying ten He-111s on the ground. Displeased with reports of so many Hurricanes and Spitfires attacking the German bomber formations, Hitler in Berlin told his commanders that he would delay his decision about Operation Sea Lion until September 14. In any case he felt he still held two strong cards: he could bomb Britain until its government gave up, or he could bomb it until the people revolted, overthrew the Churchill government, and replaced it with one that would come to terms. He and his advisers read reports from the German Embassy in the United States that said damage to London was considerable and that even American military staff believed Britain would soon have to call for terms.[24]

That same day, Murrow reported:

I've see some horrible sights in this city during these days and nights, but not once have I heard man, woman, or child suggest that Britain should throw in her hand. These people are angry. How much they can stand, I don't know. The strain is very great. . . . After four days and nights of this air Blitzkrieg, I think the people here are rapidly becoming veterans, even as their Army was hardened in the fire of Dunkerque.[25]

And the people had at least a moment of cheer. After three nights of little resistance to the bomb-dropping Heinkels and Dorniers, on this night the London searchlights flashed on, and the city's antiaircraft guns all began blasting upward at once. The noise was cacophonous, and Londoners shouted approval. They were hitting back.

In reality the antiaircraft guns did little, and in the exchange of explosives the city took by far the worst of it. Fires, blocked streets, blasted water lines, smashed railway roadbeds—all made for trouble and tragedy. There were also unexploded bombs around the city. Where they were discovered, signs went up and people could not go near. Unexploded bombs emptied commercial and office buildings, stopped railway traffic, and closed roads.

On September 12 a large unexploded bomb lodged deep in a crater in front of the imperious columned facade of London's iconic St. Paul's Cathedral. If it had exploded, it would have brought down the cathedral's front. In addition the bomb had ruptured a gas main. Leaking gas knocked unconscious the first three people on the scene. A Canadian lieutenant and a team of engineers set about working to remove the unexploded bomb, a task that extended to three days. Two trucks worked to haul the bomb out, failing twice when the bomb slipped back to the bottom of the crater. Eventually the Canadian and his team extracted the bomb and hoisted it on a truck. They surrounded it with cushions and wooden blocks to guard against rolling. A route through the city was cleared, and homes on either side for a hundred yards evacuated. Police vehicles readied themselves half a mile in front and half a mile behind the bomb-laden vehicle. Then the Canadian lieutenant alone in the truck—he would not allow any one else in it—sped as fast as his motorcade would allow through the East End. It stopped near marshy land outside the city, and he exploded the bomb there a few hours later.[26]

Another agonizing problem was the parachute mine. Developed as sea mines, they were eight feet long by two feet across and could weigh up to two thousand pounds. The Luftwaffe put them to work bombing land-based targets. The parachute would allow the huge mine to explode without first burrowing into a road, yard, or house that it struck, thus spreading its destructive power. A parachute mine could demolish whole swaths of homes. Often, however, their parachutes caught on lampposts, trees, or power lines, and the mines dangled mere feet or inches from an impact that would detonate them. Regular bomb disposal squads did not want to deal with them; they called in technicians from the Royal Navy.[27]

September 11 was a bigger day for battle than the day previous. Clouds dispersed. Generally all was quiet through the morning and middle of the clear day, and RAF pilots caught up on their rest. But at about 2:45p.m., the RDF cathode ray screens showed large formations massing over France, and the quiet was broken. A formation of 150 German bombers along with fighter escort was soon heading for London; a similar formation headed for Southampton and Portsmouth. Both bomber groups got through and bombed the cities. In London the Woolwich Arsenal was hit again. In the pleasant weather, airplanes tumbled down in smoke and flames; parachutes blossomed amid the vapor trails.

With darkness the Germans again bombed London from about 9:00 p.m. to 4:30 a.m. The bombers came in at high altitude and, although spotted by searchlights, were out of the antiaircraft guns' range. Again the East End got the worst of it, but Buckingham Palace was also hit. Newspaper censors wanted to suppress the story of the near miss to the royal family, but when Churchill heard of it, he raged, "Fools! Spread the word at once! Let the humble people of London know that they are not alone, and that the King and Queen are sharing their perils with them!"[28] The Queen later said, "Now the palace has been bombed, I feel I can look at the people of the East End straight in the eye." She could also have meant the people of Liverpool, because the port city on the Mersey River suffered from bombers again this night. In all it was a blistering day of airplane fights. For the second time, RAF losses were greater than those for the attackers, with twenty-nine Fighter Command planes shot down for twenty-five of the Germans'.

Murrow went on the air again that night with his characteristic monotone, describing, among other things, his personal reactions to bombs and how the sound alone—not the blast—could stagger him as he walked. He also related two small stories. First, despite bombs having exploded only a couple of blocks from his office, his secretary was still on hand to offer him a cup of tea as he walked in that morning. The other was of a store clerk who suggested Murrow not stock up on so many batteries for his flashlight because, the store having been in its location for 150 years, the clerk was confident that it would be in business the following month as well.[29]

Meanwhile, north of London, Bletchley Park code breakers read messages about troop, armament, and engineer movements that led some to believe an invasion was imminent. Churchill decided to address the nation that night by radio. The address was short. He warned his listeners that an invasion was possible, one that might strike England, Scotland, Ireland, or all three. He also described the buildup of barges and shipping across the channel and the North Sea. While admitting that he thought an invasion unlikely because the Germans had yet not wrested command of the air from the RAF and that doing so was "the crux of the whole war," he said that he thought if the Germans were going to invade, it would be soon. Then, as was his wont, he worked to rally the blood of the British by hearkening back to its dearest tales of steadfast Elizabeth and the resolute, one-armed, one-eyed Nelson.

> Therefore, we must regard the next week or so as a very important week for us in our history. It ranks with the days when the Spanish Armada was approaching the Channel . . . or when Nelson stood between us and Napoleon's Grand Army at Boulogne. We have read all about this in the history books; but what is happening now is on a far greater scale and of far more consequence to the life and future of the world and its civilisation than these brave old days of the past.[30]

Churchill and Dowding continued to read Ultra messages, the work of the code breakers at Bletchley Park. These reports gave a good, if not exact, picture of German intentions. They learned which Luftwaffe units might be used in the coming days, the movements of squadrons, and the abilities of the replacement and reinforcement efforts. Early decryptions on September 13 and 14 indicated a large daylight raid on London for first the thirteenth and then the fourteenth and which Luftwaffe groups would take part. Neither raid materialized, perhaps owing to weather. Still the RAF felt something big was in the offing.[31]

When the fourteenth arrived, Hitler equivocated about Operation Sea Lion. He told his commanders that Britain was hoping for aid eventually from the Soviet Union or America. He did not see Russia tilting toward

Britain any time soon, and he said the United States could not effectively rearm for years. The best way to knock Britain out of the war was a landing, but he admitted that the conditions were not right. "The enemy recovers again and again. . . . Enemy fighters have not yet been completely eliminated."[32] To an extent he blamed bad weather for slowing the annihilation of Fighter Command, but he concluded by postponing his decision about Sea Lion again for another three days.[33] He thought the British might yet crack: "If eight million inhabitants [the population of London] go crazy, that can lead to catastrophe. . . . Then even a small-scale invasion could work wonders."[34] Meanwhile RAF bombers were continuing to blast barges and other invasion equipment along the channel ports.

Also on this day in the United States, President Roosevelt signed into law the first peacetime military draft in the nation's history. The act called for a lottery system that would require up to 900,000 American men to serve in the armed forces for one year.

After the major fight on the eleventh, poor weather set in for three days. But every night London was bombed just about at will. South Wales and Liverpool were also regular targets. Airplane losses were relatively low.

Göring, however, was husbanding his resources for another day of massive attack. Despite Hitler's postponement of the decision about Sea Lion and the evaporation of his own boast to wreck Fighter Command in mere days, the Luftwaffe chief was determined to stage a huge daylight raid of London and southern ports on the fifteenth. He was not going to send all his bombers for these daylight raids, but he planned to put in just about all his fighters. By his lights, there couldn't be more than a few hundred Hurricanes and Spitfires left in Britain. He figured that the last of them would rise to meet his bombers, and his fighters would overwhelm them.

The morning of the fifteenth broke clear, a harbinger of a fine day. All was quiet for a while. But at around 11:00 a.m., the RDF scopes detected large formations rising over France. They were so large that they took time forming. The delay worked for the British, who sent their squadrons into the air. They climbed. All over southern England, Hurricanes and Spitfires roared their Merlin engines to life, bumped out to battered runways, and winged into the clear air. From Detling, Hornchurch, Biggin Hill, Tangmere, North Weald, and more, they rose in strength as never before.

Indeed the RAF pilots felt somewhat rejuvenated and refreshed. The terrible strains and losses and the blastings of the airfields from late August to September 7 had slackened in the lull of the previous week's rain. They felt better prepared today for what was coming at them.

As soon as the German planes crossed the English coast, Hurricanes and Spitfires tore into them. Some RAF fighter squadrons worked in large groups, zooming in on the slow German bombers with their guns blazing. One fleet of Dorniers was set upon by a formation of Douglas Bader's Big Wings. For once, RAF fighters, wanting to get at the enemy, outnumbered a formation of German bombers. Never had the German fliers seen so many Hurricanes and Spitfires.[35] Told again and again that the RAF was almost finished and that one more huge attack should finish them off, the Luftwaffe pilots were astonished and dismayed.

All summer long Dowding had been husbanding his squadrons, releasing them only bits at a time, the better to have some left for the morrow. Warned by Ultra a few days earlier that a big attack was in the offing, he sensed today would see that major attack, and it was the critical time to throw in most of what he had. Hundreds of Hurricanes and Spitfires attacked the German groups.[36] Over and over, just when the German aircrews had thought they had seen the last of the deadly RAF fighters, more and more came at them, firing.

About noon Sgt. Ray Holmes went after a Dornier head-on over central London. His guns were about empty, and after a short burst, they fell silent. Holmes decided to ram the German bomber: "There was no time to weigh up the situation. His aeroplane looked so flimsy, I did not think of it as something solid and substantial. I just went on and hit [it]." The German bomber broke up quickly, some of its bombs falling on Buckingham Palace and the grounds. Holmes tried to pull his Hurricane out of a spin but couldn't and bailed out. His parachute opened with such a jolt that Holmes's boots fell off. He landed on a third-story roof, slid down it into the air again, and was halted feet from the ground when his parachute caught on a piece of the roof.[37]

Knowing that the weather would be fair and that to this point much of the heavy air fighting had been waged on Sundays, Churchill motored in that morning from his rural residence at Chequers to the 11 Group headquarters at Uxbridge. His wife, Clementine, accompanied him. Commander of 11 Group Keith Park was there, ready to call the group's sections into action. By midday it was obvious to all in the group's underground operations room that the Germans were waging a major effort. Churchill saw from the lighted board that one after another the squadrons were committed. Soon all the squadrons were in the air. It was a perilous situation because after an hour's fight, they would have to descend for arms and fuel and possibly be jumped and destroyed on the ground. "What other reserves have we?" Churchill asked of Park then. "There are none," was the reply, and Park later wrote that the prime minister looked grave. Churchill later wrote, "Well I might [have looked grave]. . . . The odds were great; our margins small; the stakes infinite."[38] Park's gamble was less than it seemed. Code breakers at Bletchley had passed to Dowding, who had in turn passed to Park, an intercepted message that implied German fighters were not planning an attempt to catch British fighters on the ground that day.[39]

Up in the sky, the quick move of a hand or foot meant the difference between life and death. Planes jumping other planes were jumped themselves. Holding a plane in a gun's sight lasted only a second or two, glimpses of attacking planes even less. Pilot Sgt. William Rolls recounted one of his experiences that day:

> I saw an Me-109 coming down and it passed well over my head and appeared to be firing at the aircraft in front of me. As it climbed up again I climbed after it and at 200 yards gave a burst of about 2 or 3 seconds . . . I saw some tracer coming from behind me as well and in my mirror saw another Me-109 coming down at me. I evaded . . . there were about 20 more above with it, and I decided to leave.[40]

September 15 was the only day that the Germans sent two separate attacks against London in daylight.[41] In all the Luftwaffe flew 1,261 sorties that day, 437 of them by bombers and 809 of them by fighters, the rest by reconnaissance planes. The Germans lost sixty aircraft; Fighter Command lost twenty-six. Only on August 15 and 18 had the German losses been so high. Hardest hit were the bombers in the second wave. Some formations lost 20 and 30 percent of their totals. In all the Luftwaffe lost 6 percent of the sorties they put up that day. The British suffered 4 percent of the Spitfire sorties and 6 percent of the Hurricane sorties. Twelve RAF pilots were killed and another twelve wounded. For every RAF pilot killed or wounded, seven German airmen were killed, wounded, missing, or captured.

As was the norm, both sides claimed about three times the number they actually destroyed. The intelligence officers generally believed the pilots' claims, though on the British side they could and did count crashed planes on land anyway. They in turn passed their estimates up the chain of command to higher officials, who also believed the numbers. They were then reported in the newspapers and believed by the public. On September 16 the London *Times* reported 175 German planes shot down the day before for a loss of 30 RAF planes. In Germany the *Völkischer Beobachter* newspaper reported 79 British planes shot down for a loss of 43 German ones.[42]

The consequences of the day's aerial fighting were swift. It was obvious to the Luftwaffe aircrews involved that they had not gained daylight superiority over southern England. Luftwaffe intelligence officers could hardly deny it, and this ungainly truth found its way to the highest German military commanders. In a meeting with these men on September 17, Hitler postponed Operation Sea Lion indefinitely, though he called for preparations to continue. Enigma cryptologists intercepted a message later in the day from Berlin to Luftwaffe fields opposite Britain: they were to stop certain procedures for loading air transports. Intelligence officers interpreted this directive to mean that plans for airlifting supplies to an invasion force in England were to be suspended, an indication that a German invasion was postponed. They notified Churchill and the chiefs of staff that evening.[43]

On this same day in rough seas six hundred miles west of Liverpool, the German submarine U-48 torpedoed the four-year-old passenger ship *City of Benares*, which was carrying ninety children to Canada in an evacuation program begun the week France capitulated. The death toll included 77 children and 217 adults. Other survivors were rescued within 24 hours, but 6 children and 46 adults survived 6 days in an open boat before being rescued. Churchill, who had never liked the evacuation program in the first place, asked the cabinet to halt it. It did so unanimously.

■

Britain had long anticipated that the Italians would advance across the Libyan-Egyptian border toward the main British stronghold in the Middle East: Alexandria. Mussolini was keen on getting started. If the Italians could drive the British out of Alexandria, they would sever Britain's best link to its eastern empire and open for Italy and Germany the great petroleum fields under the Middle East sands. However, Mussolini's field marshal in Libya, Rodolfo Graziani, was most reluctant to move the Italian army, despite outnumbering the British five to one. By early September Mussolini's patience was worn thin. He cabled Graziani that if he did not move to the attack by Monday, September 16, he would be replaced. Graziani launched the invasion of Egypt on September 13.

Several battalions of British troops held the border area. They were under orders to harass the Italians and make a fighting withdrawal. The Italians moved en masse and made inviting targets, with their motorcyclists out in front, then waves of light tanks and other vehicles, along with trucks carrying infantry. A British colonel likened the march to a parade. The British lobbed their artillery shells into these masses but could not do much to slow them and retreated as they kept up their fire.

The territory here being desert and the only good means of communication a single road that ran along the Mediterranean stringing together the only appreciable towns, the Italians set their goal on the first settlement inside Egypt of any consequence: the coastal village of Sidi Barrani. In four days the Italian army covered the fifty miles from the border to get there. Then they stopped to consolidate their gains.

The 150 tanks that Churchill had risked sending to Egypt even in the face of invasion at home were just then beginning to arrive, and he urged them to be unloaded with all speed for immediate transport to the battle line. Britain was now no longer fighting on one front—that is, southern England—but on two, each requiring men, airplanes, ships, code-breaking capacity, food, and more, putting further demands on a strained effort.

Churchill still had fears for Malta as well. The island just east of the Strait of Sicily was virtually undefended yet critical to British positions in the Mediterranean. Because the British did not control the sea around the island and their ships only occasionally appeared there, the island was vulnerable to invasion by the Italians. "The danger, therefore, appears to be extreme," Churchill wrote General Ismay on September 21, and he would look around for reinforcements.[44]

After the great air battles over London and the fields of England on September 15, the Germans sent fewer bombers north during daylight. Instead they fitted Me-109s and Me-110s with one or two bombs and ordered them on swift raids against specific targets. The German fighters would release their bombs and then be free to tangle with the Hurricanes and Spitfires sent against them. There was no respite after dark, however. The Germans kept up their bombing raids by night against Liverpool and London. The capital had been bombed every night since September 7. Its residents began calling this string of night attacks the Blitz, a name that stuck ever after.

British bombers continued to target the barges, ships, and boats collected in cross-channel ports that might launch an invasion. At first a nuisance, the bombing's effectiveness increased, sinking or blasting a good many of these craft along with port railroad yards, docks, and storage areas. Frustrated, the Germans began to disperse the vessels to other places so as not to make such inviting targets.

On September 22 Roosevelt telephoned Churchill to say that U.S. intelligence had learned that the invasion would certainly begin the following day at 3:00 p.m. Churchill was skeptical but thanked the president and then telephoned Secretary of State for War Anthony Eden, who was at the time near the coastal town of Dover. Churchill asked Eden to have a look. Eden strolled out to the cliffs, scanned the channel, and then reported that he felt quite safe. The seas were choppy, and any Germans in barges would be seasick upon arrival. Churchill breathed easier.

Roosevelt telephoned the prime minister the next day to apologize. There had been a mix-up, the president said; the invasion he had been told about was actually a Japanese strike against the Vichy French colonies in Southeast Asia. Indeed the Japanese did attack the colonies on September 23. After brief fighting between Japanese and French forces, the latter surrendered. Northern Indochina fell into Japanese hands.[45]

On September 24 and 25, small raids did a great deal of damage to Spitfire factories in Southampton and Bristol. In Southampton a large bomb struck an air raid shelter, killing nearly a hundred key personnel and wounding half again as many. In part, the raids were successful because the German bombers originally went for one target but then abruptly changed course. The RDF interpreters and communicators were surprised, and fighter interference was light. Although damage to the Spitfire plants was severe, much of the work had been decentralized to other factories in the previous two months so that production was less hobbled than it would have been earlier.

On the twenty-seventh the Luftwaffe shifted its tactics of the previous ten days and again sent up large daylight raids against Bristol and London. But the Luftwaffe fighter-bomber rendezvous over London was botched, and the Germans suffered heavily. Fifty-five of their planes were destroyed for a loss of twenty-eight RAF planes. For the next two days, daylight activity was again light, but the habitual night bombings of London and Liverpool continued. On the last day of the month, however, the Germans again put up masses of bombers protected by waves of fighters above. This day they tried to draw up the Hurricanes and Spitfires sooner so they would be low on fuel when the biggest waves came, but Park's 11 Group waited. The Observer Corps' spotters on the ground confirmed that the initial waves of German planes were fighters rather than bombers. When Park did get his fighters up and in position, the German bombers were having communication problems; moreover, their fighters at first were not protecting them. One hundred and fifty of Park's Hurricanes and Spitfires zoomed in among the German bombers. Forty-eight German planes were destroyed that day for a loss to the RAF of twenty.[46]

■

Having recently figured out that the British had detected and compromised its bombing navigation system Knickebein, the Luftwaffe began working with a new kind of bombing radio wave system called X-Gerät, or "X-Apparatus." It worked generally on the same principle as Knickebein, but it used a much higher frequency and accordingly was far more accurate. The "approach beam" sent from Cherbourg, France, was only ten yards wide over England; in fact it was so narrow that a wide Knickebein beam overlapped it so pilots and navigators could find it. The beam was aimed at an English target, such as an aircraft factory, for example. The navigator used the wide Knickebein beam to find the narrow "approach beam" and then looked for three cross beams, each named for a German river. The Rhine beam warned him that he should prepare his equipment and be alert for the next two beams. The Oder beam told him he was thirty kilometers from the target and to start a special clock. The Elbe beam was fifteen kilometers from the target and told him to press a button on the clock that reversed one of the clock's hands and stopped the other. Presuming that the plane flew just as fast in the thirty-kilometer to fifteen-kilometer distance from the target as it would from fifteen kilometers out to the target itself, when the hand of the clock reached zero again, the bombs were automatically dropped. The final beam was adjusted for altitude and wind direction to help the bombs hit the target.

The X-Gerät's accuracy was a tremendous improvement over the Knickebein system. At first the British thought the narrow beams were in the 1,500 hertz (Hz) range, and they broadcast deception beams at this frequency. This countermeasure would have worked if, as with Knickebein, the German navigators relied on their ears to hear the tone of the cross beams. The Germans were really sending the beams at 2,000 Hz, although in a noisy aircraft, this signal difference would not have mattered. In fact the Germans had developed a visual instrument that displayed a pointer in the cockpit to reveal when the plane crossed an X-Gerät beam. The British only figured this development out after examining a crashed He-111 in November.

Meanwhile few German bombers could be equipped with the special X-Gerät. The system was given to "pathfinder" bombers, which, after locating a target with it, then dropped incendiary bombs to mark the spot for bombers coming along behind them.

When the British finally figured out how the system worked, they created an early Elbe beam that caused the German planes to drop their bombs too soon. To counter the countermeasure, the Germans waited to turn on their cross beams until as late as possible in a mission so the British would have less time to detect and mimic it.

■

As September progressed and bombing increasingly smashed blocks of residential neighborhoods in London and other cities, there was evidence of mounting dismay and even panic among the populace. Many people fled to spots where they thought they would be safer, such as homes or crude shelters or tents outside city centers. Later in the month, Home Intelligence reported that morale was bouncing back, either because discouraged people had already left prime target areas or because those who remained had been through enough to suspect that they could outlast the

Blitz. There was also the feeling as the autumn continued that the bombing campaign would not get any worse; furthermore, the Germans were not going to be able to make a landing in the countryside and overrun the nation. In addition people seemed more intent on survival than on revenge. Indeed those calling the loudest for reprisal bombing raids on German cities were from neighborhoods less blasted than others.[47]

Murrow broadcast on September 23:

> My own apartment is in one of the most heavily bombed areas of London, but the newspapers are on the doorstep each morning—so is the bottle of milk . . . and they are still building that house across the street, still putting in big windowpanes. Today I saw shop windows in Oxford Street covered with plywood. In front of one there was a redheaded girl in a blue smock, painting a sign on the board covering the place where the window used to be. The sign read OPEN AS USUAL.[48]

The toll in killed and wounded from the September bombings was seven times higher than that of August. About 7,000 British civilians had been killed, most of them in London, and another 10,600 had been injured.

The Free French as yet had little clout. They did not represent a government, unlike the governments in exile of Belgium, Holland, Norway, and Poland that were holed up in London. The Free French leader, Charles de Gaulle, was virtually unknown even in France, and when he had made his broadcast from London on June 18, he was merely a voice crying in the wilderness. Nor did the Free French have any sort of territorial base. But that situation was meant to change. Operation Menace was under way with a fleet of Allied ships (mostly British), 2,500 Free French fighters with tanks and artillery, and aircraft operating from an aircraft carrier. They were all headed down the eastern Atlantic for Dakar, French West Africa. Seizing the port city of Dakar, the Free French would then have a territorial base and a working government that would take control. In addition, with Dakar in Free French hands, the British and the Free French would achieve many goals. First the Germans would be denied naval bases far into the Atlantic. The British and free French could also obtain Polish and Belgian gold. The Polish and Belgian governments removed significant bullion to

France when their countries fell, and they removed it again to French West Africa when France was overrun. The final prize would be the *Richelieu*, one of the most powerful battleships in the world that for the moment was at anchor in Dakar's harbor. The expedition was meant to sail from Liverpool on August 13, with the faster troopships finishing their departures by August 23. Delays caused these schedules to be missed. This setback, of course, increased the possibility of a security leak, made more opportune by French soldiers dressed in tropical fatigues drinking beer in British pubs who were not subject to British Army discipline. "Dakar" was on the lips of more than one wag at taverns up and down Britain's west coast.

The Operation Menace plan was to leave the British ships just out of sight of the Dakar harbor and use airplanes to scatter over the city leaflets saying the Free French had come to assume authority and prevent undue German interference. French ships would then steam into port and request permission to land, hoping a peaceful transition from the Vichy French to the Free French would follow. If the authorities resisted, the British fleet was to close upon the city and bombard, as discreetly as possible, shore batteries that were putting up fire. One way or another, de Gaulle was meant to be master of Dakar by sunset.

Unfortunately for the British and Free French, there did seem to be a security leak, and the Vichy regime had caught wind of the plan. Three French cruisers and three destroyers spirited out of Toulon, the naval base in southern France; evaded the British at Gibraltar; and steamed into Dakar harbor before the British-French invasion fleet arrived offshore. Hearing this development, Churchill wanted to call off the exploit. He reckoned that the French ships had delivered stern Vichy officials and shore battery gunners to stiffen both the backbone of the Vichy colonial authorities and the harbor artillery. De Gaulle, however, was determined to proceed. He pointed out that the newly arrived French ships were not in a particularly good position for firing their guns toward the sea and that one way or another he could make good the effort of seizing the city. Churchill, who respected élan and was inclined to give leeway to commanders on the scene, relented.

The attempt was made beginning on September 23. In foggy conditions unusual for Dakar in this season, de Gaulle's representatives approached under the French Tricolor and white flag. They were rebuffed, fired upon, or arrested. Accordingly, the British ships approached. The French shore batteries opened fire and damaged some of the British ships, which attacked and damaged a French submarine and destroyer. De Gaulle landed troops at a town some distance from Dakar, whose Vichy commander rejected an ultimatum to cease resistance. More naval engagements ensued the next day, this time with the *Richelieu* taking part, and generally the Free French suffered the worst of it. It seemed as if the Vichy French were determined to make the sternest possible resistance. Churchill and his advisers, in touch with the British commanders on the scene, decided to abandon the attempt. They were not willing to risk a worse debacle as well as a declaration of war from the Vichy regime.

As it turned out, Vichy did not declare war, but the following day it did send a hundred aircraft from Morocco to bomb the British naval base at Gibraltar. Seemingly, the pilots were not keen on the mission, and most of the bombs fell into the ocean. No one was injured.

Much of the fallout from the Dakar assault was unpleasant. To the Western press, the operation looked bungled, and there was much criticism from the United States, which looked uneasily at Dakar's proximity to America. Soon, however, the invasion fleet did not feel itself finished. France had colonies farther south and east in French Equatorial Africa. Though not so strategically located as French West Africa, parts of the equatorial colonies early in the century had been under German rule. There government officials were considerably more anxious about the Germans reseizing their territories and might be more amenable to a Free French presence.[49]

On September 27 Germany, Italy, and Japan signed the Tripartite Pact, in which each pledged to come to the others' aid if any one of them was attacked by a country not involved in the European war. In other words Germany and Italy would react if the United States declared war against Japan. The import of the pact was that it made Japan both an ally of Germany's and more of a menace to the United States. Hitler favored the pact because he believed if Japan was friendlier to Germany and more hostile to the United States, it would preoccupy the United States in the Pacific. Thus the United States might leave Europe alone. The pact was celebrated with great ceremony in Berlin, and the German people were told that the agreement would bring "world peace."[50]

■

On September 29, broadcaster Murrow, after having traveled to the countryside of West Somerset for two days, broadcast as follows: "[My hotel's landlord] said, 'It's too bad some people have to live in terror and fear, being bombed every night, when nothing happens to us. If we could spread it out a bit, all share in it, maybe it wouldn't be so bad.' And then I understood what people mean when they say this country is united."[51]

Murrow followed this observation with the story that on his return trip as his train approached London, the conductor apologetically told the passengers an air raid was in progress and that he was sorry to have to turn out all the lights. Murrow finished the account of his trip by noting that when he told his taxi driver the address of his flat, the driver said, "Right you are, sir. I 'ope it's still there."[52]

Murrow's cabbie was not the only one anxious about enduring the onslaught. Indeed, Churchill's government, the Americans, and the German military hierarchy all wondered: How long could the British people hold out?

CHAPTER NINE

DIPLOMACY

The Craft of Binding Friends and Stabbing Enemies

"In fulfillment of her obligations as an ally, Spain will
intervene in the present war between the Axis powers
and Britain when the military assistance necessary
to her preparation has been granted."
—*Secret protocol of Spain and Germany, September 1940*[1]

As noted, not all of the struggles during the summer and autumn of 1940
occurred where the bullets sped and explosions thundered. There was the
hard scramble to crack the Enigma messages, the exertion to use electromagnetic radiation to best effect, and the effort to shape public opinion.
There was also the dueling of the diplomats and the diplomats' proxies.
Whole territories, even countries, might be won or lost on a promise, a tan-
trum, a word, or a missed meeting. Ambassadors, chargés d'affaires, agents,
and spies could sometimes gain what regiments or divisions could not.

THE WINDSOR INTRIGUE

About the time of Mers-el-Kébir, Churchill began wrestling with the prickly problem of the former king of England, Edward VIII. Since abdicating
the throne to marry Wallis Simpson in 1936, Edward had taken the title
Duke of Windsor, his wife becoming the Duchess of Windsor. Mainly the
two lived in France. In 1937 Hitler invited the couple to Germany. The
Duke and Duchess accepted; enjoyed the hospitality of such highly placed
Nazis as Göring, Himmler, and Goebbels; and met the führer at his Alpine

retreat. Edward and Wallis were believed by some to be favorably disposed to the German regime. When the war broke out, the duke became connected to the British military command staff in Paris. But when the Wehrmacht bore down on the French capital, Edward and his wife fled their apartment for Madrid.

Owing to the duke's perceived admiration for some aspects of the German government, German-leaning people in Britain believed he might be restored as king either for a reconstituted Britain that would negotiate a deal with Hitler or after a peace settlement. This notion did not escape the Germans. After all, they thought, Britain would be negotiating a cease-fire within weeks. The country would need a new government and a new leader. Who better than the former king who had met Hitler and had tea with Göring?

Accordingly, Edward's presence in fascist Madrid was a potential embarrassment to Churchill's government, if not a calamity. Appeasers and defeatists might rally to the former king there, or worse, German agents could whisk him to Berlin. Already there was talk that someone among the duke's entourage was a German agent. Sensitive information about Britain had already made its way from the duke to Germany during the first months of the war.

After two weeks in Madrid, Edward and Wallis moved from Madrid to Lisbon, Portugal. The British were relieved that the former king was in a neutral country rather than a fascist one whose leader owed his seat of power to the Nazis. But the couple settled in at the home of a man noted as being pro-German, where Edward voiced defeatist and harsh words for the Churchill government. The Third Reich's foreign minister, Joachim von Ribbentrop, hoped to lure Edward back to Madrid, and he cabled the German ambassador to Spain as much. Meanwhile Churchill prevailed upon the former king to accept the post of governor of the Bahamas. Wily Churchill knew the pleasures of the Bahamas would appeal to the duke's softer side, and in the Western Hemisphere, Edward would be safer from German agents and intrigue.

Although accepting this arrangement, the duke did not leave Lisbon for a month, dragging his feet over staff and petty arrangements. Some of the delay owed to Edward's request to stop over in New York City during the voyage. Churchill strongly resisted, suspecting Edward would expound defeatist views or otherwise discourage the United States from enthusiastically supporting the country whose throne he once held. In any event the delay allowed intrigue to swirl around the former king. The Germans worked as best as they could to lure the duke and duchess back to Madrid, where German diplomats could more easily prevail upon Edward to take a role in the Nazi New Order in Europe. Cables flew back and forth among Ribbentrop in Berlin, the German ambassador in Madrid, and German agents in Lisbon. One on July 11 from Ribbentrop to Germany's ambassador in Spain read: "At a suitable occasion in Spain the Duke [of Windsor] must be informed that . . . Germany is determined to force England to peace by every means of power and upon this happening would be prepared to accommodate any desire expressed by the Duke, especially with a view to the assumption of the English throne by the Duke and Duchess."[2]

Ribbentrop sent a rising young SS officer, Walter Schellenberg, to Spain with schemes to wrest Edward back to Spain, one being the offer of fifty million Swiss francs in a Spanish bank account provided Edward made remarks against present British policy. According to Schellenberg later, the Germans even had a plot to kidnap Edward near the Spanish border on a shooting holiday and spirit him to Madrid. Schellenberg himself whipped up rumors for Edward's ears that the British Secret Service was planning to assassinate him once he reached the Bahamas.

Churchill's government fought back. The British ambassador to Spain, Samuel Hoare, urged his counterpart in Lisbon, Walford Selby, to encourage the duke to take the Bahamas position. Late in July Churchill sent Walter Monckton, an old friend of Edward's, to Lisbon to keep the former king on track for the Bahamas voyage. Above all Monckton was to convince Edward that the Churchill government was determined to see the war ultimately to victory. Monckton's presence seems to have steadied the duke. Pro-German Portuguese agents attempted to stall the Windsors' departure by raising the specter of an assassination attempt again, but Monckton persuaded the duke to proceed.

Churchill had the duke and duchess's ship skip the normal stop in New York and travel directly to Bermuda, where they boarded another ship for the Bahamas. Moreover he had the British government pay the shipping line the extra expense for the detour.

Just before the duke sailed, Churchill wrote to him:

Many sharp and unfriendly ears will be pricked up to catch any suggestion that your Royal Highness takes a view about the war, or about
the Germans, or about Hitlerism, which is different from that adopted
by the British nation and Parliament. . . . Even while you have been
staying at Lisbon, conversations have been reported by telegraph
through various channels which might have been used to your Royal
Highness' disadvantage.[3]

Seemingly reluctant and equivocal to the last, the Windsors sailed for
the Bahamas on August 1.

SPAIN: THE KEY TO THE MEDITERRANEAN AND THE ATLANTIC

Through the 1930s Hitler strove to build a greater Reich, a conglomera-
tion of German-speaking peoples both inside and outside Germany. He
reclaimed the Rhineland, absorbed Austria, and manipulated the annexation of the Sudetenland from Czechoslovakia. Then he ignited open warfare in Europe, avowing to reabsorb previously controlled German land in
and around Danzig and swallowing Poland in the bargain. From his earliest days in politics, Hitler's vision was for expanding the Reich eastward
as he seized new farmland and resources from Poland and Soviet Russia.
The Reich was meant to be the dominant power on the continent and ultimately control it, since there was no way to achieve his vision for the Reich
without force of arms. The nonaggression pact with the Soviets in August
1939 allowed Hitler to conquer Poland, but then he faced a quandary: drive
into the Soviet Union or turn to grapple with France and Britain, which
had declared war against him. With the Soviets more or less neutralized
and supplying him with important war matériel, including petroleum,
Hitler decided to deal with France and Britain before turning east again.
He had expected to begin a war in the West almost immediately after
crushing Poland—that is, in the fall or winter—but delay upon delay had
put off the offensive until April, when he overran Denmark and Norway,
and in May he sent the Wehrmacht into the Low Countries and France.
Within weeks, and to the astonishment of nearly all the world except the
higher reaches of the German military, France was as swiftly defeated as
Poland had been.

With each week the world's governments assessed the changing map of Europe and their own relations to both the conquerors and the unconquered. Italy generally looked with favor toward Germany's success at arms. Although German conquests increasingly showed Italy to be a much junior partner in the Rome-Berlin Axis, Mussolini's nation could count on territorial spoils flowing from the string of German victories. On June 10, with German conquests assured in France, Italy itself launched its army into the French homeland. With this move Italy felt certain it would be expanding its power in the Mediterranean and possibly northern Africa.

Spain took a similar though more cautious approach. Having only just finished its ruinous civil war, it needed food and rebuilding. Spain's fascist dictator, Franco, was in power with no small thanks to the German Luftwaffe, which had committed considerable resources and caused serious damage to the Spanish Republican cause. Franco, in short, was indebted to Hitler. The Spanish dictator also wanted to expand his power in the Mediterranean and northern Africa. Notably he wanted to regain Gibraltar, a base in southern Spain awarded to the British in 1704 and used to good advantage by Great Britain ever since to grow as a Mediterranean presence. In addition Franco wanted to expand Spanish power in northwest Africa, his base of power before the Civil War. Because the area of northwest Africa not colonized by Spain was under French control, whatever expansion Franco coveted would be at the expense of France.

Britain could do little or nothing about Italy, which after June 10 was in the war, had divided Britain's western and eastern Mediterranean fleets, and had to be fought by force of arms. With respect to Spain, however, Britain would do everything possible to keep it from coming into the war on Hitler's side. If Spain did so, Gibraltar almost certainly would be overrun, and Germany would have more bases along the Atlantic coast from which to challenge British sea power.

Over the summer Spain held talks with Germany about joining the war against England. At first Spain was eager while Germany was reticent, perhaps because Germany thought England was about to be forced out of the war, and it could get what it wanted without Spanish help. In any event Spain expected substantial territorial gains if it did come into the war on the side of the Axis powers. Some of Spain's demands Germany could live with: Gibraltar, all of French Morocco, and an expansion of Spanish Sahara into French West Africa. What gave Germany pause were Spain's additional requests for more territory in Algeria, which was sure to upset the French, and in equatorial Africa. The latter meant cutting into Cameroon, which was a former German colony the Nazis had expected to take for themselves.

Another sticking point was that Germany wanted a naval base in French Morocco and yet another naval base in the Spanish Canary Islands.[4] Franco, however, was jealous of his territories—those in hand and proposed—and did not want Germany controlling any of them. Yet Hitler wanted those bases. According to historian Gerhard Weinberg, Hitler's hope for a naval base in the Spanish Canary Islands indicated that the German dictator's intention to wage eventual war against America, for the base would serve as a launching platform across the Atlantic.

In addition to his other demands, Franco said he needed grain because his country's supplies were short. He also told the Germans he would not lead Spain into the war until the Germans had landed in Britain, an assurance that the war would then come to a quick conclusion.

Principal in the intrigue with Spain was the head of the Abwehr, or the Wehrmacht's foreign intelligence agency, Adm. Wilhelm Canaris, who in July entered Spain disguised as Señor Juan Guillermo of Argentina. Canaris had a bizarre history.[5] Born in 1887, he rebelled against his industrialist father to join the German navy, which the young Canaris believed was the key to Germany's future as a world power. With a keen mind and adept at languages, Canaris took a liking to the Latin countries. During battles with the British navy in World War I, the cruiser on which Canaris served was scuttled in Chile in 1915 and its crew interred, Chile being neutral in the war. The twenty-eight-year-old Canaris disguised himself and escaped, traveling over the Andes to Argentina. With the help of German immigrant families and disguised as a Chilean widower whose father was supposedly Chilean and mother British, Canaris boarded a ship bound for Germany via England and Holland. The German navy, delighted to have him back, sent him to serve as a spy in Spain, a country he quickly came to love. He developed a network of spies in the country and worked out ways of supplying German U-boats from Spanish ports. Late in the war he became a successful and deadly submarine captain in the Mediterranean.

Appalled by the near Communist revolution in Germany in 1919, Canaris became a confirmed rightist. On missions to Spain and Japan, he helped the German navy's secret effort to build submarines for itself in both countries. He welcomed the ascendancy of Hitler as a tonic to chaos. By 1935 he was the head of Abwehr, a position that was roughly equivalent to that of Stewart Menzies, the head of the British Secret Intelligence Service. But Canaris soon sickened of Hitler's aggressions. He was a leader of an effort that planned to topple the führer at the moment Germany invaded the Sudetenland, but Chamberlain's appeasement unintentionally ruined the plot. A tour of Poland after the invasion convinced Canaris that Hitler's methods were abhorrent. Canaris and a few Abwehr subordinates conspired to warn the West in advance of the May 10 attacks, again in hopes a military setback would expose Hitler to discontent in Germany and make him susceptible to a coup; but the warning proved insufficient. Canaris, in short, was loyal to Germany but highly suspect of Hitler. The admiral wanted to see a German place in the sun, but he could not be sure it could win the war and viewed Hitler as a man who might well lead Germany to ruin.

Yet Canaris, being the reigning German intelligence expert on Spain, was the man the top Wehrmacht planners consulted to nudge Spain into an alliance with the Axis. Canaris seemed not averse to wresting Gibraltar from the British so it could be put to use by either the Spaniards or the Germans, and he helped both spy on British defenses there as well as draw up plans for an assault. But Canaris was far from keen on Spain entering the war on the Germans' side for several reasons. For one, he saw a Hitler-Nazi victory as doom for Germany. For another, he believed the Allies rather than the Axis would be the ultimate victors. Finally, he recognized Spain was too poor and exhausted from its civil war to be of much use to the German side anyway. When in Spain "Juan Guillermo" counseled his friends Gen. Juan Vigón, the chief of the Spanish General Staff, and Gen. Carlos Martínez Campos, the chief of Spanish intelligence, to keep Spain out of the war. He repeated these arguments in August to Franco's brother-in-law Ramón Serrano Súñer, about to become Spain's foreign minister. By one account Canaris presented his arguments for keeping Spain out of the war to Franco himself during a face-to-face meeting in August. In this version of

Canaris's intrigues, Hitler's own chief of military intelligence worked the hardest to keep Spain neutral, which was a boon to the British.[6]

Twice in September the head of the German navy, Admiral Raeder, caught Hitler's ear about strategy for the war.[7] Raeder had never been enthusiastic about the chances of success for a seaborne invasion of England. Even with the RAF quelled, the Royal Navy would still have to come down in force east and west to contest a German corridor of transportation across the channel. In Raeder's mind, the way to defeat Britain was in the Mediterranean. He would have Germany seize Gibraltar and then the Suez Canal. From the Canal, Italy could foray into the Indian Ocean, disrupting or challenging Britain's hold on India, which would bring Britain to terms.[8] Meanwhile Germany could move up through Palestine and Syria to Turkey. With Turkey in the German camp, Russia would be neutralized; invading it from Poland, as Hitler was working on, would be unnecessary. Raeder, as did Hitler, also wanted bases in the Canaries and northwest Africa. In the long run they could be used as launching pads against America, but in the short run they could forestall any U.S. or British attempt to land in Africa and take a first step against the Axis by fighting up through southern Europe.[9] Hitler was amenable to Raeder's Mediterranean ideas but told his chief admiral he first had to talk with Franco, Pétain, and Mussolini. He would undertake this task in October.

TARGETING RUSSIA AND LOOKING FOR ADVANTAGE IN THE EAST

In the east Stalin was apprehensive. He had invaded Finland in November 1939 to annex land that would help protect Leningrad and boost his power in the Baltic. What he got instead was the costly Winter War of 1939–40 and a resentful Finland that might then ally with Germany, or even Britain, in order to regain its losses under the Russo-Finnish peace settlement of March 1940. Stalin had hailed (and even helped in the Narvik area) Germany's conquest of Norway the following month for at least wrecking the possibility of Britain attacking Russia through Finland.[10]

On June 9 the Soviets signed an agreement with Japan that defined the borders of Manchuria and worked to soothe Soviet-Japanese tensions in Asia. The Soviets then expected Japan, thus relieved of needing so many troops along the Manchurian-Siberian border, to look south for territorial expansion, confront American interests, and allow the Soviet Union to concentrate on its European borders.

Accordingly, and as noted in chapter 2, in mid-June the Soviets moved into the Baltic states of Lithuania, Latvia, and Estonia. In late June the Soviets also moved to annex from Romania the Bessarabia and northern Bukovina regions. Romania drew special interest on account of its Ploiesti oil fields north of Bucharest, the most productive oil fields in Europe. Germany, Britain, and France all courted Romania for its oil, but Germany could offer arms that it had seized from Poland plus a muscular presence against Soviet aggression toward the oil fields. France and Britain could offer neither arms nor, on account of their own troubles, protections or guarantees of any kind. Stalin, in part to regain territory the Russian Empire lost in World War I, pressed his demands for the northern Romanian territories on June 26 with a two-day ultimatum: give up the regions or face war. Germany pressed Romania to make the concession in part because it had ceded influence in that area to the Soviets in their August 1939 pact and in part because it did not want fighting that might disrupt the flow of oil from Ploiesti. Romania, like Finland, had the option of fighting the Soviets, but without any friends that could offer practical help, it made the concessions. The result mirrored what happened in Finland: the Romanians feared and disliked the Soviets more than they did the Germans.[11]

Britain had hoped to temper Germany in 1939 by forging closer ties with the Soviet Union. Through the spring of 1939 this effort seemed to be working, but Germany's entreaties co-opted the British scheme when it made the mutually beneficial if cynical agreement of August 1939. Despite more than a year of the Soviets' barely concealed hostility, aggression into Poland, and the annexation of the Baltic states as well as parts of northern Romania, Britain still looked to the Soviet Union as a possible ally in the war against Germany. In late June 1940 Churchill chose Stafford Cripps to be ambassador to the Soviet Union. Cripps was raised an aristocrat but was much taken with Marxist ideology, having joined the Labour Party and become one of Britain's leading leftist politicians. Believing, naively as it turned out, that Bolsheviks honored rather than hated leftists, Cripps was meant to ease the Soviets away from hostility toward Britain and develop a friendlier policy.

The Soviets undoubtedly recalled that Churchill advocated sending British troops to Russia in hopes of defeating the Bolsheviks in the post-revolution civil war. In his letter to the Soviets accompanying Cripps as the new ambassador to Moscow, Churchill wrote:

> Geographically our two countries lie at the opposite extremities of Europe, and from the point of view of systems of government it may be said that they stand for widely differing systems of political thought. But I trust that these facts need not prevent the relations between our two countries in the international sphere from being harmonious and mutually beneficial. . . .
>
> Since [August 1939] a new factor has arisen which I venture to think makes it desirable that both our countries should re-establish our previous contact, so that if necessary we may be able to consult together as regards those affairs in Europe which must necessarily interest us both. At the present moment the problem . . . is how the States and peoples of Europe are going to react towards the prospect of Germany establishing hegemony over the continent. [Here Churchill laid out Britain's two current aims—save itself from Nazi domination and free those countries having succumbed to it] . . .
>
> The Soviet Union is alone in a position to judge whether Germany's present bid for the hegemony of Europe threatens the interests of the Soviet Union, and if so how best these interests can be safeguarded. But I have felt that the crisis through which Europe, and indeed the world, is passing is so grave as to warrant my laying before you frankly the position as it presents itself to the British Government . . . [which is ready] to discuss fully with the Soviet Government any of the vast problems created by Germany's present attempt to pursue in Europe a methodical process by successive stages of conquest and absorption.[12]

The Soviets declined to make a reply; rather, they disclosed the contents of Churchill's appeal to the Germans.

Stalin's perspective on European developments was just about as Hitler hoped it would be: more or less satisfied with the present and unfolding situation. Stalin's complacency allowed Hitler to plan at leisure his invasion of the Soviet Union for the Reich's greater glory and economic enhancement. Doing so had always been Hitler's ambition. The attack on the West was just a means of eliminating or neutralizing the Western powers at his back while he struck at Russia. Britain was not acquiescing to his expectation of making peace, but to Hitler's mind he could handle its obstinancy. Crushing the Soviet Union would, Hitler thought, have three beneficial consequences: it would achieve his dream of *lebensraum* (living space) in the east, expunge Bolshevism, and eliminate Britain's hope for a powerful ally in Europe. Thus defeating the Soviet Union would also mean Britain's defeat, because its other ally, the United States, could not arm itself fast enough to be of any assistance and would anyway be distracted by an aggressive Japan in the Pacific. Hitler had thought he might be able to invade the Soviet Union in the autumn of 1940 and conquer it in a few months, believing as he did that the Soviet military and government were practically hollow shells.[13] Britain's stubbornness upset this schedule, but it also made Hitler all the more eager to get on with the Russian invasion. During the Battle of Britain he set the assault for the spring of 1941.

Accordingly, with hopes of protecting Germany's flanks in an attack against Russia, Hitler began overtures to Finland in the north and to Romania in the south. Both Finland and Romania were meant to be in the Soviet sphere of influence as described in the Nonaggression Pact of August 1939, but Hitler paid no mind. He secretly began arms shipments to Finland, which was happy to receive weapons because it was worried about further Soviet aggressions following the Winter War. Germany also expressed interest in the important nickel mines in northern Finland that, at present, were supplying the British and important in steelmaking. Hitler also made agreements with Finland about allowing German troops to travel through the country to northern Norway.

The approach to Romania was similar and had some significant repercussions during the summer and later. Germany saw Romania not only as a protector of its southern flank in an attack on Russia but also as a vital source of oil, the flow of which had to be protected at almost any cost. Romania was in the Soviet sphere of influence, but Germany made welcome overtures. Germany guaranteed Romania's new borders, thus annoying the Soviets, and worked to settle disputes Romania had with both Hungary and Bulgaria.

Finally, in August, Mussolini told Hitler about his plans to invade Yugoslavia and Greece. Hitler was adamantly opposed. Though he could not tell Mussolini, Hitler did not want the Balkans stirred up and possibly drawing in German troops while he was trying to assemble as many soldiers as he could for an attack against Russia. He only told Mussolini that he did not want to see the Balkans agitated into warfare.

NEVER FAR FROM THOUGHT: IRELAND, THE UNITED STATES, AND JAPAN

Now that Germany had access to the Atlantic through the coast of France, Ireland became a more significant player in the European struggle. Germany could stage an invasion of Britain by first landing on the Emerald Isle. Indeed Germany might expect light opposition to Wehrmacht troops in Ireland. The Irish Republican Army, opposed to the governments in London and in Dublin, placed its highest value on the reunification of Eire by repossessing the northeast portion of the island, which was sovereign to Great Britain. Churchill was so worried about a Nazi landing in Ireland that he even made secret offers to the Dublin government to grant postwar reunification if Ireland would be an ally in the struggle against Germany.

Ireland's leader Eamon de Valera refused, sensing the danger to his country if it tilted to either Britain or Germany. His neutrality policy was that Ireland would struggle against whoever landed first, though unofficially he favored a British victory over the Germans on the sensible grounds that if Britain lost the war, Irish independence would likely be lost as well in the Nazi New Order. Churchill, having failed with his reunification gambit, as early as May began asking Roosevelt to send a military presence to Ireland. Roosevelt did not act on this suggestion.

The German attacks against the Low Countries and France in May kindled fresh anxiety in the United States. As the attacks culminated on the continent in June, Roosevelt moved from feeling he would not run for a third term to deciding he would. Thus Germany's own actions tilted both Roosevelt to the decision and the American electorate to greater support for yet another term under Roosevelt's leadership. In addition, owing to the German threat in the Atlantic and the Japanese threat in the Pacific, the United States realized it needed a larger navy. Accordingly, in the middle of July, Congress authorized the largest increase in naval shipbuilding in the nation's history, doubling the size of the fleet with modern craft. This development, in turn, troubled the Japanese, who felt they could not keep up with such prodigious production. To their thinking, if they were to go to war with America, they had better do so before the modern ships were finished.[14] Meanwhile, the destroyers-for-bases exchange and the mutual defense planning with Canada set the United States on a course aligned with the British cause.

Since May Japan could look to smoother expansion to the south. With Holland and France overrun by the Germans, the Dutch East Indies and French Indochina could be wrested without serious trouble. The Dutch possessions were all the more alluring given their petroleum and rubber resources. Given that significant matériel flowed through French Indochina to the Chinese, who were resisting Japanese aggression, seizing the territory would help Japan's war in China. Moreover the weakened and distracted British would less stoutly defend their considerable interests in Southeast Asia, such as Hong Kong, Singapore, and more.

Accordingly Japan welcomed stronger ties with Germany. Early in the summer, Hitler did not want Japan to have a free rein in southern Asia, but with Britain still in the war, he reversed this position and began talks with Japan in August. These discussions bore fruit with the Tripartite Pact signed on September 27 among Germany, Italy, and Japan. As noted in chapter 8, the pact essentially made the three nations allies and carved out spheres of interest—Europe for Germany and Italy, East Asia for Japan—in a "new order of things." If the United States tried to interfere, it would be at war with all three countries.

CHAPTER TEN

OCTOBER

How the Pieces Fell

"Mrs. C came in with the exciting news that a policeman
. . . says that apart from the East End, which is beyond all
comparison, our part of the world has had the worst damage and the heaviest casualties. We feel thrilled. The morale
around the tenement is now quite magnificent. The weak-
lings have left for the safer places, and those remaining . . .
are flatly refusing to leave."
—*Mrs. Rosemary Black, resident of the West End,*
October 1940[1]

In the early cool days of October, Hitler prepared to meet Mussolini at the
Brenner Pass, four thousand feet up in the Alps along the border of Italy
and Austria. Hitler traveled in from the north and Mussolini from the south
to the pass, where the two dictators had met six months earlier, in March,
when Hitler outlined to Mussolini his war plans for defeating France and
Britain. Now on October 4, the summer of turning the world upside down
having passed, Hitler did most of the talking. He could not reveal to Mussolini his plan to invade the Soviet Union, but he did say he was moving
some troops eastward to keep Stalin in check. Hitler spent much of his
time discussing Spanish and French issues. He told Mussolini that Franco
might be persuaded to enter the war for the reward of portions of France's
North African possessions. The great prize for the Axis would be Gibraltar and sealing Britain out of the western Mediterranean. France would

be compensated for its losses to Spain with some colonies of the British Empire—probably parts of British West Africa—when Britain finally came to terms.[2]

Hitler admitted to Mussolini the fear that if Spain declared for Germany, Britain would immediately seize the Canary Islands, Spanish territory off the coast of northwest Africa. In addition the Free French would pressure French West African colonies to abandon the Vichy regime under the theory that the colonies could better resist Spanish encroachments under de Gaulle than under Pétain. Hitler told the Italian dictator that he would also attempt to persuade Vichy France to come into the war against Britain. In any event, with success in the Mediterranean, Italy could look forward to taking Tunis and Corsica from France, as well as the city of Nice, which Napoleon III had annexed eighty years earlier. To Mussolini's foreign minister, Galeazzo Ciano—who was present—Hitler seemed to be looking at knocking Britain out of the war through blows to its power in the Mediterranean and not by invading England itself. Hitler told Mussolini nothing about his intention to send German troops into Romania to keep watch on the Ploiesti oil fields and firm his relation to this vital country, which could serve as a southern flank in his invasion of the Soviet Union.

The October 4 meeting was amicable, but eight days later Mussolini found out about German troops moving into Romania. He was furious. It looked to him as if Hitler had been deceitful only to increase his own influence in the Balkans region, which Italy considered in its own backyard. The upshot was that Mussolini would no longer consult Hitler about Italy's initiatives; he would merely launch them at will.

Shortly after returning to Berlin, Hitler and Ribbentrop invited Soviet foreign commissar Molotov to the German capital. They wanted to discuss ways the German-Soviet alliance might be made even more rewarding.

On the day Hitler met Mussolini in the Brenner Pass, Churchill cabled Roosevelt that Britain was once again sending supplies to Chinese forces resisting Japanese aggression in their country. In July Japan had demanded that Britain stop sending supplies to China along the Burma Road for three months, pending efforts at easing the China-Japan war. Because nothing had come of the negotiations, Churchill reopened the Burma Road for aid deliveries. Doing so was bound to upset Japan, which since late September had become an ally of Germany's. Churchill feared that reopening the Burma Road would provoke Japanese aggression against British colonies in Asia and asked Roosevelt to send a naval force to Singapore as a deterrent. Roosevelt did not follow up on this suggestion, but American sentiment was hardening against the Japanese. By virtue of the Tripartite Pact, Japan was now an ally of Germany and Italy. Japan had hoped the American reaction would be such anxiety over a two-front war that it would shy away from confronting Japanese aggression southward; instead, the United States cast a more jaundiced eye toward Japan's intentions.

Early in the month Göring gave up on the kind of large daylight raids he had staged in August because his bombers were proving too vulnerable to the Hurricanes and Spitfires. The Luftwaffe chief began sending his large bomber force only at night, when British fighters could scarcely find them. He reserved daylight attacks for the faster, newer Ju-88 bombers as well as fighters equipped with one or two bombs while protected by unequipped fighters above. But the daylight attacks no longer seemed as if they would materially affect the outcome of the battle. Göring hoped the night raids, principally on London, would shock and dismay the British into giving up the fight.

To Churchill, doing so was unthinkable. Rather, he was determined to take the war to the Germans, especially the Berliners. He encouraged nightly RAF Bomber Command raids on military and industrial targets around the German capital. So at night bombers flew in both directions and bombs burst in Berlin as well as in London. The British bombardiers' aim was as bad as, or worse than, that of the Germans.

■

Doggedly the pilots of Fighter Command took to the skies day after day. Although they had lost twenty fighters on the last day of September, they lost only one on October 1 and one on October 2. Daylight battles were waning.

But while the pilots could rest and recollect, they could also give counsel to their fears, and what they feared most was burning. With all of the high-octane fuel around them, catching on fire was too often their fate. Many pilots flew without goggles because they diminished their peripheral vision and without gloves because they reduced the sensitivity of their hands on the controls. The result was increased cases of burned hands and faces.

Burned fliers were sent to plastic surgeon Archibald McIndoe, who soon had a burn unit operating at Queen Victoria Hospital in East Grinstead. One day dashing heroes to ladies in any pub or dance hall in Britain, these young pilots were suddenly too horrible to look upon, and their recovery, such as it was, was long and painful. One of the burned pilots, Geoffrey Page, founded a drinking club called the Guinea Pig Club for RAF airmen who underwent at least ten surgeries at East Grinstead.[3] McIndoe worked not only on the young men's faces and hands but also on reintroducing them to society. He relaxed discipline in the wards—he allowed the men to drink—and he encouraged nearby families to take patients in for periods of time. East Grinstead became known as "the town that did not stare."[4]

Ann Standen, one of the burn nurses recalled, "It would be wrong to say we weren't horrified. . . . You didn't recoil in horror but, my God, what could be done? . . . Relatives of the patients would come to the hospital to see the men. Some took it well. Some didn't. It was a shock." She married one of her patients.[5]

■

During the first week of the month, Churchill's ire flared over two newspapers' stories that were critical of the Dakar failure and of certain members of the government. By his lights these stories were detrimental to the army's morale (one story quoted H. G. Wells as saying that without new leadership, the British army could never beat the Germans), fomented discontent among labor, and may have had the intent of moving the country toward a negotiated settlement with the Axis. Churchill fumed and suspected subversion. The War Cabinet talked the prime minister out of prosecuting the newspapers but determined someone should tell the publishers that "malicious articles" could not be countenanced. This job fell to Clement Attlee, the principal Labour Party representative in the cabinet, who talked with the editors.[6] In truth, Churchill overreacted. The papers were critical but loyal, and they placed defeating Hitler as the government's top priority. But they also believed that honest criticism would reinforce British adherence to liberties and bring about a swifter victory.[7]

On October 8 Churchill addressed the House of Commons on many topics. He declared that the damage to British cities would be made good, perhaps re-creating the cities and making them more attractive and livable than before. He remarked on how well he was received by the people in bombed areas whenever he went out among them, and he talked about the importance of supplies from the United States. He criticized the newspaper stories that had upset him days earlier and announced that Britain would resume transporting supplies over the Burma Road to the Chinese resisting Japanese troops, an action clearly to be unwelcome in Japan.

Finally, Churchill pointed out that the world could now better see the "enduring, resilient strength" of the British nation and again warned of a long war. He concluded:

> No one can predict, no one can even imagine, how this terrible war against German and Nazi aggression will run its course or how far it will spread or how long it will last. Long, dark months of trials and tribulations lie before us. Not only great dangers, but many more misfortunes, many shortcomings, many mistakes, many disappointments will surely be our lot. Death and sorrow will be the companions of our journey; hardship our garment; constancy and valour our only shield.[8]

■

Darkness now was the time of horrors. Liverpool and the cities of the Midlands continued to suffer. An average of 150 planes bombed London each night. There was not much the defenders could do. Here really was evidence of the notion "The bombers will always get through." Despite searchlights and antiaircraft guns, the German Dorniers, Heinkels, and Junkers generally ranged back to France unscathed only to return the next night and the next and the next after that. Their high explosives blasted buildings; their incendiaries—two-pound, eighteen-inch flare-like sticks—started fires. In London the warehouses of the Docklands burned with unique hellishness. Pepper made the air painful for firefighters to breathe; rum barrels exploded; sugar liquefied, flowed out onto the waters, and caught fire; rubber burned so noxiously firefighters could only douse it from a distance; and acres of lumber burned, at one location blistering paint on boats three hundred yards across the river.[9] Firemen worked continuously, but many fires still burned when the German bombers returned the following night. The firefighters understood these fires served as beacons and targets for the arriving bombers. Eighty percent of the firefighters during this time were from the Auxiliary Fire Service and had little or no experience fighting fires. They learned on the job.[10] Volunteer men worked every fourth night, women every sixth night. They died when the flames engulfed them, and they died on the streets when building walls collapsed upon them.

Londoners naturally gravitated to the Underground or Tube stations. At first the government would not allow them to be used as air raid shelters. Gas, electric, sewer, and water lines ran near them; toilet facilities were minimal; and ones near the Thames could become flooded, with horrific result. But many people went to them anyway, and the authorities could not hold them back. A common sight was people with blankets, thermoses of tea, handfuls of supplies, games for the children, and often babies, lining up to enter a subway station for the night. In places some families had their own square footage night after night. Buskers sang to them, and famous actors such as Laurence Olivier and Vivien Leigh, after an evening's work in theaters, sometimes descended to entertain them. Generally the subway trains operated through the day and stopped at midnight. Riders stepped over and around Londoners lying on the concrete platforms. But life in the stations could be miserable. Sanitation was a problem, and many shelters became infested with fleas and lice.

On the night of October 14 a bomb struck near the Balham Underground Station, one of several in London fairly near street level. The explosion severed gas, water, and sewer lines running above the station. The lights went out, and water rushed in on 600 people. Panic followed in the blackness and rising water. Rescuers managed to lead 300 out of the gloom, but 250 drowned.[11] That same night Churchill was dining at 10 Downing Street with guests when the air raid began. Recalling a large plate glass window in the kitchen section, the prime minister rose, ordered the kitchen staff to a shelter, and returned to dinner. A bomb soon struck close by, shattering the kitchen window as well as the kitchen. The bomb killed a man in a nearby building, but the kitchen staff was safe. Dinner finished, Churchill and his guests clambered to the top of the Annex to watch the remainder of the raid. The prime minister reported seeing at least five fires, including a massive one on Pall Mall and others at St. James's Street and Piccadilly.[12]

On the following night, October 15, four hundred Luftwaffe bombers dropped six hundred tons of high-explosive bombs and seventy thousand incendiaries on London. As one of the most damaging raids London suffered, whole blocks were blasted flat, and thirteen hundred civilians were killed or injured. The incendiaries began a new call to action. Rather than "To the basements," the cry for some was now "To the roofs!" There men and women would watch for the incendiaries and would either extinguish them where they fell by tossing sand on the searing chemicals or report the fires' locations. "The experience of remaining on a roof night after night under fire, with no protection but a tin hat, soon became habitual," wrote Churchill.[13] People below used government-issued hand pumps in buckets of water supplied with slender hoses. Women were a principal part of the effort; they helped squelch thousands of fires.

Not surprisingly, sleep became a luxury. Many city dwellers kept their day jobs but also served as volunteer workers afterward. Even for those not working at night, the bombing raids deprived millions of rest. A survey of Londoners during this month listed 31 percent not sleeping at all the previous night, 32 percent sleeping less than four hours, and only 15 percent enjoying six hours' sleep.[14] When graced with a half hour's unscheduled time, they often catnapped. Londoners dozed on trains and buses and at their desks during short breaks at work.

The East End continued to receive the most punishment owing to the docks, oil storage, and warehouses. It was here that antiwar sentiment had a footing before the war broke out and indeed even extended into the period of the Phony War, and signs might have read, "This Is the Bosses' War." Now such signs were gone, replaced with the likes of "Our ARP Workers Are Wonderful" and "Our Thanks to the AFS" in praise of the Air Raid Precautions and Auxiliary Fire Service volunteers. As quickly as buildings were bombed, Union Jacks sprouted among the rubble. New signs went up in place of the old. Scrawled on many walls was "London Can Take It."[15]

Mrs. Rosemary Black, a widower with a small child living in the West End, recorded her thoughts one day:

> The sight of the national flag flying over the ruins was for me the most moving thing of the whole war. I never felt so humbly and proudly thankful to be English as just then. How fine it is that after watch-

ing one's country gradually degenerating slowly but surely into the ranks of the second rate, to see it glorious again and to feel whole-hearted pride and joy in it. I was very nearly undone by the sight of a nine-inch square of faded tattered paper, obviously the smallest and cheapest flag available, fluttering from the gaping, twisted window of a burned-out tenement. For an awful moment I thought I was going to burst out crying in the middle of the public highway—what was left of it, that is.[16]

Shared danger brought people together. Where they could, people helped their less fortunate neighbors. There was less British reserve and more talk and friendliness. Everyone had a bomb story; people listened and sympathized. Disaster was not viewed as uncommon. One woman who emerged from a shelter in the morning to find her home destroyed went to work as usual. She considered it part of her war duty.[17]

Of London's 8.5 million people, only about 4 percent descended to the subway tunnels, 9 percent used public shelters, and 27 percent used the Anderson shelters or ones provided by an apartment block. The remaining 60 percent of Londoners stayed in their homes, descending to their base-ments or crouching under the stairs.[18] Children, meanwhile, were evacu-ated to live in the countryside. By the middle of October almost half a mil-lion children had been moved out of the city.[19]

Digging through wrecked homes for trapped people became major work. Some diggers came to be known as body sniffers, for they could smell people below—dead or alive—and direct others where to dig. If they were digging with little hope of finding someone alive, they would take shelter when a new air raid sounded, but most often if they thought they were digging for a child, they kept to their work no matter the danger from a new wave of bombs.[20]

One day Churchill heard a very large explosion south of the Thames during daylight and asked that he and Chancellor of the Exchequer Kings-ley Wood, who had been meeting with him at 10 Downing Street, be driven to the site. When they arrived they saw little Union Jack flags already stuck defiantly in the rubble. Area residents recognized the car and came out to see the prime minister. Soon a large crowd had gathered. Churchill gazed upon a crater forty yards across and twenty yards deep, the former location of two dozen small homes. He reported in his memoir *Their Finest Hour* that the people were "in a high state of enthusiasm . . . cheering and manifesting every sign of lively affection, wanting to touch and stroke my clothes. . . . I was completely undermined, and wept. . . . They were tears not of sorrow but of wonder and admiration."[21]

Unexploded delayed-action bombs continued to be a problem. Where they lay, signs went up forbidding their approach. In their vicinities they disrupted transportation, office work, or what passed for ordinary life. The Unexploded Bomb (UXB) Disposal Squads, composed of volunteers, were dispatched to the bombs and tasked with digging them out and defusing them. This work was dangerous indeed, and life expectancy was short. Churchill, who saw many of the UXB technicians when he went about the country viewing bomb damage, said their faces looked different from those of others, more gaunt and haggard. "Grim" was a word, he said, that should be reserved for them. One of the squads was made up of the Earl of Suffolk, his female private secretary, and his elderly chauffeur. They successfully defused thirty-four bombs. All three were killed working on the thirty-fifth.[22]

All the British city dwellers' grit and the RAF fighters' endurance paid a large mid-month dividend: on October 12 Hitler admitted failure. He called off Operation Sea Lion for the autumn, possibly to be reconsidered again in the spring or summer of 1941. Instead he ordered that, where practical, Wehrmacht units move east for a decisive offensive against the Soviets proposed for May 1941. Preparations for Sea Lion would continue only to the extent to fool Britain into thinking an invasion was still in the cards. But the führer called for the bombing of England to continue. Although the Wehrmacht was relieved of puzzling over invading Sussex in order to concentrate on plotting against the Soviets, Hitler thought the Luftwaffe bombers might yet crack the British government or its people.

On this same day Mussolini gave vent to sentiment that would end up costing the Axis dearly later. Il Duce declaimed to Foreign Minister Ciano, "Hitler always faces me with a fait accompli. This time I am going to pay him back in his own coin. He will find out from the papers that I have occupied Greece. In this way the equilibrium will be re-established."[23]

Through the middle of the month, night after night the bombing of London and other British cities continued apace. Mainly people were defiant, tilting even to the cheerful and humorous. "Open for business . . ." read a sign on one bombed store, "even more open than usual." By and large, people tried to get to and perform their jobs; indeed many felt that failing to do so was a kind of victory for the Luftwaffe. The subways ran and buses plied the thoroughfares, though rubble frequently stopped them. When buses did not arrive, workers walked miles to their offices or factories. Taverns, shops, and restaurants attempted to keep regular hours as well.

Theaters, long emblematic of London living, also tried to remain open. If German bombers were heading for the capital, theater managers might— without interrupting the production—hold up a sign saying "Air Raid in Progress" so patrons could consider leaving for shelters, but most did not.[24] Only one theater in London claims never to have closed throughout the Blitz: the Windmill. Located off a street near Piccadilly, it was meant to be a rouser for the young men in uniform because women would pose nude, though motionless, in different kinds of artistic tableaux. The young women, plaster dust wafting down on them during some raids, came to be regarded as symbols of defiance.[25] Pictures of them clothed in little more than tin helmets and scanty military gear turned up on barracks' walls. Turnover was rapid. Windmill women went on to serve as WAAFs, in the Women's Royal Navy Service, or in the Women's Territorial Service, a branch of the army.

The government, which had forecasted casualties far in excess of actual numbers, had also thought there might well be three psychological victims for every physical one. But it wasn't happening. People blasted out of their homes and people living in crowded shelters held up well. Suicide rates were lower than during peacetime.[26] And there were, of course, occasional deeds of breathtaking bravery. In late September King George established the George Cross, an award for extraordinary valor demonstrated by civilians. Women and teenagers were so decorated, and a high number of recipients were from the UXB squads.[27]

There was no disguising, however, the astonishing damage to London and the dire suffering in the neighborhoods. By the end of October, 300,000 Londoners were homeless. Many others lived in homes with windows blown out, walls bashed, or roofs collapsed, all becoming colder with the advancing season. That month 6,334 British were killed in the air raids,

643 of them children.[28] And for each one killed, about thirty-five people lost their homes.[29]

■

Piqued at having been kept out of the loop on several occasions and being averse to Roosevelt's tilt toward strongly backing the British cause, U.S. ambassador Joseph Kennedy flew to New York via Portugal, landing in Lisbon on the twenty-seventh. Roosevelt, who might well have wished to keep Kennedy in London where he would not be a foil to Roosevelt's leadership,[30] sent Kennedy a telegram in Lisbon to come to the White House for dinner and an overnight stay as soon as he could after landing in New York. It was late in the presidential campaign, and Roosevelt feared Kennedy might publicly stump for Willkie. The Republican contender was gaining on Roosevelt, and it was known that one reason owed to Catholics switching from the Democrats. If the Irish-Catholic Kennedy came out for Willkie, Roosevelt might lose the White House.[31]

At dinner the night Kennedy arrived for the overnight stay, Roosevelt poured on the charm for which he was famous. He said he was sorry about Kennedy being kept out of certain negotiations and State Department affairs and professed not to know about some of them. Then Roosevelt strongly hinted that he would support Kennedy for president in 1944 if Kennedy stood by Roosevelt now. Two days later Kennedy addressed the nation by radio, admitting that he had had differences with the president over policy but strongly endorsed him as a president to keep in a time of crisis.[32] He resigned his ambassadorship shortly thereafter and did not return to Great Britain.

■

On October 20 Churchill wrote to Neville Chamberlain, who had resigned from the cabinet earlier in the month because of his ill health from cancer. Churchill wanted to extend the courtesy of sending Chamberlain occasional intelligence reports so he could stay abreast of the war's developments. In his opinion, Churchill told the former prime minister, the Germans had made a major mistake in bombing London in general rather than concentrating on factories "and in trying to intimidate a people whom they have only infuriated. I feel very hopeful about the future, and that we shall wear them down and break them up. But it will take a long time."[33]

■

Churchill's attitude toward Vichy France was hopeful if realistic. He encouraged the United States and Canada to maintain important ambassadors with the Pétain government. He felt victory over Nazism should arise from the French people as well as the countries actively at war with Germany. Churchill supported de Gaulle's Free French in their efforts to destabilize the German occupation and the Vichy government. But de Gaulle resented any of Churchill's back-channel contacts with the Vichy government, feeling emphasis should be on the Free French alone. Moreover de Gaulle felt in order to maintain his prestige among the French people, he had to maintain a certain haughtiness toward the British. Churchill found this attitude vexing but understandable.[34]

Despite what would foster de Gaulle's resentment, on October 19 Churchill cabled his ambassador in Spain, Samuel Hoare, about communicating with Vichy France through its ambassadors in Madrid. Churchill asked Hoare to soothe Vichy sentiments by saying that Britain would set aside bygones and work with anyone willing to fight the Nazis. "Convey," wrote Churchill, "that we will stop at nothing. Try to make Vichy feel what we here all take for certain, namely, that we have got Hitler beat . . . and that his doom is certain."[35]

On the twenty-first Churchill addressed the French people by radio. He spoke in French, and if the reception was good on French receivers, his French listeners could hear bombs exploding over the Annex, from which Churchill was speaking. The prime minister meant to rally the French people against both the Nazi occupation and the Vichy regime. He was not above the kind of propaganda that had been filling European airways since before the war began:

Not only the French Empire will be devoured [by Germany and Italy] but Alsace-Lorraine will go once again under the German yoke, and Nice, Savoy and Corsica—Napoleon's Corsica—will be torn from the fair realm of France. But Herr Hitler is not thinking only of stealing other people's territories. . . . I tell you truly what you must believe when I say this evil man, this monstrous abortion of hatred and defeat, is resolved on nothing less than the complete wiping out of the French nation, and the disintegration of its whole life and future.[36]

The speech lasted about ten minutes and was quite a rouser.

Frenchmen—rearm your spirits before it is too late! . . . Never will I believe that the soul of France is dead! . . . Remember . . . that our whole people and Empire have vowed themselves to the task of cleansing Europe from the Nazi pestilence and saving the world from the new Dark Ages.

Churchill intended to do more than rally Frenchmen's hearts. The British Admiralty in particular was afraid the Vichy government would declare war on Britain.[37] This act would have committed the sizable number of French ships then within Vichy harbors at Toulon and in Vichy-controlled colonies to enter the naval war against the British. Churchill was attempting to sway the French so that the Vichy regime would not make such a move.

The prime minister, however, did not rely on the speech alone. The day before, he had cabled Roosevelt about Britain's anxiety over the Vichy regime's intentions and asked the president to communicate in the strongest language possible the U.S. government's antipathy toward the Vichy regime allowing the French fleet to be used against the British. Roosevelt did so, writing: "If the French Government now permits the Germans to use the French fleet in hostile operations against the British fleet, such action would constitute a flagrant and deliberate breach of faith with the United States Government." Roosevelt went on to tell Vichy France that if it handed over what was left of the fleet, it would "permanently remove any chance that this Government would be disposed to give any assistance to the French people in their distress . . . [and] make no effort when the appropriate time came to exercise its influence to ensure to France the retention of her overseas possessions."[38]

On this same day, the twenty-first, Liverpool suffered its two hundredth air raid. The port city was being bombed almost every night. Other cities were suffering, too: Sheffield, Hull on the Humber River, Nottingham, Manchester, Birmingham, and the coastal cities in the south all continued to be targeted for bombs and fires. Catastrophes and tragedies were no less painful there than in London.

On the twenty-sixth the Luftwaffe inflicted one of its longest air raids upon London, lasting until three o'clock in the morning. German aircraft also struck Birmingham and Coventry in the Midlands and Bristol and South Wales in the southwest. In October more than 6,000 British civilians lost their lives to the Luftwaffe bombers, and another 8,700 were seriously wounded.

The British suffered losses at sea as well. October saw the greatest number of ships sunk in the war up to that time, representing more than 400,000 tons, or four times the tonnage of new ships being built.[39] Not only were German U-boats at work around the western approaches to the British isles, but heavily armed raiders masquerading as merchant ships also were at work in the Atlantic. One raider, with the help of Russian icebreakers, had steamed through the Arctic Ocean north of the Soviet Union and out into the Pacific.

Near the end of the month the pocket battleship *Admiral von Scheer* eluded British ships to enter the Atlantic via passage between Greenland and Iceland. Owing to keeping capital ships close to Britain for repelling an invasion or sending them to the Mediterranean to defend against the Italian navy, few warships escorted convoys from Canada and the United States. Thus the *Scheer* posed a dreadful threat. The German battleship made good its menace within the first few days of November when it descended around dusk on the thirty-seven ships of convoy HX 84 several days out of Halifax, Nova Scotia. The principal warship escorting the convoy was the *Jervis Bay*, an ocean liner built in 1922 and fitted with World War I guns in 1939. The *Jervis Bay* was no match for the powerful *Scheer*, but its captain, Edward Fegen, decided the best course was to head straight for the German battleship while the merchantmen of the convoy dispersed into the growing darkness. The sea fight lasted an hour until the *Jervis Bay*, with its captain and two hundred of its sailors dead, was battered beyond its capacity to resist. The *Scheer* made no attempt to pick up the *Jervis Bay*'s sixty-five survivors. It pursued ships of the scattering convoy and sank five of them; however, the sacrifice of Fegen and his ship saved many others. Much at a risk to itself, a Swedish freighter *Stureholm* in the convoy returned and rescued the *Jervis Bay* sailors.[40] The *Scheer* sailed to the West Indies, South Atlantic, and Indian Ocean, destroying Allied ships.

Such destruction of shipping was taking its toll. In a week in June Britain imported 1.2 million tons of supplies, but during the last week in July the import figure was down to 750,000 tons. August showed improvement, but average weekly totals for October were 800,000 tons.[41]

U-boats were an even greater threat than ships like the *Scheer*. In the middle of the month, German submarines struck at two convoys with special deadliness. Working only for the second time in a coordinated group they called a wolf pack, five U-boats found the thirty-five ships of convoy SC 7 out of Nova Scotia bound for Britain's northwestern ports. Lumber, grain, steel, iron ore, petroleum, and trucks were the major cargoes, and the British escorts were lightly armed sloops and corvettes. The wolf pack first discovered the convoy on the sixteenth and began three days of destruction as the convoy slowly wended its way into the northwestern approaches to Britain. The worst came on the night of October 18–19 when the U-boats were coordinated by Rear Admiral Dönitz himself and his staff in Lorient, France. Much of the work was from U-boats not outside the convoy but, cloaked in darkness, on the surface and mingled among the Allied ships. Counterattacks by the British sloops and corvettes were generally uncoordinated and ineffective. They never learned that for the most part the submarines were on the surface that night. Sixteen merchantmen were lost in as many hours. In all, twenty ships of the thirty-five in the convoy and their eighty thousand tons of shipping were sunk.

Into this area of destruction as the sun rose on October 19 steamed convoy HX 79, forty-nine ships strong out of Nova Scotia. Its escort had been two armed merchant cruisers, but they had since departed for other duty. The U-boats that had devastated SC 7 now saw this rich new assemblage, and from Lorient, Dönitz again coordinated the four U-boats that still had torpedoes. Fearing an attack on HX 79 similar to what had befallen SC 7, the Admiralty rushed destroyers to the scene. They arrived before nightfall. But as darkness fell at least two of the submarines worked their way between the escort vessels and cargo ships and began torpedoing with abandon. Twelve ships were rent with explosions and sank. In all, the Allies lost sixty-three ships in October, thirty-two of them from these two convoys alone.[42]

■

With a land invasion of Britain becoming increasingly remote, at least until spring, Hitler looked to invade Russia and win the war he had ignited. He believed that if he could overrun Russia to a line from Archangel in the north to Astrakhan on the Caspian Sea thirteen hundred miles south, he would capture immense resources for Germany and end Britain's hope of an alliance with the Soviets against Nazism. Of course it all had to be done before the United States could enter the fighting and its forces made effective. He put his top military men to work on the plan.

But Hitler's navy chief still saw a way for defeating Britain: knock it out of the Mediterranean. As noted by this scheme, the Axis would not only press the British forces out of Egypt but also capture Britain's western Mediterranean base at Gibraltar.

A major problem with the Mediterranean idea was that Germany lacked the force to execute it alone. It would need the cooperation and likely the contribution of Spain, Vichy France, Italy, or a combination. Spain could ease the means of capturing Gibraltar, Vichy France could help hold west and north Africa while fighting to reseize the Gaullist parts of equatorial Africa, and Italy was needed both for its navy and the thrust to the Suez Canal. The trouble was that each of these countries had territorial goals that they meant to win at the others' expense. Spain wanted colonies from Vichy France. The Vichy regime, if it came into the war, would want to preserve its territories against Spain or take new ones from that country. Italy expected territorial expansion at the expense of Vichy France. All of their needs could not be met.[43]

Spain was vital to British interests. First, at any time Franco's army could have erected long-range guns on the landside of Gibraltar and bombarded the Rock. British military units might have been able to hold out in caves, but they could not have maintained the harbor for their warships. Accordingly the British kept a force of five thousand men and ships, enough to transport them for the purpose of seizing the Spanish Canary Islands if Gibraltar was denied them. The Canaries could act as a base, as Gibraltar was, to combat German U-boats in the Atlantic and as a way station for transports and warships from Britain around the Cape of Good Hope to India, Australia, and Asia. Another threat was that Franco would allow German troops passage through his country to occupy both French and Spanish Morocco as well as French West Africa. By virtue of their conquest of France, the Germans were already on the northern slopes of the Pyrenees. On the one hand, the British, of course, worried that Franco felt obliged to Germany and Italy for helping him defeat the Republicans in the Civil War. On the other hand, the British could count on Franco's exhaustion with war and his inclination toward domestic repair rather than outward expansionist glory to keep him from making damaging deals with Hitler.

On October 20 Hitler set out in his special armored train called *Amerika* to meet with both the Vichy government and Franco. On the twenty-second, he met Vichy prime minister Pierre Laval at Montoire near the city of Orléans in the German-occupied zone of the country. Laval was a Nazi sympathizer and began discussions with Hitler about closer relations between Germany and the Vichy government. Two of Laval's objectives were an easing of the reparations France was paying to Germany on account of the German invasion and eventually a better deal concerning African colonies than it might otherwise expect once the war was settled. Hitler responded that these matters depended much on the Vichy regime's cooperation in the months ahead as well as the time it took to defeat Britain. Hitler suggested a meeting with Pétain a few days hence, and Laval promised to arrange it.

About this same time the Vichy government began instituting anti-Semitic laws.[44] Jews who were not French were in the most danger. Many French families began to hide or harbor Jews.

The Laval meeting concluded, Hitler's train continued south to the Atlantic town of Hendaye on the French-Spanish border, where he met Franco on the twenty-third. Hitler's objective was to cajole Franco into the war against Britain. He was impatient to end the struggle with Britain quickly, and Spain could reinforce the European array against the island nation, which, Hitler boasted, was just about beaten anyway. Hitler suggested Spain enter the war on January 10 and launch a coordinated attack on Gibraltar twenty days later.

Once seemingly eager to enter the Axis compact and wage war on England when its defeat seemed weeks away, Franco had since become recalcitrant. At Hitler's entreaties, the Spanish dictator professed all of the difficulties he and his foreign minister Serrano Súñer had raised over the summer, as well as trotting out their outsized demands for joining the fighting. A main point for Hitler was for either the Germans or the Spanish to overrun or neutralize Gibraltar. But he had little to offer el caudillo (the leader). He could not promise too much by way of new colonies because these would be wrenched from France, which Hitler was also courting. Hitler and Franco, who had never met, parleyed for nine hours in the salon of Hitler's armored train. They did not like each other, and after the meeting both uttered unflattering comments to aides. Ribbentrop stormed: "That ungrateful coward! He owes us everything and now won't join us!"[45] Hitler said he would rather have several teeth pulled rather than negotiate with Franco again.

The next day, October 24, Hitler returned aboard *Amerika* to Montoire, where Laval was as good as his word and produced the aging Marshal Pétain. As with Franco, Hitler cajoled for his active participation in the war against Britain. But just as with his session with Franco, "care" was the watchword. He could not promise much or risk angering Italy and Spain. Pétain, who had only recently heard the strong message from Roosevelt, equivocated. He said he would have to consult his country and convene the National Assembly before he could effect a declaration of war on Britain. Moreover he wanted some guarantees about retaining French colonies once the peace negotiations began. Pétain did, however, confirm the Vichy regime's collaboration with Hitler's Reich. He said that the Vichy military would resist all attempts by Britain or other countries to invade any portion of France or its colonies. By the end of the talks, the Germans and the French had drawn up a paper: "The Axis Powers and France have an identical interest in seeing the defeat of England accomplished as soon as possible. Consequently, the French Government will support, within the limits of its ability, the measures which the Axis Powers may take to this end."[46] Both parties agreed to keep this agreement secret. Roosevelt and Churchill, who knew about the meeting, could only assume the worst.

This same day the United States and Britain finalized their own secret agreement by which the United States would fully equip ten British divisions with American-made weapons so the divisions would be ready for combat by 1942. In addition the United States was filling other war orders for Britain for large amounts of ammunition, explosives, and aircraft engines.[47]

Meanwhile de Gaulle was at work for his exile movement. On October 27 from equatorial Africa, he broadcast the formation of the Free French Empire Defense Council and invited all French colonies still loyal to the Vichy regime to switch to the Free French cause. He called on French men and women wherever they might be "to attack the enemy wherever it shall be possible, to mobilize all our military, economic, and moral resources . . . to make justice reign."[48]

As Hitler's *Amerika* approached the French-German border after his meeting with Pétain, Hitler got wind of Mussolini's intention to attack Greece from Italy's enclave in Albania. In August Hitler had warned Mussolini against such a move as stirring up the Balkans. Now more than ever, Hitler did not want trouble in this region that would disrupt his moving the Wehrmacht east and his other preparations for the invasion of Russia. Moreover Britain had guaranteed the Greek borders; with Greece in the war, Britain could once again move onto the continent by putting its navy in Greek ports, its airplanes on Greek airfields, and its infantry along the rugged mountain passes. Hitler's movement of troops into Romania without consulting Mussolini was now coming due as Il Duce sprang his own surprises on the führer. Once inside Germany Ribbentrop telephoned Ciano in Rome and asked for a meeting between the Axis dictators. They settled on October 28 in Florence.

Mussolini had made his decision to invade Greece by October 15. During a meeting with his military leaders at the Palazzo Venezia that day, he had outlined his plan: move down the Ionian Sea coast, occupy Thessaloniki (Salonika) on the Aegean, compromise British power in the Mediterranean, and occupy the whole country.[49] Envious of Hitler's rapid conquests in western Europe, Il Duce wanted to make his own in southern Europe. Mussolini drew up an ultimatum to be presented to the Greek prime minister at 3:00 a.m. on the twenty-eighth. It declared that Greece had taken a nonneutral stance toward Italy and that Italy, in order to guarantee Greece's neutrality during the present war against the British, would station Italian troops to occupy strategic parts of the country. "Wherever Italian troops meet with resistance, it will be crushed by force of arms, and the Greek government will be held responsible for the consequences," the document read.[50]

Indeed this astonishing paper was presented at three o'clock in the morning. The Greeks' reply to the Italian representative was that Greece would resist an invasion with all the resources it could command. Partly its defiance owed to its agreement with Britain, made when Italy invaded Albania in April 1939, that Britain would come to Greece's aid if Italy should attack it.

Churchill's foreign secretary, Anthony Eden, at the time of the Italian invasion was in Khartoum, Sudan, learning about conditions in the Middle East. Churchill cabled him to return to Cairo as quickly as possible and attempt a strong British presence in Crete, the large Greek island south of the mainland partway to Britain's stronghold in Alexandria, Egypt. Two days later the British navy was settled into Suda Bay, the best naval harbor in Crete.

Britain was keen to send aid to Greece, not only to stop Italian aggression and further encroachment into the Mediterranean toward Alexandria but also to demonstrate to Turkey that Britain was standing up to the Axis. British forces were stretched thin, however, in holding a line west of Alexandria against the larger Italian army there. What it could supply to the Greek forces near the Albanian border was meager indeed. Yet Britain would try and began with bombers and fighter aircraft to counter Italian superiority in the air. In any event the Greeks were proving tough to dislodge from their strongholds along the rugged Greek-Albanian border.

The day of Italy's invasion, Hitler met Mussolini in Florence late in the morning. True to his word after his pique following Hitler's Romanian surprise earlier in the month, Mussolini greeted the German dictator at the train exclaiming, "Führer, we are on the march! Victorious Italian troops crossed the Greco-Albanian border at dawn today!" Hitler concealed his fury. The invasion is exactly what he had sped south to prevent.[51] To Hitler's way of thinking, the weather might deteriorate, the Greeks might be stubborn, the Balkans might denigrate into mischief and war at a time when stability was at a premium, and British bombers operating from Greek airfields would be close enough to bomb the Ploiesti oil fields. But now the Italian die was cast.

Containing himself against this disappointment, Hitler briefed Mussolini on all the discussions he had had with Franco, Laval, and Pétain. He also told Il Duce that Russia's foreign commissar Molotov was traveling to

Berlin for talks within a couple of weeks. At these talks they would see if Germany and the Soviets could make some headway on Ribbentrop's idea that the Soviets should join the Tripartite Pact, thus becoming a fourth Axis power. The general notion was to give each of the four powers a sphere of influence, with Russia's including India. The outcome of the talks would determine if Hitler would hold to his desire of conquering Russia, though he told Mussolini nothing of this possibility. In any event Hitler wanted to keep his options open. Meanwhile he had asked his military leaders to draw up plans for seizing Gibraltar whether Spain was an official ally or not (Operation Felix), overrunning unoccupied France (Operation Attila), and conquering Greece (Operation Marita).

With the Florence talks concluded, Hitler took *Amerika* north again through the Alps. He had been rebuffed three times in less than twice as many days by Franco, Pétain, and now Mussolini. The possibility of knocking out Britain with a continental coalition of Germany, Spain, Vichy France, and Italy that concentrated on the Mediterranean was losing its bloom. The full flush of June had indeed begun to whither. Hitler felt the best option left was a lightning campaign to crush Russia.

CHAPTER ELEVEN

POSTLUDE

"In War: Resolution. In Defeat: Defiance. In Victory:
Magnanimity. In Peace: Good Will"
—*Winston Churchill in 1948 writing the "moral"*
of his six-volume memoir on World War II[1]

With the passage of October into November, one thing was certain: there would be no land invasion of Britain for a time, at least until spring. The days grew shorter, the nights longer, the weather more tempestuous, and the channel rougher. The great threat raised with the fall of France was temporarily dispelled. Britain might yet be strangled by Germany sinking its supply ships, destroying its factories, and waging terror from the air, but these campaigns, if successful, would swell by increments. To this point in the war and for the time being, Churchill's proclamation of June 18, "Hitler must break us in this island or lose the war," was holding true. Bletchley Park had deciphered Enigma messages that confirmed the postponement of Sea Lion. Although messages indicated the Germans continued to make preparations through October, early in November a German order to units near the French coast to return to storage any equipment for loading barges indicated the Germans would not soon be coming by sea.[2] The British could heave a sigh for one passed danger at least.

On November 3, for the first time since September 6, no German bombers appeared over London. Some were headed east, out of France and Belgium, to prepare for the coming great struggle with Soviet Russia.

Hundreds, however, remained. The worst of the Blitz was yet to come. The Germans always held out the possibility that the Luftwaffe could pound British factories and cities until either Churchill called for talks or the people rose up to remove Churchill's government from office. The Luftwaffe, of course, by now was used to flying at night, and it had no other huge duties until the invasion of Russia. So the bombings continued, and the decisions made in the late summer and early fall of 1940 played themselves out in the late fall and early winter. Night bombings of London had become a habit, and the Luftwaffe meted out yet more damage to Midland cities and ports. Meanwhile U-boats attempted to build on their huge destructions of late October. These were good times for German submarine men.

Hitler was justified in being furious at Mussolini's vainglorious, ill-conceived, and unilateral attempt to overrun Greece. Within days disciplined and tough Greek soldiers, defending their homes and families, stopped the Italian legions in the rugged northern mountains of Greece. They began to push the Italians rearward to the Albanian border. As Hitler had feared, British planes flew to Greek airfields. As yet they were meant to help repel the Italians, but the way had been opened for the British bombers, which would be within striking distance of the Ploiesti oil fields in Romania.

On November 5 Franklin Roosevelt was reelected president of the United States. Churchill was greatly relieved. On the sixth he sent a congratulatory telegram to the president that read in part:

> I did not think it right for me as a foreigner to express any opinion upon American politics while the election was on, but now I feel you will not mind my saying that I prayed for your success. . . . We are entering upon a somber phase of what must evidently be a protracted and broadening war, and I look forward to being able to interchange my thoughts with you in all that confidence and good will which has grown up between us. . . . Things are afoot which will be remembered as long as the English language is spoken in any quarter of the globe, and in expressing the comfort I feel that the people of the United States have once again cast these great burdens upon you I must avow my sure faith that the lights by which we steer will bring us all safely to anchor.

Without saying so directly, Churchill was immensely grateful that he did not have to attempt to forge a new and vital relationship with a succeeding president, who would have been Willkie. "To close the slowly built-up comradeship, to break the continuity of all our discussions, to begin again with a new mind and personality, seemed to me a repellant prospect," he wrote later.[3]

Just three days after the election, Roosevelt handed down a general rule regarding armaments manufactured in the United States: half would remain in the country for its own defense program, but the other half would go to the British and the Canadians. He also said the United States would build three hundred merchant vessels for the British to make up for ones lost to submarines and bombings, as well as send other reconditioned World War I warships. The United States itself would bear the present cost. On the same day, the British government approved an order of twelve thousand aircraft to be manufactured in the United States, on top of the eleven thousand already on order.

This purchase suited American manufacturers, of course, but people knowledgeable of British finances wondered how Britain was going to pay. Its year of war expenses had already drawn down the British Treasury to the point where the bottom was in sight. Churchill wrote later: "Even if we divested ourselves of all our gold and foreign assets, we could not pay for half we had ordered, and the extension of the war made it necessary for us to have ten times as much."[4]

To this point Britain had been paying for its armament orders with cash. It was compelled to do so owing to U.S. neutrality laws. A provision passed in 1937 allowed armament sales only to belligerents who could pay cash (the argument being that selling on credit tied the United States too closely to the borrowing country) and could arrange for transport. This stipulation, of course, in practice limited sales only to France and Britain, because Germany and Italy could not send any ships across the Atlantic owing to the British navy.

Once the U.S. presidential election was over, Churchill worked with ambassador to the United States Lord Lothian, who was then in England, on a long letter to President Roosevelt detailing Churchill's view of what the war would bring in 1941. Churchill said it was "one of the most important I ever wrote." In this long letter the prime minister implored the president for matériel, describing warships (especially destroyers), aircraft (especially heavy bombers), and three million tons of merchant shipping. He urged Roosevelt to ask Ireland for permission to put U.S. bases on its shores so that the United States might protect Atlantic traffic, noting again that Irish cooperation might lead to an Ireland free of the British enclave of Northern Ireland. Churchill then raised the issue of payment and noted:

> While we will do our utmost, and shrink from no proper sacrifice to make payments . . . I believe you will agree that it would be wrong in principle and mutually disadvantageous in effect if at the height of this struggle Great Britain were to be divested of all saleable assets, so that after the victory was won with our blood, civilisation saved, and the time gained for the United States to be fully armed against all eventualities, we should stand stripped to the bone. Such a course would not be in the moral or economic interests of either of our countries.[5]

This letter reached Roosevelt while he was on holiday aboard the cruiser *Tuscaloosa* in the Caribbean. He mulled it over, and by the time the cruiser returned to American waters, the president was ready with his answer. He would lend and lease the supplies to Britain, which would return the equipment or in-kind at the end of the war, and dollar amounts would not be tallied. Explaining this action to the nation, Roosevelt likened the process to a man assisting a neighbor whose house is burning; when his neighbor needs the garden hose, he doesn't ask the man for money but rather allows him to use the hose to put out the fire and then return it when the emergency has passed. Roosevelt then made one of his strongest statements on behalf of American support for the British cause: "The best defense of the United States is the success of Great Britain defending itself. . . . [W]e should do everything possible to help the British Empire to defend itself."[6] The Lend-Lease Act was under way, and Congress approved it—not perhaps in the least because it went through the House as H.R. 1776—in March 1941.

■

Göring's bombers continued to drone over British cities and heave upon them bombs and incendiaries. The most infamous bombardment was the night of November 14 when X-Gerät beams guided 450 bombers to the Midlands city of Coventry, home of important aircraft engine and machine tool factories. The British radio wave experts had not yet devised a good countermeasure to the X-Gerät beams, and the German planes honed in accurately. They loosed five hundred tons of high explosives and thirty tons of incendiary bombs on the hapless city. So many fires were started that firefighters had no chance of dealing with them all. A firestorm ensued, and a hundred acres of central Coventry were destroyed. Almost five hundred citizens were killed. Of seventy thousand buildings in the city, sixty thousand were destroyed or badly damaged. Twenty-seven important factories would be out of operation for months. Even the German pilots, used to seeing devastation, were speechless. They soon had a slang word for the total destruction of a city, *Koventrieren* (to Coventrate or devastate with aerial bombing). Coventry's fifteenth-century St. Michael's Cathedral became—and, roofless and naked, still is—a symbol of wanton destruction from airplanes.

Enigma decryptions pointed for a few days to a major raid during the coming full moon, but the messages used code numbers for the target cities: 51, 52, and 53. No one could be sure to which cities they referred. In the late afternoon of the fourteenth, X-Gerät beams were found crossing over Coventry, but this discovery was still not considered conclusive evidence. Other intelligence pointed to London, and it was there that Churchill prepared to watch for the bombers. He neither knew the target of the approaching air fleet—they first struck at about 7:30 p.m.—nor concealed such information in an effort to keep Ultra secret.[7]

■

Diplomatically the most important meeting of the month was the Molotov visit to Berlin during November 12 and 13. The Germans were feeling out the Russian foreign commissar on the idea of the Soviet Union joining the Tripartite Pact, becoming an active German ally in the war, and finding reward by swallowing up portions of the British Empire. Britain, Hitler assured Molotov, was as good as beaten. Further, as one of the proposed four powers, Russia would also have a sphere of influence reaching south toward and perhaps into India. Japan would have East and Southeast Asia; Italy would have portions of North and East Africa, flowing out into the Indian Ocean; and Germany, aside from its New Order in Europe, would find resources and expanded living space across central Africa. Although Hitler could not say as much to the Russian commissar, if Molotov could be seen as content to allow Germany free rein on the continent by forging and accepting a Four Powers Pact, then Hitler would consider calling off or at least delaying his cherished intent of overrunning Russia from the west.

While in Berlin, Molotov did indeed seem vaguely disposed toward the idea of establishing an active alliance with Germany, though he had some barbed and annoying questions for both Hitler and Ribbentrop. When he returned to Moscow, he and Stalin drew up their own demands for such a prospective alliance. The Soviet Union, they said, wanted increased influence in the regions of the Bosporus and Dardanelles straits and the Persian Gulf, greater control in the Baltic, and German troops out of Finland, a country within the Soviet sphere of influence under the August 1939 Nonaggression Pact.

Molotov's sober visit to Berlin, and the demands that returned two weeks later from Moscow, convinced Hitler that Stalin was intent on meddling in territories Hitler wanted for himself, mainly Finland and southeast European countries, and that Stalin's interest in the Bosporus-Dardanelles region and the Persian Gulf were dangerous. Rather than diverting Hitler from his plan to invade Russia when good weather appeared in 1941, the Soviet talks and demands reinforced Hitler's desire to pursue them. By December 18 he had a formal, top-secret memo about the invasion drawn up for his military leadership.[8] And notwithstanding Soviet disquiet over increasing German influence in southeast Europe, before the month was out, Germany signed Hungary, Romania, and Slovakia to the Tripartite Pact. These ties were meant to thwart the Soviets in southeast Europe and steady the Balkans in the face of the Greco-Italian war.

During November Britain grew more aggressive in the skies over the continent. In the second week of the month, Bomber Command sent planes over Munich, Dresden, Danzig, and Essen, the latter being home to large steelworks. On the thirteenth, knowing in advance of Molotov's visit to Berlin, it bombed the German capital, sending Ribbentrop and Molotov into underground shelters. Molotov wondered aloud to Ribbentrop why they were sweating out British bombs when Hitler had declared Britain all but out of the war, a comment that fueled German discomfort about the entire visit. On the fifteenth British bombers pounded industries in Hamburg, killing 233 civilians,[9] and four days later the vast armaments factories of Skoda at Pilsen, Czechoslovakia.

The Blitz of London continued month after month. Describing a night bombing in December, journalist Ernie Pyle wrote:

> Shortly after the sirens wailed I could hear the Germans grinding overhead. In my room, with its black curtains drawn across the windows, you could feel the shake from the guns. You could hear the boom, crump, crump, crump, of heavy bombs at their work of tearing buildings apart. . . . About every two minutes a new wave of planes would be over. The motors seemed to grind rather than roar, and to have an angry pulsation like a bee buzzing in blind fury. . . . [The bombs] were intermittent—sometimes a few seconds apart, sometimes a minute or more . . . This sound was sharp, nearby, and soft and muffled, far away. They were everywhere over London.[10]

In all, in London and other British targets, the German bombings killed forty-three thousand British civilians, or twice as many people as the V-1 and V-2 rocket attacks would kill in 1944–45.[11]

On November 9 Neville Chamberlain died of cancer. Although Churchill had strenuously opposed Chamberlain's policy of appeasement, he had made Chamberlain a cabinet member in his government. After the former prime minister resigned in October owing to the cancer, Churchill continued to send him state papers so that Chamberlain could be current on the war efforts.

On November 12 Churchill paid Chamberlain tribute before the House of Commons with reverberations that might now well reflect on Churchill himself:

> History with its flickering lamp stumbles along the trail of the past, trying to reconstruct its scenes, to revive its echoes, and kindle with pale gleams the passion of former days. What is the worth of all this?

The only guide to a man is his conscience; the only shield to his memory is the rectitude and sincerity of his actions. . . . . Whatever else history may or may not say about these terrible, tremendous years, we can be sure that Neville Chamberlain acted with perfect sincerity according to his lights and strove to the utmost of his capacity and authority, which were powerful, to save the world from the awful, devastating struggle in which we are now engaged. . . . Herr Hitler protests with frantic words and gestures that he has only desired peace. What do these ravings and outpourings count before the silence of Neville Chamberlain's tomb? Long, hard, and hazardous years lie before us, but at least we enter upon them united and with clean hearts.[12]

Spain never entered the war. Gibraltar was never attacked. The French Vichy government never formally joined the German side. The French fleet never fell into German and Italian hands. Indeed two and a half years after these events—on November 27, 1942—French sailors scuttled scores of their ships to keep them from the Germans and Italians.

After guiding Fighter Command through the Battle of Britain, Hugh Dowding was relieved of command on November 24 for disagreements with superiors over tactics and nighttime fighter development. He never held equal responsibility for the British cause thereafter. He retired from the RAF in July 1942 and wrote books on spiritualism. He died in 1970.

Between July 10 and October 31, RAF Fighter Command shot down 1,733 Luftwaffe aircraft, killing or capturing about 3,100 crewmen. In the same period, it lost 915 airplanes.[13]

About 500 RAF fighter pilots were killed during the Battle of Britain: 398 British, 29 Poles, 20 Canadians, and other nationalities in fewer totals.[14] Compared to the great horrors yet to come, these numbers are puny, but they echo down the ages.

In the five months of June through October 1940, the British Army was driven weaponless off the Continent, and the French army disintegrated before the screaming Stukas and the flanking grinding panzers. The French Third Republic collapsed into occupation and the accommodationist Pétain government. Outside Britain much of the world saw the "wave of the future" about to engulf Britain also, or at least to compromise Britain into an accommodating peace. Russia encouraged and abetted Germany, sending much-needed war materials. Isolationists in the United States restrained their government from being of much aid.

But the British people rallied to their eloquent if pudgy prime minister and took the imperialist old soldier's voice for their own. They were an island nation, unconquered in almost a thousand years and not about to let that record fall without the fiercest fight. They had written the Common Law and forged courts of rights, and they were not about to see those trampled by any foreign tyrant. They would fight. They were bombed; they saw their sons fly up daily to fall down in flames; they saw their hospitals, churches, and schools smashed; they saw their babies and mothers and elderly blown apart in their homes, and their young women in uniform die at their posts; and they said all this was preferable to seeing Europe—indeed the world—succumb to a regime of race hatred and savagery. Nor would they parley with such a regime. Rather they would struggle to expunge it. If liberal government was to be saved, they would have to be the ones to save it. They knew this would be a day far off, and that to reach that day first they could not allow themselves to be defeated. That was the work of these five months.

In June–October 1940 the world lay in the balance. Many millions believed the future lay with fascism and Nazism, if not by acquiescence then by conquest. Britain had a choice to make, and it said no. Much pain, and many blessings on the future lay pregnant in that decision. The scales tipped in these months, if ever so slightly, and hope could cast its cold rays upon a new and different future.

NOTES

Introduction

1. Adolf Hitler, *Mein Kampf*, trans. Ralph Manheim (Boston: Houghton Mifflin, 1971), 138–39.

Chapter 1. Prelude

1. It is a poem Winston Churchill had memorized as a child and, as he reported later, recalled in 1935; author unknown. Winston S. Churchill, *The Gathering Storm* (Boston: Houghton Mifflin, 1948), 122–23.
2. John A. Garraty and Peter Gay, eds., *Columbia History of the World* (New York: Harper & Row, 1972), 992.
3. William Shirer, *Rise and Fall of the Third Reich* (New York: Simon & Schuster, 1990), 29–30.
4. R. R. Palmer and Joel Colton, *History of the Modern World*, 3rd ed. (New York: Knopf, 1965), 702.
5. Ibid., 702.
6. Ibid.
7. Shirer, *Rise and Fall*, 58–59.
8. Ibid.
9. See www.germanculture.com.ma/library/history/bl_weimer_republic .htm.
10. Shirer, *Rise and Fall*, 62.
11. Ibid., 112.
12. Ibid., 118.
13. Palmer and Colton, *History of the Modern World*, 807.
14. Shirer, *Rise and Fall*, 136.

15. Ibid., 192.

16. Ibid., 224.

17. Ibid., 241.

18. Churchill, *Gathering Storm*, 143.

19. The Nazis were trying to legitimize themselves by demonstrating their link to German heritage. The first two Reichs were the Holy Roman Empire of 962–1806 and the German monarchy of 1871–1918.

20. A pocket battleship was about the size of a cruiser but with firepower more akin to that of a battleship.

21. John Keegan, *The Second World War* (New York: Penguin Group, 1989), 104–5.

22. "Anglo French Supreme War Council," *Wikipedia*, http://en.wikipedia .org/wiki/Anglo-French_Supreme_War_Council; and Churchill, *Gathering Storm*, 576.

23. Gerhard L. Weinberg, *World at Arms: A Global History of World War II* (New York: Cambridge University Press, 1994), 134.

24. "Battle of France," *Wikipedia*, http://en.wikipedia.org/wiki/Battle_of_ France, and Keegan, *Second World War*, 60.

25. Martin Gilbert, *Winston S. Churchill*, vol. 6, *Their Finest Hour, 1939–1941* (Boston: Houghton Mifflin, 1983), 143.

26. Weinberg, *World at Arms*, 125.

27. "Winston Churchill: 'Blood, Toil, Tears, and Sweat,' May 13, 1940," *Internet Modern History Source Book*, http://www.fordham.edu/halsall /mod/churchill-blood.html.

28. Weinberg, *World at Arms*, 127.

29. Winston S. Churchill, *Their Finest Hour* (Boston: Houghton Mifflin, 1949), 56–57.

30. Norman Moss, *19 Weeks: America, Britain, and the Fateful Summer of 1940* (Boston: Houghton Mifflin, 2003), 131; and Churchill, *Finest Hour*, 63.

31. Moss, *19 Weeks*, 137–43.

32. Ibid.

33. Churchill, *Finest Hour*, 82.

34. Ibid., 111.

35. Ibid., 101–2.

36. Hugh Sebag-Montefiore, *Dunkirk: Fight to the Last Man* (Cambridge, MA: Harvard University Press, 2006), 298–301, 501. On evidence from the two survivors, the SS officer in charge was tried for the massacre after the war and hanged.

37. Ibid., 437–38.

Chapter 2. June: Collapse

1. Churchill, *Finest Hour*, 115.
2. "Dunkirk Evacuation," *Wikipedia*, http://en.wikipedia.org/wiki/Dunkirk_evacuation#cite_note-mm-10.
3. Churchill, *Finest Hour*, 145.
4. Ibid.
5. Gilbert, *Their Finest Hour, 1939–1941*, 92.
6. Churchill, *Finest Hour*, 147.
7. Ibid., 148.
8. Gilbert, *Their Finest Hour, 1939–1941*, 89; and Cesare Salmaggi and Alfredo Pallavisini, eds., *2194 Days of War* (New York: Mayflower Books, 1977), 62.
9. Gilbert, *Their Finest Hour, 1939–1941*, 92.
10. Churchill, *Finest Hour*, 122.
11. Moss, *19 Weeks*, 166.
12. Gilbert, *Their Finest Hour, 1939–1941*, 92.
13. Moss, *19 Weeks*, 170.
14. Gilbert, *Their Finest Hour, 1939–1941*, 97.
15. Moss, *19 Weeks*, 170–71.
16. Churchill, *Finest Hour*, 152–58.
17. Father of the future U.S. president John F. Kennedy.
18. Churchill, *Finest Hour*, 185.
19. Ibid., 193–94.
20. Ibid., 222.
21. Ibid., 201.
22. Moss, *19 Weeks*, 178. Jean Monnet after the war became a prime mover in the creation of the European Common Market, officially known as the European Economic Community, the predecessor of the European Commission.
23. Churchill, *Finest Hour*, 208–9.
24. Ibid., 208.
25. Moss, *19 Weeks*, 180.
26. Ibid., 182.
27. Ibid., 183.
28. Churchill, *Finest Hour*, 229.
29. Ibid., 217.
30. Shirer, *Rise and Fall*, 738.
31. Moss, *19 Weeks*, 184.

32. Churchill, *Finest Hour*, 225–26. Churchill appropriately quotes this speech in his memoir of this time, which he called *Their Finest Hour*, written in 1949. Immediately after the quote in his memoir, he admits that to the world these words may have seemed mere bravado before an attempt at a negotiated peace. He wonders that others may not have condemned him and even applauded if he had guided Britain to a gentle peace in expectation of Germany turning on Soviet Russia as both were intent upon destroying each other. Then he added, "Future generations will find it hard to believe that the issues I have summarized here [i.e., a brokered peace and its advantages] were never thought worth a place upon the Cabinet agenda, or even mentioned in our most private conclaves."

33. Ibid., 218.

34. Mandel was returned to Vichy France, then handed over to the Germans in November 1942. They sent him to concentration camps, then returned him to Paris and had him murdered in July 1944.

35. Shirer, *Rise and Fall*, 741.

36. Churchill, *Finest Hour*, 134.

37. John H. Waller, *The Unseen War in Europe: Espionage and Conspiracy in the Second World War* (New York: Random House, 1996), 153–54.

38. Gilbert, *Their Finest Hour, 1939–1941*, 100.

39. Ibid.

40. Shirer, *Rise and Fall*, 742–43.

41. Ibid., 744.

42. Ibid., 746. It was later destroyed in an Allied bombing raid.

43. Martin Gilbert, *The Second World War: A Complete History* (New York: Henry Holt, 1989), 102.

44. Ibid., 105.

45. Ibid.

46. Salmaggi and Pallavisini, *2194 Days*, 67.

47. Churchill, *Finest Hour*, 227.

48. Ibid., 228–29.

49. Weinberg, *World at Arms*, 143.

50. Moss, *19 Weeks*, 231.

51. Richard Overy with Andrew Wheatcroft, *Road to War* (London: Macmillan, 1989), 264–65.

52. Shirer, *Rise and Fall*, 760. Emphasis is Jodl's.

Chapter 3. The Race to Read the Codes

1. Stephen Budiansky, *Battle of Wits: The Complete Story of Codebreaking in World War II* (New York: Simon & Schuster, 2000), 135.

2. Information for this chapter derives from: Budiansky, *Battle of Wits*; Hervie Haufler, *Codebreaker's Victory: How the Allied Cryptographers Won World War II* (New York: New American Library, 2003); Francis Russell, *Secret War* (Alexandria, VA: Time-Life Books, 1981); Ronald Lewin, *Ultra Goes to War: The First Account of World War II's Greatest Secret Based on Official Documents* (New York: McGraw-Hill, 1978); and David Kahn, *The Codebreakers: The Story of Secret Writing* (New York: Macmillan, 1967). Winston Churchill makes no mention of code breaking in his memoir of this period. Revelation of the reading of German Enigma machine messages was not revealed until the 1970s. Security about the code breaking was so tight, despite the thousands of people having worked at Bletchley Park during the war, that for twenty-five years word never leaked out. Code breakers even feared that under anesthesia during an operation or the like they might blurt out the secret, but it never happened.

3. Lewin, *Ultra Goes to War*, 26.

4. Haufler, *Codebreakers' Victory*, 50.

5. Weinberg, *World at Arms*, 549. Many of the German code-breaking records captured at the end of the war are still classified, so we do not know entirely how successful they were in reading Allied messages.

Chapter 4. July: Fire and Wait

1. John Lukacs, *The Duel: 10 May–31 July 1940: The Eighty-Day Struggle between Churchill and Hitler* (New York: Ticknor & Fields, 1991), 164.

2. Ronald Kessler, *Sins of the Father: Joseph P. Kennedy and the Dynasty He Founded* (New York: Warner Books, 1996), 214, 217.

3. Lukacs, *The Duel*, 190–94.

4. Gilbert, *Their Finest Hour, 1939–1941*, 630–31.

5. "French Navy," *Wikipedia*, http://en.wikipedia.org/wiki/French_Navy.

6. With respect to battleships, battle cruisers sacrificed either armor or gun size for speed.

7. For disposition of the French fleet, see Churchill, *Finest Hour*, 233.

8. Gilbert, *Their Finest Hour, 1939–1941*, 589.

9. Churchill, *Finest Hour*, 235.

10. Ibid., 234.

11. Ibid., 235.
12. Henry H. Adams, *Years of Deadly Peril* (New York: David McKay, 1969), 194.
13. Ibid., 194–95.
14. Ibid., 202.
15. Ibid.
16. Ibid., 206.
17. Churchill, *Finest Hour*, 236.
18. Gilbert, *Their Finest Hour, 1939–1941*, 641.
19. Ibid., 642.
20. Roy Jenkins, *Churchill: A Biography* (New York: Farrar, Straus & Giroux, 2001), 625.
21. Churchill, *Finest Hour*, 238.
22. For more information on Operation Catapult and Mers-el-Kébir, see Churchill, *Finest Hour*, 224–39; A. B. C. Whipple, *The Mediterranean* (Alexandria, VA: Time-Life Books, 1981), 23–45; and Adams, *Years of Deadly Peril*, 176–212.
23. Lukacs, *The Duel*, 162.
24. Hitler, *Mein Kampf*, 620.
25. Edwin P. Hoyt, *Hitler's War* (New York: Cooper Square, 2001), 150.
26. Shirer, *Rise and Fall*, 751.
27. Hitler, *Mein Kampf*, 620.
28. Leonard Mosley, *Battle of Britain* (Alexandria, VA: Time-Life Books, 1977), 24.
29. Shirer, *Rise and Fall*, 766.
30. Stephen Budiansky, *Air Power: The Men, Machines, and Ideas That Revolutionized War, from Kitty Hawk to Gulf War II* (New York: Viking, 2004), 137.
31. Ibid., 222.
32. Robert Wernick, *Blizkrieg* (New York: Time-Life Books, 1976), 116.
33. Churchill Centre and Museum at the Cabinet War Rooms, http://www .winstonchurchill.org/learn/speeches-of-winston-churchill/1940 -finest-hour/126-war-of-the-unknown-warriors.
34. Shirer, *Rise and Fall*, 753.
35. Lukacs, *Duel*, 176.
36. Gilbert, *Second World War*, 110.
37. Shirer, *Rise and Fall*, 754.
38. Churchill, *Finest Hour*, 260; and Salmaggi and Pallavisini, *2194 Days*, 72.

39. Churchill, *Finest Hour*, 258.

40. Ibid., 262.

41. Tim Clayton and Phil Craig, *Finest Hour: The Battle of Britain* (New York: Simon & Schuster, 1999), 241.

42. Battle of Britain Historical Society, www.battleofbritain1940.net/0001 .htm.

43. Moss, *19 Weeks*, 200.

44. Churchill, *Their Finest Hour*, 279.

45. For information on the Home Guard and defenses, see Mosley, *Battle of Britain*, 30, 42–45; and Moss, *19 Weeks*, 195–99.

46. Gilbert, *Their Finest Hour, 1939–1941*, 618.

47. Mosley, *Battle of Britain*, 23.

48. Richard Hough and Denis Richards, *Battle of Britain: The Greatest Air Battle of World War II* (New York: Norton, 1989), 114.

49. Richard Overy, *Battle of Britain: The Myth and the Reality* (New York: W. W. Norton, 2000), 46; and Hough and Richards, *Battle of Britain*, 56.

50. Hough and Richards, *Battle of Britain*, 125–27.

51. Ibid., 100.

52. Ibid., 130–31.

53. David E. Fisher, *Summer Bright and Terrible: Winston Churchill, Lord Dowding, Radar, and the Impossible Triumph of the Battle of Britain* (New York: Shoemaker & Hoard, 2005), 139–40.

54. Hough and Richards, *Battle of Britain*, 136.

55. Franklin D. Roosevelt, *Roosevelt and Churchill: Their Secret Wartime Correspondence*, ed. Francis Lowenheim, Harold Langley, and Manfred Jonas (New York: Saturday Review Press, 1975), 107–8.

56. Weinberg, *World at Arms*, 154.

Chapter 5. Radar, Radio Waves, and the Race for Air Superiority

1. Budiansky, *Air Power*, 187.

2. Fisher, *Summer Bright and Terrible*, 57.

3. Robert Buderi, *Invention That Changed the World: How a Small Group of Radar Pioneers Won the Second World War and Launched a Technological Revolution* (New York: Simon & Schuster, 1996), 53.

4. He added the hyphen to his name in 1942 when he was knighted and has ever since been known as Robert Watson-Watt.

5. Is it more than a coincidence that the term reads the same left to right as right to left, mimicking a wave and its echo?

6. Hough and Richards, *Battle of Britain*, 328.

7. "Battle of Britain," *Wikipedia*, http://en.wikipedia.org/wiki/Battle_of _Britain.

8. For information about the development of RDF, see Buderi, *Invention That Changed the World;* Hough and Richards, *Battle of Britain;* and David E. Fisher, *A Race on the Edge of Time: Radar—the Decisive Weapon of World War II* (New York: McGraw-Hill, 1988).

9. The author of the Oslo Report was revealed in 1989 to be Hans Ferdinand Mayer, a scientist at the Siemens Company in Germany. He died in 1980.

10. Russell, *Secret War*, 137.

11. Budiansky, *Air Power*, 248.

12. Russell, *Secret War*, 138–39.

Chapter 6. August: The Mailed Fist

1. Moss, *19 Weeks*, 260.

2. Shirer, *Rise and Fall*, 765.

3. Mosley, *Battle of Britain*, 91.

4. John H. Thompson and Stephen Randall, *Canada and the United States: Ambivalent Allies*, 3rd ed. (Athens: University of Georgia Press, 2002), 152.

5. Fisher, *Summer Bright and Terrible*, 61–63.

6. Hough and Richards, *Battle of Britain*, 38.

7. Budiansky, *Air Power*, 215.

8. "Hugh Dowding," *History Learning Site*, www.historylearningsite.co .uk/hugh_dowding.htm.

9. R. J. Mitchell died of cancer in 1937. A 1942 movie about him was called *First of the Few*.

10. Hough and Richards, *Battle of Britain*, 387.

11. Overy, *Battle of Britain*, 160.

12. Battle of Britain Historical Society, www.battleofbritain1940.net/0005 .html.

13. Hough and Richards, *Battle of Britain*, 117; and Overy, *Battle of Britain*, 54.

14. Overy, *Battle of Britain*, 57.

15. For information on the aircraft, see Mosley, *Battle of Britain*, 52–55; and Hough and Richards, *Battle of Britain*, 32–45.

16. Mosley, *Battle of Britain*, 48.

17. Hough and Richards, *Battle of Britain*, 112.

18. Mosley, *Battle of Britain*, 52.

19. Ibid., 50.

20. Fisher, *Summer Bright and Terrible*, 134–35.

21. Ibid., 142–43.

22. Overy, *Battle of Britain*, 30; and Mosley, *Battle of Britain*, 74–85.

23. Mosley, *Battle of Britain*, 47.

24. "The Pilots That Took Part," Battle of Britain Historical Society, www
.battleofbritain1940.net/0004.html.

25. Moss, *19 Weeks*, 213–14.

26. Josef Frantisek was killed on October 8. At the time he was the Royal
Air Force's leading ace with twenty-eight German planes shot down.
See Hough and Richards, *Battle of Britain*, 186-187.

27. Fisher, *Summer Bright and Terrible*, 158; and Virginia Bader, conversation with author, 1993.

28. Douglas Bader bailed out over France in 1941 and spent the rest of
the war in POW camps, though he attempted escape twice. German
fighter aces, familiar with his renown, befriended him, helped him get
replacement legs from England, and showed him their planes.

29. Mosley, *Battle of Britain*, 91–92.

30. Hough and Richards, *Battle of Britain*, 359.

31. Fisher, *Summer Bright and Terrible*, 163–64.

32. Churchill, *Finest Hour*, 418.

33. Michael Curtis, *Verdict on Vichy: Power and Prejudice in the Vichy France
Regime* (New York: Arcade, 2003), 73; and Churchill, *Finest Hour*, 508.

34. Hough and Richards, *Battle of Britain*, 141–44.

35. Ibid., 359.

36. Ibid., 154.

37. For aircraft losses by day, see ibid., appendix I.

38. Frederick William Winterbotham, *The Ultra Secret* (New York: Harper
& Row, 1974), 48.

39. Winterbotham, *Ultra Secret*, 46–53.

40. Hough and Richards, *Battle of Britain*, 329.

41. Ibid., 347.

42. Ibid., 346–47.

43. Ibid., 329.

44. Ibid., 348.

45. Budiansky, *Air Power*, 238.

46. Gilbert, *Their Finest Hour, 1939–1941*, 736.

47. Hough and Richards, *Battle of Britain*, 204–5.

48. Ibid., 211.

49. Ibid., 345.

50. Ibid., 336–37.

51. Ibid., 200.

52. Overy, *Battle of Britain*, 84.

53. Hough and Richards, *Battle of Britain*, 233.

54. The Churchill Centre and Churchill War Rooms, www.winston churchill.org.

55. Winston S. Churchill, *Blood, Toil, Tears and Sweat: The Speeches of Winston Churchill*, ed. David Cannadine (Boston: Houghton Mifflin, 1989), 192.

56. Gilbert, *Their Finest Hour, 1939–1941*, 743.

57. Leonard Mosley, *Backs to the Wall: London under Fire, 1939–45* (New York: Random House, 1971), 117.

58. Gilbert, *Their Finest Hour, 1939–1941*, 121.

59. Hough and Richards, *Battle of Britain*, 362.

60. Overy, *Battle of Britain*, 80; and "Battle of Britain Campaign Diary," *Battle of Britain*, http://www.raf.mod.uk/Bob1940/august31.html.

61. Shirer, *Rise and Fall*, 800.

Chapter 7. Cracking a People's Will to Fight

1. Lukacs, *The Duel*, 160.

2. Horst J. P. Bergmeier and Rainer E. Lotz, *Hitler's Airwaves: The Inside Story of Nazi Radio Broadcasting and Propaganda Swing* (New Haven, CT: Yale University Press, 1997), 200–202.

3. Ibid., 210–12.

4. Ibid., 101.

5. Born in Brooklyn, New York, to British-born parents, Joyce grew up in England. Captured after the war, he was tried and hanged for treason by the British in 1946.

6. Bergmeier and Lotz, *Hitler's Airwaves*, 213.

7. Ibid., 213–14.

8. The aristocratic Mitford sisters drew attention throughout the 1930s. Nancy became a writer. Pamela married and divorced a millionaire. Unity revered Hitler and unsuccessfully tried to kill herself when Britain declared war on Germany. Jessica became a Communist and a writer.

9. Richard Thurlow, "Britain: The British 'Union of Fascists,'" in *Fascism Reader,* ed. Aristotle Kallis (London: Routledge, 2003), 241–48.

10. Overy, *Battle of Britain,* 12.

11. Ibid., 99–100.

12. United States Holocaust Memorial Museum, "German American Bund," *Holocaust Encyclopedia,* April 2010, http://www.ushmm.org/wlc/en/article.php?ModuleId=10005684.

13. A. Scott Berg, *Lindbergh* (New York: G. P. Putnam's Sons, 1998), 402.

14. Ibid., 405, 406, 409.

15. Kenneth Sydney Davis, *FDR, the War President, 1940–1943: A History* (New York: Random House, 2000), 89.

16. Samuel Eliot Morison, *Oxford History of the American People,* vol. 3, *1869 through the Death of John F. Kennedy* (New York: New American Library, 1972), 353.

17. Albin Krebs, "William Stephenson, British Spy Known as Intrepid, Is Dead at 93," *New York Times,* February 3, 1989.

18. Moss, *19 Weeks,* 244.

19. Ibid., 247.

20. Joseph P. Lash, *Roosevelt and Churchill, 1939–1941: The Partnership That Saved the West* (New York: W. W. Norton, 1976), 283n.

21. William Stevenson, *A Man Called Intrepid: The Secret War* (New York: Lyons Press, 1976), 9.

22. Ibid., 114.

Chapter 8. September: From under the Rubble

1. Anonymous. Quoted in Desmond Flower and James Reeves, eds., *The War, 1939–1945: A Documentary History* (Cambridge, MA: Da Capo Press, 1997), 132.

2. Moss, *19 Weeks,* 301–2.

3. Ibid., 315–16.

4. Hough and Richards, *Battle of Britain,* 250.

5. Gilbert, *Their Finest Hour, 1939–1941,* 770.

6. Ibid., 772.

7. Shirer, *Rise and Fall,* 779–80.

8. Hough and Richard, *Battle of Britain,* 241.

9. www.worldwar-2.net/timelines/war-in-europe/european-air-war/european-air-war-index-1940.htm.

10. Overy, *Battle of Britain,* 80. The Luftwaffe lost about the same number

of fighters and as many again in bombers during roughly the same period.

11. Shirer, *Rise and Fall*, 777.
12. Ibid., 780.
13. Hough and Richards, *Battle of Britain*, 241, 262.
14. Moss, *19 Weeks*, 294.
15. Churchill, *Finest Hour*, 312; ibid., 312–13; and Gilbert, *Their Finest Hour, 1939–1941*, 122.
16. "The Chronology: Sunday, September 8th–Monday, September 9th, 1940," *The Battle of Britain*, www.battleofbritain1940.net.
17. Gilbert, *Their Finest Hour, 1939–1941*, 124.
18. Moss, *19 Weeks*, 306.
19. Mosley, *Battle of Britain*, 36–37.
20. Gilbert, *Their Finest Hour, 1939–1941*, 776.
21. Shirer, *Rise and Fall*, 780.
22. Moss, *19 Weeks*, 320.
23. Edward R. Murrow, *This Is London* (New York: Simon & Schuster, 1941), 160.
24. Shirer, *Rise and Fall*, 769n.
25. Murrow, *This Is London*, 163.
26. Moss, *19 Weeks*, 324–25; and Mosley, *Backs to the Wall*, 177.
27. Mosley, *Backs to the Wall*, 180.
28. Mosley, *Battle of Britain*, 139.
29. Murrow, *This Is London*, 173–74.
30. Gilbert, *Their Finest Hour, 1939–1941*, 778.
31. Alfred Price, *Battle of Britain Day: 15 September 1940* (London: Greenhill Books, 1990), 137–38.
32. Shirer, *Rise and Fall*, 771.
33. Hough and Richards, *Battle of Britain*, 365–66.
34. Gilbert, *Their Finest Hour, 1939–1941*, 125.
35. Price, *Battle of Britain Day*, 49.
36. Ibid., 129.
37. Ibid., 55–58.
38. Gilbert, 784–85.
39. Moss, *19 Weeks*, 343.
40. Price, *Battle of Britain Day*, 40.
41. In Great Britain, September 15 is celebrated as Battle of Britain Day.
42. For this and the numbers in the previous paragraph, see Price, *Battle of Britain Day*, 115, 119, 126.

43. Moss, *19 Weeks*, 345.
44. Churchill, *Finest Hour*, 472.
45. Ian Kershaw, *Fateful Choices: Ten Decisions That Changed the World, 1940–1941* (New York: Penguin Press, 2007), 124.
46. Hough and Richards, *Battle of Britain*, 296.
47. Overy, *Battle of Britain*, 101–5.
48. Murrow, *This Is London*, 183.
49. Churchill, *Finest Hour*, 473–94; and Weinberg, *World at Arms*, 160.
50. William Shirer, "The Hour Will Come When One of Us Will Break," in *Reporting World War II: Part One: American Journalism, 1938–1944* (New York: Library of America, 1995), 137.
51. Murrow, *This Is London*, 191.
52. Ibid.

Chapter 9. Diplomacy: The Craft of Binding Friends and Stabbing Enemies

1. Heinz Höhne, *Canaris*, trans. J. Maxwell Brownjohn (Garden City, NY: Doubleday, 1979), 434.
2. Frances Donaldson, *Edward VIII* (New York: Lippincott, 1974), 389.
3. For information on the Duke of Windsor, see Gilbert, *Their Finest Hour, 1939–1941*, 698–707; Weinberg, *World at Arms*, 143–44; Philip Ziegler, *King Edward VIII* (New York: Knopf, 1991), 362–75; Donaldson, *Edward VIII*, 383–402; and J. Bryan III and Charles J. V. Murphy, *The Windsor Story* (New York: Morrow, 1979), 456–66.
4. Weinberg, *World at Arms*, 177.
5. For the life of Canaris, see Höhne, *Canaris*.
6. Waller, *The Unseen War in Europe*, 155–56.
7. Shirer, *Rise and Fall*, 813.
8. Ian Kershaw, *Hitler: 1936–1945 Nemesis* (New York: W. W. Norton, 2000), 327.
9. This strategy is, of course, the one the Allies chose, putting it into effect in 1942.
10. Weinberg, *World at Arms*, 134.
11. Both Finland and Romania eventually allied with Germany and protected the northern and southern flanks during Germany's invasion of the Soviet Union in June 1941.
12. Churchill, *Finest Hour*, 135–36.
13. Weinberg, *World at Arms*, 179.
14. Ibid., 155.

Chapter 10. October: How the Pieces Fell

1. Mosley, *Backs to the Wall*, 168–69.
2. Keegan, *Second World War*, 131.
3. Mosley, *Backs to the Wall*, 202–3.
4. "Guinea Pig Club," *Wikipedia*, http://en.wikipedia.org/wiki/Guinea_Pig_Club. Club membership grew to more than six hundred by the war's end. Reunions were frequent and continued into the twenty-first century. McIndoe was knighted for his work in 1947.
5. Hough and Richards, *Battle of Britain*, 342.
6. Gilbert, *Their Finest Hour, 1939–1941*, 831.
7. James Curran and Jean Seaton, *Power without Responsibility: The Press, Broadcasting, and the New Media in Britain*, 6th ed. (New York: Routledge, 2003), 58–59.
8. Gilbert, *Their Finest Hour, 1939–1941*, 833.
9. Mosley, *Backs to the Wall*, 142.
10. Ibid., 141.
11. Mosley, *Battle of Britain*, 147.
12. Churchill, *Finest Hour*, 346–47.
13. Ibid., 371.
14. Mosley, *Battle of Britain*, 145.
15. Mosley, *Back to the Walls*, 171, 189.
16. Ibid., 171–72.
17. Moss, *19 Weeks*, 335.
18. Ibid., 327.
19. Gilbert, *Their Finest Hour, 1939–1941*, 130.
20. Mosley, *Backs to the Wall*, 175.
21. Churchill, *Finest Hour*, 348–49. Churchill did not give a date for this incident.
22. Ibid., 362–63.
23. Weinberg, *World at Arms*, 209.
24. Mosley, *Backs to the Wall*, 206.
25. Ibid., 204.
26. Moss, *19 Weeks*, 335ff.
27. George Cross Database, www.gc-database.co.uk/decoration.htm.
28. Gilbert, *Their Finest Hour, 1939–1941*, 135.
29. Moss, *19 Weeks*, 329.
30. Lash, *Roosevelt and Churchill 1939-1941*, 238.

31. Kenneth Sydney Davis, *FDR: Into the Storm 1937–1940* (New York: Random House, 1993), 58.

32. Davis, *FDR*, 619.

33. Gilbert, *Their Finest Hour, 1939–1941*, 854.

34. Churchill, *Finest Hour*, 509. Churchill wrote later: "[De Gaulle] had to be rude to the British to prove to French eyes that he was not a British puppet. He certainly carried out this policy with perseverance. He even one day explained this technique to me, and I fully comprehended the extraordinary difficulties of his problem. I always admired his massive strength."

35. Ibid., 526.

36. Ibid., 510–12.

37. Ibid., 512.

38. Roosevelt, *Roosevelt and Churchill*, 117.

39. Keegan, *Second World War*, 118.

40. Gilbert, *Second World War*, 138.

41. Churchill, *Finest Hour*, 602.

42. See "Convoy SC7," *Wikipedia*, http://en.wikipedia.org/wiki/Convoy _SC_7; and "Convoy HX 79," *Wikipedia*, http://en.wikipedia.org/wiki /Convoy_HX_79. These two days ended up being the most destructive of the Battle of the Atlantic for the entire war.

43. Kershaw, *Fateful Choices*, 81–83.

44. Tellingly, the Vichy government replaced the previous motto of France, *Liberté, Egalité, Fraternité* (liberty, equality, fraternity) with *Travail, Famille, Patrie* (work, family, country).

45. Shirer, *Rise and Fall*, 814.

46. Ibid., 815.

47. Gilbert, *Their Finest Hour, 1939–1941*, 136.

48. Gilbert, *Second World War*, 134.

49. Churchill, *Finest Hour*, 532.

50. Salmaggi and Pallavisini, *2194 Days*, 81.

51. Shirer, *Rise and Fall*, 816.

Chapter 11. Postlude

1. Churchill, *Finest Hour*, front matter. So simple and yet so elegant. Could anyone other than a person who had already written a million words have crafted these thirteen?

2. Gilbert, *Their Finest Hour, 1939–1941*, 138–39.

3. Churchill, *Finest Hour,* 553–54.
4. Ibid., 558.
5. Ibid., 566.
6. Ibid., 568.
7. For the Coventry attack, see Russell, *Secret War,* 139; Churchill, *Finest Hour,* 376–77; Time-Life Books, *Luftwaffe* (Alexandria, VA: Time-Life Books, 1982), 96–97; Gilbert, *Second World War,* 142; Lewin, *Ultra Goes to War,* 100–104; and Gilbert, *Their Finest Hour, 1939–1941,* 913–15.
8. For the Molotov negotiations, see Kershaw, *Hitler,* 332–34; Shirer, *Rise and Fall,* 1053–62; and Churchill, *Finest Hour,* 579–85.
9. Gilbert, *Their Finest Hour, 1939–1941,* 143.
10. Ernie Pyle, "This Dreadful Masterpiece," in *Reporting World War II,* 148.
11. Moss, *19 Weeks,* 306.
12. Churchill, *Finest Hour,* 550–51.
13. Hough and Richards, *Battle of Britain,* 310.
14. Norman Franks, *Battle of Britain* (London: Bison Books, 1981), 61.

BIBLIOGRAPHY

Adams, Henry H. *Years of Deadly Peril*. New York: David McKay, 1969.

Berg, A. Scott. *Lindbergh*. New York: G. P. Putnam's Sons, 1998.

Bergmeier, Horst J. P., and Rainer E. Lotz. *Hitler's Airwaves: The Inside Story of Nazi Radio Broadcasting and Propaganda Swing*. New Haven, CT: Yale University Press, 1997.

Bryan, J., III, and Charles J. V. Murphy. *The Windsor Story*. New York: Morrow, 1979.

Buderi, Robert. *Invention That Changed the World: How a Small Group of Radar Pioneers Won the Second World War and Launched a Technological Revolution*. New York: Simon & Schuster, 1996.

Budiansky, Stephen. *Air Power: The Men, Machines, and Ideas That Revolutionized War, from Kitty Hawk to Gulf War II*. New York: Viking, 2004.

———. *Battle of Wits: The Complete Story of Codebreaking in World War II*. New York: Simon & Schuster, 2000.

Churchill, Winston, *Blood, Toil, Tears and Sweat: The Speeches of Winston Churchill*. Edited by David Cannadine. Boston: Houghton Mifflin, 1989.

———. *The Gathering Storm*. Boston: Houghton Mifflin, 1948.

———. *Their Finest Hour*. Boston: Houghton Mifflin, 1949.

Clayton, Tim, and Phil Craig. *Finest Hour: The Battle of Britain*. New York: Simon & Schuster, 1999.

Curran, James, and Jean Seaton. *Power without Responsibility: The Press, Broadcasting, and the New Media in Britain*. 6th ed. New York: Routledge, 2003.

Curtis, Michael. *Verdict on Vichy: Power and Prejudice in the Vichy France Regime.* New York: Arcade, 2003.

Davis, Kenneth Sydney. *FDR: Into the Storm 1937–1940.* New York: Random House, 1993.

———. *FDR, the War President, 1940–1943: A History.* New York: Random House, 2000.

Donaldson, Frances Lonsdale. *Edward VIII.* New York: Lippincott, 1974.

Fisher, David E. *A Race on the Edge of Time: Radar—the Decisive Weapon of World War II.* New York: McGraw-Hill, 1988.

———. *Summer Bright and Terrible: Winston Churchill, Lord Dowding, Radar, and the Impossible Triumph of the Battle of Britain.* New York: Shoemaker & Hoard, 2005.

Flower, Desmond, and James Reeves, eds. *The War, 1939–1945: A Documentary History.* Cambridge, MA: Da Capo Press, 1997.

Franks, Norman. *Battle of Britain.* London: Bison Books, 1981.

Garraty, John A., and Peter Gay, eds. *Columbia History of the World.* New York: Harper & Row, 1972.

Gelb, Norman. *Dunkirk: The Complete Story of the First Step in the Defeat of Hitler.* New York: William Morrow, 1989.

Gilbert, Martin. *The Second World War: A Complete History.* New York: Henry Holt, 1989.

———. *Winston S. Churchill.* Vol. 6, *Their Finest Hour, 1939–1941.* Boston: Houghton Mifflin, 1983.

Haufler, Hervie. *Codebreakers' Victory: How the Allied Cryptographers Won World War II.* New York: New American Library, 2003.

Hitler, Adolf. *Mein Kampf.* Translated by Ralph Manheim. Boston: Houghton Mifflin, 1971.

Höhne, Heinz. *Canaris.* Translated by J. Maxwell Brownjohn. Garden City, NY: Doubleday, 1979.

Hough, Richard, and Denis Richards. *Battle of Britain: The Greatest Air Battle of World War II.* New York: W. W. Norton, 1989.

Hoyt, Edwin P. *Hitler's War.* New York: Cooper Square, 2001.

Jenkins, Roy. *Churchill: A Biography.* New York: Farrar, Straus & Giroux, 2001.

Keegan, John. *The Second World War.* New York: Penguin Group, 1989.

Kershaw, Ian. *Fateful Choices: Ten Decisions That Changed the World, 1940–1941.* New York: Penguin Press, 2007.

————. *Hitler: 1936–1945 Nemesis*. New York: W. W. Norton, 2000.

Kessler, Ronald. *Sins of the Father: Joseph P. Kennedy and the Dynasty He Founded*. New York: Warner Books, 1996.

Laqueur, Walter. *Fascism: Past, Present, Future*. New York: Oxford University Press, 1996.

Lash, Joseph P. *Roosevelt and Churchill, 1939–1941: The Partnership That Saved the West*. New York: W. W. Norton, 1976.

Lewin, Ronald. *Ultra Goes to War: The First Account of World War II's Greatest Secret Based on Official Documents*. New York: McGraw-Hill, 1978.

Lukacs, John. *The Duel: 10 May–31 July 1940: The Eighty-Day Struggle between Churchill and Hitler*. New York: Ticknor & Fields, 1991.

Morison, Samuel Eliot. *Oxford History of the American People*. Vol. 3, *1869 through the Death of John F. Kennedy*. New York: New American Library, 1972.

Mosley, Leonard. *Backs to the Wall: London under Fire, 1939–45*. New York: Random House, 1971.

————. *Battle of Britain*. Alexandria, VA: Time-Life Books, 1977.

Moss, Norman. *19 Weeks: America, Britain, and the Fateful Summer of 1940*. Boston: Houghton Mifflin, 2003.

Murrow, Edward R. *This Is London*. New York: Simon & Schuster, 1941.

Overy, Richard. *Battle of Britain: The Myth and the Reality*. New York: W. W. Norton, 2000.

————. *Road to War*. With Andrew Wheatcroft. New York: Random House, 1990.

Palmer, R. R., and Joel Colton. *History of the Modern World*. 3rd ed. New York: Knopf, 1965.

Pyle, Ernie. "This Dreadful Masterpiece." In *Reporting World War II: Part One: American Journalism, 1938–1944*, 147–49. New York: Library of America, 1995.

Price, Alfred. *Battle of Britain Day: 15 September 1940*. London: Greenhill Books, 1990.

Roosevelt, Franklin D. *Roosevelt and Churchill: Their Secret Wartime Correspondence*. Edited by Francis Lowenheim, Harold Langley, and Manfred Jonas. New York: Saturday Review Press, 1975.

Russell, Francis. *Secret War*. Alexandria, VA: Time-Life Books, 1981.

Salmaggi, Cesare, and Alfredo Pallavisini, eds. *2194 Days of War*. New York: Mayflower Books, 1977.

Sebag-Montefiore, Hugh. *Dunkirk: Fight to the Last Man*. Cambridge, MA: Harvard University Press, 2006.

Shirer, William. "The Hour Will Come When One of Us Will Break." In *Reporting World War II: Part One: American Journalism, 1938–1944*, 104–38. New York: Library of America, 1995.

———. *Rise and Fall of the Third Reich*. New York: Simon & Schuster, 1990.

Stevenson, William. *A Man Called Intrepid: The Secret War*. New York: Lyons Press, 1976.

Thompson, John H., and Stephen Randall. *Canada and the United States: Ambivalent Allies*. 3rd ed. Athens: University of Georgia Press, 2002.

Thurlow, Richard. "Britain: The British 'Union of Fascists.'" In *Fascism Reader*, edited by Aristotle Kallis, 241–48. London: Routledge, 2003.

Time-Life Books. *Luftwaffe*. Alexandria, VA: Time-Life Books, 1982.

Waller, John H. *The Unseen War in Europe: Espionage and Conspiracy in the Second World War*. New York: Random House, 1996.

Weinberg, Gerhard L. *World at Arms: A Global History of World War II*. New York: Cambridge University Press, 1994.

Wernick, Robert. *Blitzkrieg*. New York: Time-Life Books, 1976.

Whipple, A. B. C. *The Mediterranean*. Alexandria, VA: Time-Life Books, 1981.

Ziegler, Philip. *King Edward VIII*. New York: Knopf, 1991.

INDEX

ABOUT THE AUTHOR

A graduate of Princeton University, Brooke C. Stoddard has served as a writer and editor at Time-Life Books and a book project editor at National Geographic. For several years he was editor of *Military Heritage* magazine, and he wrote about the year 1940 for *World War II History* magazine. His work has appeared in the *Washington Post, Historic Preservation,* and other periodicals. He lives and works in Alexandria, Virginia.